"I wish my parents had read this book befo
—*Jordan Roberts, Producer*

"This beautiful book shares the sensitive tale of a mother and son and their journey through Erikson's stages of development. It's a brave book that shows what each of us is called upon to struggle with at each stage of growth—not only in our own lives but also those of our children. Parents, mental health professionals, and anyone interested in human development will benefit from this heartfelt book. They will find healing and hope in its pages. A valiant contribution."
—*Jina Carvalho, Communications Director, The Glendon Association and The Santa Barbara Response Network*

"It's not hyperbole to say that Sally Raymond's groundbreaking book is helping save humanity one reader at a time. Sally informs her audience about how to raise happy, healthy children, how to face any adversity with courage, and how to visualize a psychologically healthier world for us all. With grace, insight, a splash of humor, and a fierce commitment to life, she takes us on a journey that is changing lives. Whether writing, speaking, or by helping her clients walk one more step, Sally thrills, enlightens, and astonishes as she shines a clear light on the way forward."
—*Michael Frick, Founder, Speaking.com*

"This book is a lifesaver for children and adults. If you are struggling to stay alive, or know someone who is, this book is for you. If you are a parent concerned about your child's capacity to survive the insane challenges before them, this book is essential! If only my parents had read this book when I was a child . . . it would have saved me from further abuse and decades of hard work recovering from trauma."
—*Keely Meagan, Author, Healer, and Child Abuse Survivor*

"Sally's raw honesty in this epic book on parenting and loss is a big wake-up call for us all as adults and parents to own our mistakes so we can move forward with love and courage. This book is a powerful tool for knowledge and healing, not only when or before we lose our kids to suicide, but also when we lose ourselves on this rough journey called life."
—*Muna al-Sheikh, LMFT, and Palestinian Advocate for World Peace*

"Sally Raymond's story of her son Jon is deeply moving and profoundly painful. Her guide for parents of troubled children can be used as a guide for everyone on developing empathetic, caring relationships with family and friends. Mindful listening, loving without judgment, and being aware of distress signals will help all of us to support one another."
—*Joan Levinson, Artist, Writer, and Editor*

The Son I Knew Too Late

The Son I Knew
Too Late

~

A Guide to Help You Survive and Thrive

Sally A. Raymond

DELFINAS PUBLISHING
Santa Barbara, California

DELFINAS PUBLISHING
Santa Barbara, California

Frontispeice: Mélancolie (2012) © Albert György.
gyorgy-albert@hotmail.com

Printed in the United States

ISBN: 978-0-578-64396-0 (paperback) | ISBN: 978-0-578-64397-7 (ebook)
Library of Congress Control Number: 2020902540

To every child
Who is born a genius
If simply allowed to be

Contents

~

ERIK ERIKSON'S EIGHT STAGES
OF HUMAN DEVELOPMENT

Stage	Age	Virtue Instilled	Psychosocial Crisis	Significant Relationship	Existential Question	Significant Issues
1	Birth–1 year	Hope	Trust vs. Mistrust	Primary Caregivers	Can I trust this world?	Bonding, Safety, Comfort, Nurture, Touch, Approval, Joy, and Play
2	1–3 years	Will	Autonomy vs. Shame and Doubt	Primary Caregivers	Can I be me?	Mobility, Toilet Training, Mastering Skills, Asserting Independence, Learning Limits, Gender Identity
3	3–5 years	Purpose	Initiative vs. Guilt	Family and Age-Mates	Can I do, move, and act on my own?	Selfhood in Family, Solo Exploring and Cooperative Play, Toys and Tools, Secret Erotic Feelings, Gender Preference
4	5–12 years	Competence	Industry vs. Inferiority	Neighborhood and School	Can I befriend, cooperate, study, organize, play, and learn?	Individuation, Sense of Humor and Self-Control, Building Skills, Developing Work Ethic
5	12–18 years	Fidelity	Identity vs. Role Confusion	Peers and Role Models	Who am I? Where and with whom do I belong?	Finding Unique Identity, Fitting in Peer Group, Exploring Sexuality, Testing Career Paths
6	18–26 years	Love	Intimacy vs. Isolation	Relationships: Mutual Intimacy, Friends, and Colleagues	Can I love and be loved?	Finding Fulfillment in Relationships with Family, Colleagues, and Friends
7	26–65 years	Care and Contribution	Generativity vs. Stagnation	Family, Elders, Career, Workmates, Avocations, and Community	Can I make my life count?	Caring for Self, Family, Elders, Friends, and Colleagues; Contributing to Work, Community, and Earth
8	65 years on	Wisdom	Ego Integrity vs. Despair	My Life, My Kin, Humankind, Faith / Spirit	Is it okay to have been me?	Final Life Review, Being a Wise Shepherd to Younger Generations

Haunted

~

SINCE MY SON Jon's suicide, I remain haunted by him, by his life, and by his decision to end that life a little after 9:00 p.m. on March 29, 1991. On that Good Friday night, with spring blossoming under a silent sky lit by a dazzling full moon, Jon sped down Highway 49 in California, leaving his seat belt—this one time—unbuckled. Suddenly, with one perfectly timed jerk of the wheel, he threaded his car into a narrow carve-out, then straightened to gun it all the way into a looming concrete soundwall.

Jon died on impact. Fifteen days earlier we had all celebrated his birthday. He had turned twenty-three.

Jon was sure he died alone. He was, oh, so wrong. That night I, and the world I knew, died with him. Soon I would learn that I was just one of many lives shattered with his against that soundwall.

Although I knew Jon had at times been depressed, I also knew he was a fine person who had done everything right to ensure a strong, positive, and successful life. After four condensed years of intense study and just after turning twenty-one, Jon had graduated with both his BS and MS in theoretical mathematics from an elite school. He, more than most, had all the right stuff to guarantee a future worth living for.

That was the Jon I knew, a son who, along with his younger brother, Alan, made me the world's proudest, happiest, luckiest mom. At the time Jon died, I had just completed my counseling degree and was only one test away from earning my license as a marriage and family therapist. But no amount of psychological training could teach what Jon would teach in the toughest possible way—that moms love to swim in the cup half full, always buoyant, focused on hope and love and life. Our child's death by any means—especially by suicide—is unimaginable. And that is exactly what can make us blind, unavailable to our children at the very moments they need us most. Unwittingly, I must have abandoned Jon when his cup seemed empty so that he felt lost and alone. How did I blind myself to seeing and addressing his pain? That is the question Jon's suicide has forced me to ask forever.

But before Jon died, I had no idea there even was such a question. Bits and pieces of Jon's pain began to be revealed only in the days that followed. Each new piece introduced a fresh shock, all of them together begging ever louder for answers. There was no choice but to leave all I knew as true about myself, him, or us. I would have to seek out Jon's truths—to follow the clues that might help me understand how and why my son had suffered so much that his own life story ended in the most impossible, unspoken postscript, "and then I killed myself."

The First Clues

I am sitting in a car driven by the boyfriend I tried to break up with over a week ago, on Good Friday, the very night Jon died. Under the same huge moon that witnessed Jon's final drive, I returned home and later fell into bed. Awakened the next morning by a ringing phone, I stood naked to pick up. I heard three simple words.

"Jon killed himself."

Each word hit like an executioner's bullet. My body slowly bent at midpoint, shuddering. A retching began that turned vocal, one word only repeating: "No... no ... *no ... no ... noooo!*" Everything I knew, everything I was, obliterated. I pitched forward, wheezing and choking to the floor and lay, writhing.

For a week I have remained locked in my bedroom, unable to eat, sleep, turn on the light, or do anything but curl up on the bed, sometimes screaming and crying incoherently, sometimes mute and immobile, staring into emptiness.

Now, riding toward Jon's memorial service, I am an empty shell. A ghost on a leash.

I glance toward the backseat at my younger—now only—son, Alan.

His too-white shirt and too-black pants starkly accent stilts instead of legs. In a week's time he has lost a lot of weight. His face looks frozen, pallid, even sick. My younger son is suffering, I realize, as much as I am.

Everything blurs.

What did I do to my sons? Am I the reason Jon is dead? Acrid questions arise to flay me.

Just then Alan pipes up, quietly, sadly, "You know, he tried to do this before…"

"What?" I cry out. *What in the world is he saying?*

"Jon tried to kill himself before."

"What? When? What are you talking about?"

"When we were little, Tracy was babysitting while you were at work. Jon told me to come with him. He got a box and took it out to the tree in front of the house. Then he went into the garage and got a rope. He threw the rope over a branch, got on top of the box, and tied one end to the tree and tied the other end around his neck. Then he told me to kick out the box. I didn't know what he was doing, I guess, so I did what he said. Jon fell a little and just hung there."

Aghast, I cry, "Oh, my God! He was hanging himself! Why did you do it?"

"I didn't know any better."

"Oh, God! What happened?"

"I guess Tracy saw us from the front window. She ran out, grabbed him, pulled the rope off his neck, and said never to do that again."

Shock waves roll through me. My mind takes a journey back in time, imagining my beautiful little towhead dangling from our gnarled Brazilian pepper tree. I double over and nearly wretch.

"Why didn't I ever hear about this?" I heave. "How old were you?"

"Oh, I don't know, maybe four or five, I guess."

Stop this grilling, I tell myself. *Alan has just told the truth, sharing something huge he was carrying. How long did Jon's suffering go on? If Alan was five, then Jon was seven! Seven? My God! Ever since, Jon must have thought I knew and just didn't care!*

Too overwrought to realize it then, I have just received my first clue.

We arrive at a place new to me but one my children have visited many times. It is their stepmother's parents' estate, high on the bluffs overlooking the cobalt Pacific. The day is too beautiful and perfect: sunny, balmy, and clear, the seventh of April.

I try to step out of the car, but my feet won't move. The boyfriend's hand extends to help me out.

Shrinking back, I look down. *No. Please, no.*

For days I've kept my suffering private, alone, walled off from others. Now I must face everyone, at once, with all of it.

The hand hovers, waiting.

Sharp inhale. Beyond all anguish, deep within, someone is admonishing: *Be strong for him. Honor him. You who birthed him, loved him, held and cared for him, watched him rise—only you can do him the justice he so richly deserves. If there was ever a time to honor him, it is now. Stand up! Stand up for Jon! This is the last chance you will have.*

My hand takes the one extended. In slow motion my body unfolds and stands.

We walk forward in silence, heads down, shadow people following shadows ahead. Other shadows slip in behind. Without him, who or what am I? Hollowed out, I am just a place marker. The real me has vacated, gone to search for him.

In my mind I see the shimmery infant held by green latex gloves high above my white-sheeted moon of belly. "Congratulations, Mrs. Raymond," the doctor booms, "you are the proud mother of a fine baby boy!" Finally! Finally! Our firstborn, our own dearly awaited cherub—a boy! Exactly as we wanted.

Atop this sea cliff, people stand in strained, subdued clusters across a perfectly manicured lawn. Each cluster knows a Jon unique to them. I glance around, seeking the only person in the world who would know everyone here.

With a shock I remember. Jon won't be coming.

But his friends have gathered from near and far—friends from kindergarten and high school and college, along with their families. Also relatives: Jon's stepdad, my second ex, with his new wife. Jon's dad and stepmother with Jon's dear grandma, along with every member of his father's extended family. A distant cousin on his father's side with her preteen daughter, Anna, a shy, dear girl whom she quietly introduces me to. Anna's mother shares that Jon lived with them for several weeks just months ago. My relatives are also here, notably, Jon's staunchest ally and my family's matriarch, seventy-eight-year-old Great-Aunt Amelia. My coworkers are here supporting me, and so many others I know but haven't seen in years.

Clutching the single sheet of words I must somehow deliver, I grow increasingly frantic. I can't speak this. Even if I do begin, I'm sure to fall apart. *Oh, God, please help!*

Dressed in black, a quite mature Tracy walks up and stands by me. She's driven over two hundred miles to be here, and it's been years since we last met. Our irrepressible, nearly live-in babysitter for eight years, the girl I used to call my surrogate daughter. But right now, my mind is full of just one thing—Alan's stunning revelation in the car.

"Tracy, why didn't you tell me that Jon tried to hang himself back when he did and you rescued him?"

She looks at me quizzically a moment, remembering, then says, "Oh, you were under so much stress back then, I didn't want to add to it."

"Tracy, I needed to know that! Jon probably thought I didn't care, when I simply had no idea."

Just then Jon's dad walks up holding a glass of wine in each hand and carefully extends one out to me. This is a no-alcohol event, with no reason to celebrate. What in the world is he doing? "Thought you might like a drink," he offers easily. Floored, I just stand, speechless.

But beside me, Tracy's dark eyes flash. "Oh, you're finally going to *give* her something?" she asks acidly. That's our Tracy—unswerving loyalty to me and the boys. She was a tween back then, too young to comprehend the full gravity of what Jon was doing—and she absolutely saved his life.

A great-uncle of Jon's on his dad's side approaches. "You know," Leo begins genially, as if continuing a dialogue begun moments ago instead of twenty-five years, "I only met Jon once, about a year ago. But after talking to him for five minutes, I realized that here really was someone who could save the world." Our eyes meet and hold as his words echo through my mind. Mute, I think, *Yes, I do believe Jon could have.* Then my eyes fall, and I am devastated anew. It's too late.

"You know," he continues, "I had been thinking he would be the perfect person to do our family's genealogy. I was going to ask him next time we met." His voice trails away, and I am undone yet again. Jon would have adored such a meaningful, cool task. *If only Jon knew. This alone could have changed everything. He would still be here.*

Jon's forever friend from junior high, Todd, steps toward me, along with his mom, who was one of Jon's favorite schoolteachers. Todd has flown here from MIT, where he is a rising star. Quietly he tells me that the night before Jon died, Jon called him from California, and they talked over two hours. Jon, he shares, seemed fine.

Fine? Huh? Then what could have happened?

Sweet and staunch Laurel, Jon's high school classmate and friend he brought to our home and tutored in calculus, comes up alone, her eyes seeking mine. She confides sorrowfully, "I . . . was waiting for him." My heart breaks. If he'd only known! Jon already had the perfect girl and never lived long enough to find out.

The music starts, and I go numb, hearing the first of three songs I chose for Jon's memorial. "Climb ev'ry mountain, search high and low, Follow ev'ry highway, ev'ry path you know." The surging music Jon's brother and I were hearing at home after I returned that fateful night, both of us watching *The Sound of Music*—while a few hundred miles north, Jon was driving his car into a freeway soundwall. Too late would I realize that every day Jon lived, he certainly did follow his dreams, did climb every mountain. Lost in agony, I sense him calling me to do the same.

Next comes the second song we heard that night: "So long, farewell, auf Wiedersehen, good night . . . I hate to go and leave this pretty si-ight. . . Goodbye! Goodbye . . . Goodbye!" I glance up to see a lone seagull riding the air currents above the cliff, cocking one eye down at us. Is that Jon? It could be. I named my infant son after Richard Bach's hero, Jonathan Livingston Seagull. Dipping one wing, the gull wheels and disappears. With a start, I realize that the bird's story really did become Jon's—even to its ending.

The pastor steps to the podium and speaks, then invites up all who want to share. It is time. Slowly I rise and numbly walk toward the lectern. Seeing the array of familiar faces before me, I feel a strange resolve forming within. *I cannot fail. I will not fail you, Jon. I love you now and always. This is for you.*

I read the first words, look up, and speak out strong:

I want you to really look around you, and look at one another. You are all mirrors of Jon's many facets. You are the incredible people Jon picked to know, love, and be with.

Please don't let Jon's life or this moment be forgotten. Every day, live the principles that you recognize Jon embodying. Make connections here and always that you nurture and keep alive. Jon was always looking for love, warmth, and family connections. This is what I believe Jon meant to convey in this life. He could only be so brilliant in a warm, supportive, loving, and honest environment. He's not alone. It's now left to us to do the same. Recognize the truth he lived here on earth, and honor that truth by doing something about it—every day that you live.

It was an honor to be his mother.

I stumble back to my seat as tears blur the audience into watercolors. Jon's best friend from first grade, Paul, is the next to walk to the podium. He wears small, round, John Lennon glasses. Worn to hide any tears, their smoky lenses make his eyes look like twin spinning black holes. As he speaks, the glasses keep slipping off their perch to dangle in odd angles off his nose. Each time, a little more vexed, he nervously repositions them, just to have them slip again. He is talking about how angry he feels at being left because he expected and needed Jon to be there throughout his life.

Suddenly, my mouth curves up. I can almost see Jon standing beside his lifelong friend, teasing him like always, flicking his finger to send the glasses off-kilter again and again. *Hey, lighten up*, he might say, *You may think I'm gone, but you know what? I'm right by your side, now and always, because I love and need you too.*

Paul ends with a potent summary: "Jon was the most *who he was* of anyone I have ever known."

His words hit me like a sucker punch. Like this is the most essential truth about Jon ever. But what does it mean? What?

The girl I was just introduced to, sweet little Anna, walks to the podium. She faces us, looks up, and says a forlorn "I just lost my pinochle partner."

Again am I undone, sensing in her words another clue. Something happened here—but what?

Other people rise and speak. The memorial ends with the last song Jon's brother and I heard that night, "Edelweiss." For Jon truly was that rare being, like that sweetest and purest flower in all of the Alps.

As the final notes die away, people begin to rise. My elderly but unstoppable Aunt Amelia comes up with determination in her step. Squaring off in front of me, she pins me with those shrewd Italian eyes. "So," she begins, "just *what* was he supposed to do for an *encore?*" Her shoulders shrug futilely as her hands rise and spread apart, empty. "Get *married?* Have *kids?*" She snorts and looks me straight in the eye. "Wasn't he . . . *done?*"

I can only stare, but my mind is roaring back, *NOOOOO! Jon was just BEGINNING!*

Before she turns away, her chin lifts, and in a breaking voice she adds, "Did he *have* to get an A in *everything?*" Mute and stunned, I watch her walk off, still one hundred percent loyal to Jon, even to his horrendous last choice. There is no way I can ever agree—or match—such unconditional love.

A few hours later I am standing atop another cliff above the Pacific beside my second ex-husband, Scott, who is flanked by Jon's dad and stepmom. Before us spreads a gently rolling carpet of green. Partway down the hill is a large mound covered in green cloth. As we near the mound, a sharply etched, coffin-size cut in the earth appears and darkly gapes.

Please God, no. Another shock wave hits.

Jon's ashes are boxed and already placed in the hole.

We stop a few feet away. I want to scream, jump in, end this torture. A wrenching sorrow crescendos within and starts spilling out my mouth.

"Jon, Jon, oh, my dear son, there is no way I can or ever will say goodbye to you. When I saw you being lifted to my sight that very first time, I remember how surprised I was by my first thought: 'Here is the one who will teach me all I need to know.' And, oh, yes, how you surely did teach me, Jon, every day of your life from that moment on. First you taught me what love truly is, then you taught me to be the best by being always the best yourself. This cannot be the end of all your lessons."

I have no control over the words. They just keep spilling out.

"Jon, I will be back, and I promise to look for you always. I must understand your truth, what happened to bring you here. I will keep listening, will never abandon you or walk away. Jon, I love you so much. I always have and always will. I promise to return here to share with you, learn from you, and find every way to honor you always."

Finally the gush of words begins to soften and still. The only sounds left are the gentle breeze around us and the distant hum of cars on the freeway.

Slowly, without anyone else speaking, we turn and walk back up the slope. I am surprised to feel my ex holding my hand. At the car I look back at that horrid green mound to fix the scene in my mind. I need to find my way back. For here is my new touchstone, my new home. I will return every year on Jon's birthday and deathday to clean his grave and share with him what I have done lately to keep my promise.

Digging for More Clues

For months I wandered in a fog. Jon was gone. Without him, I had no self, no life either. Whatever agony he had felt was over—I hoped—in a flash, but mine would flay me forever. So I fled with Jon. An empty husk stayed behind, going through the motions.

Day after day I drove to work with tears streaming down my cheeks. At the time I was working as a therapy intern, spending my days at a residential facility for schizophrenics, returning home at night to my grief. Close to licensure when this happened, I had to keep going, to finish that last test and stay solvent. But even more, I needed the work for my own sanity—to focus for eight hours a day on helping others. Work provided a respite, the only antidote to an endless roll of grief and pain.

When the internship suddenly ended less than two months later, I had no escape. Without a license, I couldn't get another job. Now the house

I occupied 24/7 was no longer a home, much less the home I'd known for over twenty years, full of life, laughter, and good memories. Now every room, every wall, floor, window, and view seemed loaded with land mines. All my sweet memories had turned toxic, to torture and ambush me at will. My body weakened, and I grew sick.

Though not yet an official therapist, but with all the therapeutic skills and training, I had to become my own first client. I made myself two promises. Evenings, I would study for licensure as I could between the hours of numbing grief. By day I would restore my house, turn it into a celebration of Jon's life—not as it was now, a mausoleum full of his death.

I tore into the restoration, opening the home to more sun, repainting every door and wall. I learned to tile, then set tiles everywhere—counters, floors, outside. For the yard where my boys had played, I designed a new lawn, put in sprinklers, and replanted all my roses in happier locales. With the work, my body strengthened.

And as I turned over dirt and installed new windows, something else kept happening. Bits and pieces of memories surfaced in each square foot. At first each just broke my heart once more, but then my therapist self took over, had to explore it. Under a bed I found Jon's old grade school papers. At the pepper tree out front I stared and stared, pondering what happened that day to make Jon get that rope. As I cleaned out closets and drawers, the therapist in me kept asking simple questions: *What really happened here? What was Jon's experience—his lived reality, the stories I as his mom missed or never understood in full?*

Six months later, full of trepidation, I took my test for licensure and passed. Though now a full-fledged psychotherapist, I couldn't stop wondering what Jon's real story was. What of his story could be found and understood? What could be salvaged from his loss?

I found a new position and after work each day kept searching for Jon's truth. I started writing down each snippet of memory that surfaced. Stories began to emerge that were different from those I first believed—stories full of hard truths and moral lessons. The night a baby awakened us, and his father wordlessly took off down the hall toward his room. The colorful jungle sheets on Jon's bed that night Jon would not stop crying. His report cards, all A's. The school picture of my adolescent son staring back at the camera hollow eyed.

Writing a story down, I would reach a new realization, hit a new wall of fresh agony, and simply flee. Months might go by before I could bear to return to my desk to sit down, remember more, and write again. But there was no choice. I had to know *his* story. I felt like an anthropologist, on a dig of our life together. Each time I finished a story, I threw it in a file drawer, shut it tight, and walked away.

Finding the Road Map

Years went by this way. One Saturday I sat on the floor of my home office, feeling hopeless and upset, sure I had failed to keep my promise to Jon. Behind my back was that drawer I never opened except to drop in another story and run.

There was only one thing to do—confront my failure in full. I slowly turned to face that drawer, reached for the handle, and pulled. Without looking, I plunged in my hand. To my amazement, out came handful after handful of stapled stories. Soon I was surrounded on the floor by print-outs. Without thinking, I began putting them into chronological order. The stack kept rising until it nearly reached my chest. Then I counted them—more than ninety stories, arrayed in order from Jon's birth to his untimely death. Stories not only of Jon's soaring success but also of his pain and disappointment, stories not just about the supportive relationships in his life but also about connections and encounters that undermined him—a sadder, truer version of Jon's life than I, as just his mom, had understood while he was alive.

Yet now that mom was also a therapist, and that new therapist self began asking some new and surprising questions: *Can I rebirth Jon through these sadder, truer stories in a way that allows him to be present and meaningful to others? Can I honor his life in a way that will be of benefit to others? How can Jon's life and sacrifice help others survive what he did not?*

Simply asking these questions seemed to summon an instant answer. As part of the training to become a psychotherapist, I'd been required to read Dr. Erik Erikson, known as the "Father of Psychosocial Theory." I had devoured Erikson's writings, especially his deceptively simple chart outlining Eight Stages of Human Development. Erikson said that every human life evolves through eight stages from birth to old age. In each stage we face a new growth crisis, and we resolve that crisis through our interactions with others in one of two directions: toward either a positive or a negative result. We internalize that result and carry it forward, for good or ill, into the next stage. A growth challenge can be resolved in a way that builds on what came before and supports our ongoing development, or it can be resolved in a way that undermines or inhibits the maturation process and limits or perverts our sense of self. Each stage of growth thus includes a psychological pitfall to be avoided and a psychological strength to be gained.

Erikson saw that every person faces the same psychological crisis at the same stage of development. In revealing the human developmental process as universal, and in making explicit the psychological challenge inherent in each stage, Erikson gave us tools for facing the core challenges at every stage of life. No longer do we need to wander blindly through our own process of maturation. Erikson's road map provides a long perspective, showing us where we begin and where we are going—or, more powerfully, greater control in helping us get where we want to go.

With Erikson's chart in hand, we can be more conscious and empowered, better able to guide ourselves and our children forward while avoiding the various pitfalls along the way. When we use Erikson's chart to look back on our lives, it gives us the keys to begin to heal our past and reshape our future.

Jon was over eighteen when I first read Erikson's work, fervently wishing I'd had such a simple map in hand decades earlier when my sons were infants. With it I could have identified the current issue each son was facing and helped to steer each of them true. Though other developmental theorists, such as Piaget, Bowlby, and Kohlberg, made great contributions, I found Erikson's chart to be the one key I wish I'd had to be a better parent. It would have given me the tools to recognize whether I was supporting or hindering my sons' ability to grow and flourish.

Erikson's chart also gave me the tools to be a wiser shepherd of my own life. I could reflect back through earlier stages and finally recognize debilitating messages I fell prey to as a child, internalizing those messages and later reflexively passing them on to my sons. Armed with its knowledge, I could stop repeating past errors, admit them in full, and seek to repair the damage done. I could consciously keep becoming a clearer, more responsible mom and good shepherd to Jon, to Alan, and to others.

After Jon's suicide, and far too late to repair the unhealed damage, Erikson's road map of human development helped me unearth and understand these newer, sadder stories of Jon's life. With Erikson's help, I realized how much of Jon's pain I could have prevented or healed—and how much of the pain of others can similarly be addressed and healed.

Now I could understand more of what Jon internally experienced at each stage of his too-brief life. I could sense exactly how the wounds he experienced predisposed him to some eventual overwhelming calamity—because too often those wounds were left unaddressed and remained inside him to fester and undermine his progress. At the time I saw only my young son rocketing straight to the stars, while internally and out of my sight, Jon kept losing psychological ground.

With Erikson's simple chart showing the internal crisis we face at each stage in life, I could have been a clearer and more supportive mom. Knowing what was key to Jon's positive development at every age, I would have known better how to support his best development and help him preserve his internal stability.

Because Erikson showed that we become stronger and more capable depending on the kinds of relationships and experiences we have at each age, I realized I could fit Jon's stories within Erikson's simple, comprehensive road map. Together, stories and road map could clarify and enhance each other, showing readers how to live well and long and avoid Jon's fate.

This was how to make the best use of the lessons that cost Jon his life.

Young People and Suicide

Jon was at the time one of four thousand young people in this country each year who end their own lives. Today that number approaches six thousand. Long the tenth leading cause of death nationwide, suicide recently rose to be the second leading cause of death among American youth ages fifteen to twenty-four. Only accidental injuries kill more American youth than the number of young people killing themselves.

These totals are unprecedented, but underneath them lies yet another horrendous fact: today about two million American youth, every year, are making serious suicide attempts. Even little children are attempting and completing suicide—in 2013, about three hundred children aged five to twelve. In tragic testimony to this terrible new development, "Pediatric Depression" is a new category appearing in the latest version of the diagnostic manual for mental health professionals. The yearly cost to society from attempted suicides is estimated at $6.5 billion. That figure does not include the many young casualties of suicide attempts consigned to live the rest of their lives permanently disabled. In this country alone, it is estimated that 85 percent of the total population is now affected by suicide.

Much of suicide's devastating legacy could be avoided if people knew how to help themselves, their children, and others weather life's ultimate challenges. Yet the National Alliance on Mental Illness (NAMI) states on its website that while "reducing suicide risk factors is one of the primary goals of effective suicide prevention strategies . . . unfortunately, very little is known about the treatment of suicidal youth."

Erik Erikson's work suggests that when the core emotional challenge at each stage of life is resolved in positive ways, a young person can move forward in life with more stability, clarity, and confidence. Traumas do not have to build up, threatening to destabilize their lives and demoralize our precious, fragile young. The truth is a simple one—*resolving core dilemmas at each stage of life development can prevent suicide.* It can grow young people who have confidence in themselves and others, who know how to calm themselves in crises, and who have the emotional tools needed to resolve life's challenges in favor of life rather than death.

Life Is Calling You

Each stage of life from birth on introduces us to new experiences and ushers us on to a new synthesis. Outside of our awareness, life is always preparing us for greater life. Only by looking back after a lot of living can we have enough perspective to see all the ways that what we first saw as our most adverse events over time helped us reach positive ends. Our problems and pain truly served an ultimate positive purpose.

If you trust anything, trust life. Life wants life—whole life, full life—and has honed itself over the millennia to give us just that.

I don't want another person to suffer as Jon did or do what he did. No matter what tragedy befalls us, no matter how badly we've been treated or how poorly we've resolved earlier life stages, at any moment all of that experience is able to be recalled, felt in full, reworked, and integrated. Every prior hurt can be healed, here and now. There is no need for any past experience to continue to diminish or depress our lives. Only by believing these painful experiences are shut in the past do we guarantee that they remain stuck in their original state, raw and explosive. When we keep them repressed outside of our awareness, we give them the power to erupt into the present whenever triggered and, if they do explode, to wreak untold damage on ourselves and others.

Instead, we can—when we finally feel very safe—turn and face our original wounds. Once we recognize them, understand them in full, and then integrate them into our conscious life story, our wounds can empower us rather than limit or destroy us. Released to consciousness, our past wounds transform into great allies for our enhanced growth and power. The truth really does set us free.

Everything we survive, we can heal. Often later on, with the benefit of time and the clear, seasoned acuity of hindsight, we can realize how some terrible experience transformed to some equal benefit. From our pain, something crucial shifted, something new was learned. For pain is a teacher. Each bad or ugly experience contains equal transformational power for greater truth and freedom. I witness the process time and again in my therapy office—first the wounding is revealed, and then eventually comes the healing. And each time we resolve a past hurt or heal a past wound, we are released into new life with greater awareness and possibilities.

Pain arises as an error message: something is wrong, needing to be addressed, and it is asking us to resolve it. And resolve it we can and will, if we stay alive. With time and trust and the benefit of a clearer perspective, each challenge can be surmounted, each problem resolved, each wound healed. If we stay open, we can trust life to bring us to the other side of every trial. Trust that this is your very own process too.

Life Is Calling Your Family

Just as our own personal wounds can be healed, so can the wounds that inevitably happen in the day-to-day life of a family. Many of the crises that eroded Jon's psyche and sense of well-being received their toxic hurt because we as a family did not know how to deal with them. His father and I were young, naive parents. Jon was our firstborn. We did not have the tools to address and heal the assaults and wounds that young Jon experienced.

Our family crises were not unique. We experienced things that many families experience—divorce, a child's challenges in school, a toxic and abusive neighbor. Most of Jon's crises were exacerbated by our own ignorance and unhealed early-life traumas. In this too we were not unique. Every parent brings their past crises, whether healed or still raw, into their parenting.

This book is written so that you can have the tools to heal your own unresolved pain, first of all, and be able to help yourself and your children resolve the core challenges faced at each stage of life. Understanding Erikson's stages of life can help parents calm themselves or their children when crises hit. It can help all readers talk themselves or others "down off the ledge."

Placing our own, our children's, or others' struggles within the larger vision of Erikson's stages helps all of us and especially parents grow empathy for their own child-selves and for their own children. We learn to see the world through the eyes of a young person at each stage of life. We learn what matters to a child as they grow, why some challenges leave emotional scars, and how those scars can be healed so they do not undermine the child's forward movement in life. Through the lens of Erikson, every parent can learn new ways of listening and talking with their children. They can learn what things are helpful to say—and what are unhelpful—depending on the child's place in Erikson's stages. Parents can learn how to heal family traumas, what kind of positive relationships a child needs at his or her particular stage, and how to build family life that supports children and adults at each age of development.

Unique Stories, Common Challenges

The genius of Erik Erikson is his assertion that each of us faces certain predictable challenges simply by being alive. Each of us goes through the same sequence of emotional challenges, though the details of that challenge look different for each individual. Some life experiences trigger deep and overwhelming feelings because they touch the core emotional challenge of a particular stage of life. The common hope to be found in Erik Erikson's theory is the hope that, though we as individuals live out our own unique life stories, each of us faces the same core emotional crises at the same age in the same sequence throughout our lives. This knowledge in itself gives us power to use to our own and others' benefit.

In this book you will find Erik Erikson's Eight Stages of Human Development explored through the unique experiences of Jon Raymond's life. Though Jon's story may be unique, the tools and life skills he needed to resolve his core emotional challenges are the same ones that every individual needs at a similar stage of development.

In this way, Jon's story is not at all unique. He passed through the same stages of life as every one of us does. He needed to resolve the same core emotional challenge that life asks each child to resolve at that same stage. By knowing what Jon needed at each stage of life, we, his parents, could have helped him resolve the core issue of that stage. And by seeing the example of one child and young person, you, the reader, can glimpse what every child and young person needs to resolve the core emotional challenge of that age and move forward in life with confidence.

Each chapter of the book addresses one stage of life. In the first half of the chapter I delve into Jon's experience at that stage of life, noting what went wrong and what went right, reflecting on what Erikson had to say about that developmental age. In the second half of each chapter, you will learn how to put Erikson's theory to work—how to negotiate and resolve that age's challenge in positive ways and, if wounding has occurred, how to help yourself or your child heal those old wounds and move forward in life with hope.

This book is written so that you will have the tools that neither Jon or nor I, as his mother, had to help him. Though adverse events inevitably happen in a child's life, they need not cloud a child's identity or slow their forward progress. With knowledge and love, we can help ourselves, our children, and others to survive, heal, and thrive at every stage of life.

Decades have passed since that moonlit night when my twenty-three-year-old son Jon crashed his car into that soundwall. The pain of his death will never leave me. Yet it is my hope that through his life and sacrifice, Jon can help give others the keys to live a rich, long, happy, productive, and fulfilling life.

Born in heartbreak, this book is supremely a book of hope.

Colic

〜

STAGE 1. INFANCY

Age	Virtue Instilled	Psychosocial Crisis	Significant Relationship	Existential Question	Significant Issues
Birth–1 year	Hope	Trust vs. Mistrust	Primary Caregivers	Can I trust this world?	Bonding, Safety, Comfort, Nurture, Touch, Approval, Joy, and Play

"WAHHHH. Waaaaaaaaaah. WaaaaaaaAAAaaaaah. WaaAAAAAAAA...."

Tiny Jon's wails went on and on. Ragged. Endless. Tortured. Nothing I could do soothed him. We had waited five years to have him. Had done everything possible to prepare and welcome our baby into our lives. But he arrived so terribly alien, so unhappy and uncomfortable—nothing like the baby books described. At birth he began crying and, except when he was sleeping, didn't stop.

Something was wrong, but what? Jon couldn't say. Desperate to comfort him, I brought him to his new pediatrician, a doctor I picked for his forty years of experience: a spare, tall, and rather elderly doctor with a long face. "It's just colic—stomach upset," he assured me. "Some newborns have problems with their plumbing. Stomach's immature. Lasts a couple of months—three months tops."

I wanted to believe him. Each time I called, more frantic than before, the doctor's answer was the same. "It's just colic. He'll be fine in about three months." Three months? Easy for him to say!

The doctor ordered medication. Instead of providing the promised relief, it constipated him. With his internal problems compounded, Jon only cried harder, longer.

Nurse him, and he cried. Burp, bathe, or hold him, pick him up, put him down, bounce or rock him, and he cried. Change him, and he cried. Tuck him in bed and leave, and he cried. My mother tried to help. Remembering her own difficulties with me, she announced, "Your milk is no good. Put him on formula." I resisted for three months, finally caved, and put him on a bottle. He kept crying.

The only thing that worked even slightly was a rubber pacifier, his binky. Whenever he dropped or spit it out, night or day, in a panicky flash I would spring up to reinsert it. Snatching an hour or two of sleep in twenty-four hours, I felt lucky. Baby slept less than that.

Then there was hubby. "Can you hold him while I make dinner?" I made the mistake of asking exactly once.

Dad's answer was terse. "You deal with the kid. I bring home the bread." My breath caught. While I stood absorbing this news, he walked into the living room and snapped on the TV. I knew of his zero tolerance for any problem I might have, but I never imagined it applied to our baby too. Now I knew— a hurting baby was entirely my problem. He would have none of it.

My mission was clear—somehow I had to pacify both a new dad and our distressed infant son. Separately. From then on, no matter which one I tended, I felt torn in the middle and always half wrong. And even that was just my problem. Back then there were no hands-free slings to hold babies against you while you worked. To cook or clean, I had no choice but to lay Jon down, where he would lie looking so stranded, helpless, and needy. My little home, sweet new baby, handsome husband, and all my dreams seemed to be twisting into one big nightmare.

One especially miserable afternoon, I called my pediatrician for the nth time to be told he wasn't in. The secretary gave my distraught call to his younger colleague.

"Colic?" a mellow, resonant male voice confirmed. "Okay. Here's what you do. Go into your kitchen. Take a ten-ounce glass out of the cupboard. Fill it with wine. Take a teaspoon out of the drawer. Dip it in the wine. Feed that to the kid—then you drink the rest."

For the first time in months, I laughed.

"Do it," he commanded, and hung up.

Renewed and slightly giddy, I followed the doctor's prescription. Two things happened in quick succession. That teaspoon of wine put little Jon sound asleep for hours while I sipped and passed out.

For the first time since giving birth, I awoke refreshed but riddled with guilt. No way would I turn my beautiful baby boy into an alcoholic! I put the doctor's recommendation behind me and never again yielded to that temptation—even though now I knew full well what really did work.

Three long, miserable months finally passed. Little Jon was still crying. I dialed the pediatrician.

"He's still crying as hard as ever, and you said colic would be gone by now," I complained.

"Well, maybe it's the four-month colic, or even the five-month—"

I hung up on him. Helpful friends steered me to another pediatrician, described as middle-aged, sharp, and very cool. I called his office with my story. Staff gave me an appointment the same day.

Already I felt better.

Dr. Kinsley had a tyke-friendly waiting room full of sturdy, colorful wooden toys. Soon a smiling nurse escorted us into an examining room. Moments later, in swept the doctor, affable, assured, and clear-eyed. After peering over his glasses to greet me, he turned his full focus on Jon as I updated him with our miserable story. Without looking up, he asked me to lay the baby on a table and undo his clothes. I did. The doctor began his examination, checking, pushing, and probing.

"Ah, how interesting," he said at one point as if to himself. "Look!" he said. "Feel right here." His big fingers were aligned along the middle of Jon's right collarbone. I put my fingers where his were. "Feel that bump? That's a broken collarbone. The bump means it's started healing."

A shock wave went through me, sending me reeling. I seemed to be floating over the scene below.

Broken collarbone?

"Not . . . not . . . colic?"

"No. This is what's been hurting him all along," the doctor stated with easy finality. "The weakest bone in the body, collarbones are first to break

21

during birth—which is sometimes required for a baby to be born at all. But see here? It seems to be healing straight. From now on, just keep all pressure off those shoulders when you handle him, and he'll soon be fine."

The doctor's discovery made instant, perfect sense out of three horrible, chaotic months. But instead of bringing relief, the truth felt unbearable. A gun to the head would have been more merciful. From now on I would live knowing that since his birth, I had failed my very own baby. All I did to comfort, care for, love, and help him either reinjured or hurt him worse. Jon's entrée to life and for months afterward was inescapable suffering—at my own hands.

No wonder he cried.

Sorrow welled up then, deep and immense—beyond words or even tears. Slowly, gently, I dressed Jon, avoiding his right arm and shoulder. Tenderly, I lifted him up and laid him back in his carrier. For the first time I noticed the wariness that shaded those huge blue eyes looking back at me.

Erikson's Stage 1:
Trust vs. Mistrust (Birth–1 Year)

According to Erikson, starting with birth until twelve months, our first and truly foundational issue is whether we learn to trust or mistrust. At birth and for many years after, our well-being and indeed our very life is entirely in another's hands. We are utterly dependent in every moment on our first relationship. Without at least one consistently present, caring significant other, babies cannot survive. To be left alone is terrifying and, if prolonged, can mean death. We exist between our own helpless, needy body-self and our primary, all-powerful caretaker—usually our mother. Crying is the only way we have to call our caregiver close to soothe our fears and to feed, protect, and care for us. Attachment to our caregiver is literally a matter of life and death.

It follows that our first life crisis is all about trust. *Am I safe here? Delighted in, cuddled, and loved just as I am? Do I and my needs matter? When I cry, do you come? Am I understood, soothed, suckled, and kept comfortable? Can I be me and learn to trust this body, this caretaker, others, and this world? Or instead do I feel unsafe—alien, misunderstood, or unwanted? Am I left in sorrow, misery, or terror? Is it not okay to be me here, and must I mistrust instead?*

Each encounter adds more evidence either for or against trust. The conclusion every tiny but fully sentient baby reaches through these interactions over time becomes neurologically wired into their forming identity and reactions. From then on, especially when activated by distress, those circuits fire as originally programmed to shape future responses. For good or ill, these reactions, for each of us, subtly carry our infantile reality forward into our future relationships and life experiences. Learning we can trust tends to buoy us on our pilgrim's progress through life. Learning we must mistrust acts to alienate us from others and life—our own life included—which helps to isolate and undermine us.

The evidence we collect as infants affects us the rest of our life. Learning we can trust the world and ourselves in it is a key first discovery. Trust allows our tiny, forming ego to feel safe, calm, and open—free to interact with life and to enjoy and learn from experiences in ways that create a stable, resilient identity. Trust lays the foundation for strong and secure relationships in the future. Trusting others and feeling connected to them allows us to trust ourselves and our own good judgment. Trust helps to free us to be who we are, to find trusted allies along the way, and to blossom into our full potential. Without trust, we tend to retreat inside ourselves and become more fearful, closed off, and shut down. Either way, the style of relating formed out of our first relationship tends to keep us reacting similarly with others as we grow.

Trust is the basis for hope. Studies of suicide suggest that mistrustful experiences at this formative time, if left unaddressed or unresolved, can weigh a child's psyche down, leading to a chronic, despairing sense of unworthiness, alienation, and hopelessness and increasing the eventual risk of suicide. Chronic mistrust tends to inhibit our growth. It curbs our exploration and increases our odds of living a more circumscribed life.

To grow up well—to become free, resilient agents—we need that bedrock of trust that Erikson said is developed in the very first year of life. When we resolve our first developmental challenge in favor of trust, we have the foundation we need to feel calm in life; to participate in creative, happy play; to learn how to reason reflectively; to develop satisfying relationships; and to continue to mature in mind and body.

Jon in Stage 1

Jon's beginning should have been ideal. We'd been married for five years and were happy and secure, excited about a family and ready to start one. The pregnancy had been healthy and peaceful, and Jon was the dearly wanted firstborn as well as the eagerly awaited first grandchild on both sides of the family. Yet Jon arrived doubly traumatized—first by a broken collarbone suffered during birth and then by the resulting physical pain that went undiagnosed for months. Any movement, including handling from his caregivers, could exacerbate it.

What else could he learn but that from his first moment outside the womb he was not safe? He was in continual pain, and no one understood him or helped him feel better. What else could he do but shy from the touch of those who loved him?

Though Jon survived this beginning—he seemed to heal and develop quickly and well after those first four months—still, his body and subconscious remembered being delivered into months of pain. And I, as his primary caretaker, was the most obvious perpetrator of that pain. Could he trust me, his mom, to care for him in the best possible way? His own body had subjected him to months of pain; could he trust this body? By extension, could he trust life itself?

The wariness that Jon learned at the start would continue. Throughout babyhood, childhood, and into early adolescence, Jon nearly always would physically shy or flinch from touch, hugs, kisses, or caresses. His body seemed to be on guard against human contact. I watched it all with sadness and sorrow. I felt helpless to know what to do except not push it.

One day when Jon was perhaps twelve or thirteen and I felt sure he could understand, I finally told him the truth, offering the story with heartfelt apologies.

"Well," he began tentatively after my confession, in that reedy adolescent voice he had begun growing into, "I'm glad to know where I got it ... but now, what do I do about it?"

Good question. I had no idea. This was long before any of my training in psychology and even longer before the internet. No book I knew of delved into any problem like this.

"I don't know, Jon," I answered truthfully. "But," I added, "the first step has got to be simply knowing what really happened—that it's not your nature or how you have to be. Just a reflex from having to live your first months hurting from an undiagnosed broken collarbone, experiencing me—or anyone—as someone who didn't help and could make you hurt even more. Which is the last thing I would ever do had I any idea of what was really wrong. If Dr. Kinsley had been your first pediatrician, he would have caught it and you would never have to feel or react this way."

He heard me out then went back upstairs to his homework. We never spoke of it again. I didn't know what else to say. As far as I could tell, nothing much changed. Jon remained physically and emotionally removed, his super-logical brain leavened by a wonderfully keen and droll sense of humor. For I always knew that deep inside, Jon had a marshmallow heart. Nobody cared more than Jon did about everyone and everything.

Today I know that telling him what really happened was the first right step to help him know that his reactions were symptoms and not "who he was." But much more can be done. Had I known more at the time, I could have begun helping him feel more comfortable with physical touch. It would have been important to make it very safe and to give him full control over how much touch, when, where, what kind, and how long.

For example, children or young people who tend to avoid touch can sometimes enjoy and feel soothed by having their skin brushed with a soft brush. In increments, they might learn to tolerate head or foot massage. What is important always is to proceed at the child's pace so that they feel safe and learn to build confidence in the process of tolerating touch.

Jon's birth trauma did not have to predispose him to a life of shying away from touch. His was a classic case of a Stage 1 crisis failing to be resolved in a positive way. His very first core challenge, beginning at birth, was settled in favor of mistrust rather than trust.

But it didn't have to be this way. Let's take a deeper look at early-life traumas that can lead to feelings of mistrust and how to heal the crisis of trust.

Birth Trauma

Most people who suffer birth trauma have no idea they are among the walking wounded. They and those around them assume their reactions are "just who they are," when these reactions are simply visceral responses stemming from some early, preverbal, traumatic experience, including birth trauma. A small but growing body of research suggests when early traumas are recognized, addressed, and resolved, children from newborns to adolescents can be released to grow more fully into their potential than was once thought possible. (See the Castellino Prenatal and Birth Therapy Training in the Resources.)

Now we know that through labor and delivery—and indeed long before birth—we are sentient beings with a much greater felt sense of the world than was once recognized. Up until birth, we grew in the shelter of the dark and living womb, listening, learning, sensing, and reacting, becoming more aware and responsive and ready for a world "out there." Labor initiates a rude and shocking upheaval. Ever-quickening waves of compression bear down to evict the helpless yet aware infant from its safe haven. The experience can be a scary and crushing one for both mother and baby. Few newborns escape some form of birth trauma, and certainly not babies delivered by cesarean section, who experience a different but equally overwhelming trauma.

Besides the relentless compressions of labor, newborns can experience additional trauma. Hearing their mother scream in labor (as Jon certainly did) or being forcibly turned, as in a breech birth, or having forceps applied or getting a head stuck in the pelvic girdle or experiencing an umbilical cord winding around the neck, reducing or cutting off the oxygen supply—these and more can leave indelible imprints on the newborn's life and psyche. Or, as in Jon's case, the collarbone may snap, as it is designed to do if needed for birth to occur at all.

What is now clear is that our first core crisis of development may arise out of the process of birth itself. Being released headfirst into some unimagined, too-bright universe, suddenly separate and dizzily free, is no reassuring initiation into life beyond the womb. Delivered to an alien world helpless, needy, and in peril, we have good cause to wonder from the start: Will we physically survive? Can we trust our caretaker and the world we have been delivered into?

Healing Trauma, Building Trust

For infants, as for anyone, trauma creates shock and dissociation, leaving discontinuities in our felt sense of self—gaps where time, meaning, and perhaps even our own identity are suspended, hung in the balance. Even after we acquire language, trauma delivers a profound shock to the system—we shut down, are disoriented, can't think or speak. When trauma stems from birth or very early life experience, before we have language or can form conscious memories, our dissociation can be profound. In extreme cases, it can result in mental disintegration or failure to thrive physically. Infants might become listless or have no interest in sucking or might lose weight.

Mistrustful, traumatic experiences early in life that we cannot make conscious sense of remain unconscious but viscerally held within, able to create explosive problems in the future. Even many years later, if we encounter the same feelings the original trauma generated, those raw feelings can erupt in the present. When they do, they can generate an instant overreaction to the current situation. Their power derives from having been contained underground for so long, festering out of sight. (For more information, see the works of Bessel van der Kolk listed in the Resources.)

Time is required to heal early-life traumas so that we can mature to a point where our body grows more capable and we feel safe enough to release them to consciousness. Only then can we begin to face, understand, and resolve them. However, until we reach that point, early shocks such as birth trauma remain unremembered, buried deep in our bodies, where they can subconsciously influence our responses, possibly underlying dysfunctional reactions such as addiction, obesity, or anorexia. We and others typically believe this is just how we are wired, when that may not be true. These reactions may instead be symptoms of some split-off trauma that is needing to resurface so we can finally face it, understand

27

it, and make it a conscious part of our life story. Then we will know that our reactions are not who we are but rather, as in baby Jon's example, are reflexes stemming from some trauma that happened to us long ago.

Once the trauma is known, then we have a choice—to remain its victim or to gain power over it. We take back our power when we finally face what happened and work through it, which was impossible while the trauma was still unconscious. Facing it and integrating it frees us to make more informed choices that help us move into our healed and whole potential.

Healing Birth Trauma

We now know that even trauma from the preverbal stages of infancy can be healed. Even before a baby is born, expectant mothers can build a foundation of safety to minimize the trauma of the coming birth process. In the womb, as a growing fetus hears its mother (and others) singing simple, repeated refrains or reading rhyming stories aloud or talking calmly and laughing, all of these become familiar and reassuring sounds. The more these are replayed after birth, the more they give babies the cue to return to the peace of their experience in utero. Giving newborns quiet, dim light and soothing sounds calls up that idyllic haven before birth where they felt safe, held, and centered in perfect bliss.

In addition to comforting sounds, newborns need close physical connection to their mom and to their welcoming dad, siblings, and others. Following the overwhelming experience of birth, they need skin-to-skin contact so that they can remain physically connected, hearing the heartbeat and other soothing sounds to be able to calm down, sleep, or begin to suckle.

Babies will alert their loving parents or caregivers to birth trauma, for babies are constantly communicating through their body, face, eyes, mouth, and voice. What they say through either action or inaction can provide cues for healing. To heal birth trauma, caretakers need to watch with loving and informed attention.

In order to heal, babies—and adults as well—will physically act out a trauma they experienced but could not cope with at the time. In effect, babies tell us what happened by showing or reenacting their experience. Aware parents notice and remain nearby to watch and encourage a baby who may be reenacting some difficult experience. They let the baby know through their loving attention and simple responses that the baby's experience matters and is being felt and understood.

For example, an infant may be traumatized in childbirth by experiencing its head stuck and forcibly reshaped by contractions to finally fit through the mother's pubic bones. Months or more after birth, the infant may reenact that experience, perhaps by scrunching up and crying in apparent physical distress when all else seems well. Healing can take place when caregivers first notice and realize the baby is communicating. They can pay attention and participate empathetically by gently touching, caressing, and making encouraging or soothing sounds. They stay nearby to feel what the baby feels throughout a reenactment.

When we sense that others care enough to feel in full what we experienced—when we sense that we are understood, that we matter, and that we are known and connected—then we no longer feel alien, helpless, terrified, or in pain. That's when a traumatic experience can recede into the past, because it is over; it is no longer happening. We are on the other side of it—understood and cared for. Surrounded by caregivers who feel for us, we are welcomed into a new life. Then we feel safe and can begin to trust. For that is love, and love is healing.

Healing continues as caregivers help the child sense that their terrifying experience is over. Through their continued love and caring attention, mother and father and other loving caregivers reassure the infant that his or her trauma is in the past, and it is now safe to open up to a stable, happy, and secure life. The baby learns that her caregivers do understand and support her and are really there for her. In this way can tiny, shocked, and traumatized infants begin to open up and feel loved and secure. They have found a safe haven, and they can trust it.

Beyond what parents can do by observing with compassion, many body-mind and somatic therapies are available to help babies, children, and parents address and resolve early traumas. Even the most embedded and traumatic feelings of disconnection can be reworked and finally resolved—no matter how old or young an individual. (For specific recommendations, please see the Resources section at the end of the book.)

Parenting Styles and Trust

How babies get treated by their primary caregivers can also lead the developing baby to feel a bottom-line sense of trust or mistrust. Dr. Daniel Siegel, a child psychiatrist, suggests that each infant responds to how they experience their primary caretaker, forming their own ability or inability to bond emotionally with others accordingly.

In *The Developing Mind*, Dr. Siegel cites a study in which researchers observed babies' responses to a situation in which their mother said goodbye and left them in a strange room for a few minutes and then returned. Babies might respond in one of four different ways to this separation and reunion.

The researchers identified those four styles of connection as: a secure style, an avoidant style, an ambivalent/resistant style, and a disorganized/ disoriented style. In each case the baby's style of connecting with or disconnecting from their parent reflected the parent's own style of connection. In other words, the babies were reflecting back how they experienced their parent's treatment.

The secure baby (65 percent of those studied) reflected sensitive and "secure/autonomous" parents who accurately read their baby's emotional signals and quickly and consistently responded. Babies of secure parents felt safe and cared for, and they naturally learned to explore the world independently. They learned to believe and trust their needs would be met, resolving the first stage's trust-or-mistrust challenge in favor of trust.

Avoidant babies (20 percent of those studied) reflected primary caregivers who appeared emotionally distant, neglectful, or dismissive of their baby's needs. These babies learned not to trust their parent to always care and be there to meet their needs. They didn't feel safe, and therefore they stayed detached. In the research study, when their mother reappeared after leaving the room, these babies tended to ignore her return and not approach her. They were less free in exploring their environment on their own. As they grew they tended to be more logical and analytic rather than sensory and intuitive, and they often seemed unemotional and socially inept.

Ambivalent/resistant babies (10 to 15 percent of those studied) tended to be generally insecure or distressed and to explore their surroundings very little. They remained physically remote and anxious, unable to be calmed or comforted by anyone, including their parent. Their parent often seemed preoccupied or not present—unfocused, distracted, and moody. These babies had learned not to trust their needs would be met.

Disorganized/disoriented infants (10 to 15 percent of those studied) displayed symptoms of trauma. They could be angry or depressed or freeze in place, or they could simultaneously approach and avoid their parent, or else they could go physically inert and be nonresponsive. Their parents appeared erratic, dramatic, frightened or frightening, or else passive or intrusive. These babies were severely compromised, unable to trust they could get their needs met in any way at all.

In each case, in order to survive the baby was responding to the parent's own style of behavior and connection. That is, babies respond to the parent according to how they experience the parent, and parents show their babies the kind of connection or disconnection they themselves were shown as infants. This research suggests that how we internalize and recall our own bonding experiences with our parents in infancy can predict, in turn, how we will parent. Without seriously reflecting on our own parenting and making conscious corrections as needed when we become parents, we tend to simply reenact (or project) our own experience of our parents onto our children.

As a baby encounters and copes with their primary caretaker's parenting style, the baby begins to answer the question of trust or mistrust and to reflect it in their personality characteristics—for better or for worse.

Doing Our Own Emotional Work

Because babies pick up their caregivers' ways of connecting or disconnecting from others, it is important for all adults, whether parents or not, to reflect upon and heal their own early memories. Without seriously reflecting on how our parents related to us, we tend to simply reenact our own experience of our parents with our children or any others in our care.

Of course, any time is right to do this work, but pregnancy and childbirth are the perfect time to begin or continue this work. The best gift any baby can have are two mature and secure parents who have done their own emotional work and know better than to fall prey to repeating their own parents' dysfunctional patterns.

Spend time reflecting on how your parents connected—or didn't connect—with you when you were tiny. If you can't remember those years, engage your parents, siblings, or relatives in conversation about those times. Doing so will help you gain perspective and will bring memories out of the shadows. Making what happened to you conscious again is the only way to heal or change unhelpful patterns.

Becoming aware of your parents' patterns gives you the opportunity to consider what it was you needed then and to make better, more conscious choices in how you relate to your children. As opportunities appear in life, you can choose to improve on your own past bonding experiences. In this way parents can learn to make conscious and positive, healthy choices for themselves and their children in each new moment. As we evolve into securely connected, responsive parents, we can give our children a better experience and, in turn, a better world.

Trust Yourself, and Trust Your Children

Celebrate your baby's entry to life with joyous, happy moments together. Laugh with your children. At every opportunity, bond with them. Express your delight, awe, and happiness at their presence in your life—when you are diapering, bathing, rocking, or feeding them and when you are playing with them or showing them off to family and friends. Slather your children with happy, approving attention. Express your appreciation for them through tender words, touch, looks, and cuddles. In every way, let your children know they are wanted and cherished and that you are thrilled with every little expression or move they make. Weaving a powerful web of comfort, love, delight, and trust between the two of you is the strongest foundation any parent can give their child.

Trust your newborn. Babies are telling the truth as best they can, showing us in movement, responses, feelings, facial expressions, sounds, eye contact, and more. Deeply empathize with their feelings and reactions. Allow yourself to enter into their experience, and let this guide your responses and choices. The process of healing can begin anytime parents pay heartfelt attention to their child and respond to what the child is communicating.

Trust yourself. When it comes to your children's welfare, trust your own instincts even when they differ from the views of authority figures. Professionals too are humans, and humans are fallible. They may be biased, they can misjudge, or they may make hasty mistakes. No human is God or even close. A good authority—one you can trust—is one who truly listens to understand and is not quick to judge.

If your baby is in distress, do not give up searching for answers, and do not be intimidated by anyone else, including professionals or well-meaning parents, friends, and spouses. Do not rest until your baby does. You are your infant's entire source of protection and well-being, your baby's first relationship. More critically, you are his or her sole representative out in the world. The role of protector is one to commit yourself to and carry out again and again. From infancy on, safety and well-being are the keys that free children to explore, learn, and become.

Colic is both overused and misdiagnosed in newborns—a default diagnosis and catchall when nothing else is found. Doctors may diagnose colic to pacify frantic new moms whose newborns are crying. What some expert calls colic might be stomach upset—or, as in Jon's case, it might be the residual effect of misunderstood or misdiagnosed birth trauma. Or it might be something else entirely. Seek second and third opinions, ideally from professionals in different fields. Consensus across differing domains of expertise helps to increase the chances of accuracy.

Question social mores. They change as we learn more, and we always do. Conventional wisdom may not apply to the situation you are facing, so be fearless in searching for more complete answers.

If you err, err on the conservative side—on the side of conserving the well-being of your child. Always support your child's health, safety, and happiness. Not only is that in the best interest of the child, it is in your best interest as well. It provides you lasting peace of mind that you did your best no matter what the outcome. Then your children can trust you—and when they can trust you, they become able to trust themselves, their bodies, their feelings, their own knowing, and life as well.

—

TEACHINGS, AIRBAGS, AND SAFETY NETS

- From birth until twelve months, our first and truly foundational issue is whether we learn to trust or mistrust.

- Each encounter adds more evidence—either for or against—the question of trust, becoming neurally hardwired over time into our forming identity.

- Once we are born, our attachment to our caregiver or caregivers truly is a matter of life or death in each moment. How our caregivers connect with us (or don't connect) in our first year is deeply imprinted on us and affects us for better or worse ever after.

- Without a reassuringly constant emotional bond with caregivers and others, babies sense they are stranded—that they don't matter and can't survive. Over time, such babies can exhibit a failure to thrive.

- Trust frees us to feel safe, calm, and open—free to interact with others and to learn from our experiences so that we can build a stable, resilient identity and blossom into our full potential.

- Without trust, we tend to retreat inside—to be more fearful, closed off, and shut down.

- Parenting begins the moment you know you are pregnant. Pregnancy is a wonderful time to do your own healing. Do your research into your own family history so you can become aware of family patterns that might need healing.

- Continue to reflect on your own early memories of connecting with your parents so that you can make more conscious choices about how to connect with your children.

- Pregnancy is also the time to begin connecting with that developing being inside who all too soon can hear, feel, intuit, remember, respond, and learn.

- Before your baby is born, take parenting classes with your spouse or partner or coparent. Get recommendations for good classes from your pediatrician or other new parents, or go online to local resources such as Adult Education, Planned Parenthood, Child Protective Services, Child Wellness Clinics, Domestic Violence Solutions, or others.

- Colic is both overused and misdiagnosed in newborns—a default diagnosis and catchall when nothing else is found. Colic may be something else entirely. The same is true for other diagnoses as well, for doctors too are human. Seek out second and third opinions whenever there is question.

- Err on the conservative side—on the side of conserving the well-being of your infant.

- You are your infant's entire source of protection and well-being, your baby's first relationship. More critically, you are his or her sole representative out in the world. The role of protector is one to commit yourself to and carry out again and again.

- Bracket authority figures and current social mores. If something is not working, question the conventional wisdom.

- Trust yourself as a new parent, and trust your baby. Your infant is telling the truth as best she or he can, in their expressions, vocalizations, tones, eyes, face, and movements.

- Listen to your baby with all your senses, and respond from your heart. This is how your child learns to trust you first, himself or herself next, then the world beyond. Together you weave a relationship in which your baby learns trust and security.

- Be patient, consistently responsive, and joyous with your new baby as you care for and play with her or him. Every chance you get, let your baby know you are thrilled and delighted that she or he is here, alive, together with you. The safer and more secure a baby's initiation into life, the freer that baby is to respond, absorb, explore, and learn.

- Doulas, midwives, and birth assistants along with preschool and nursery school directors and staff are wonderfully insightful people who are well seasoned in child and parenting challenges and who can recommend parenting resources in your community.

- Make a list of experts, caregivers, and role models in and beyond your family to consult as needed, such as physicians, friends, and neighbors, along with their contact information. Keep a list of resources for every sort of infant need or issue, and add to it over time.

- Much parenting information is available online. Keywords to use in searches on babies and parenting include "enhancing bonding and attachment," "what babies really need," "the family as a social nervous system," "body morphology and life experience," and "attunement."

- Many somatic techniques are available and can be adapted for babies' healing, including energy field therapy (EFT), body brushing, and baby massage. Do an online search for "prenatal and birth therapy" for more, and check out the Resources section at the end of this book.

- Remember that once your child is born, she or he has only you to know and trust. And you are the one who knows your child best.

Trouble

～

STAGE 2. EARLY CHILDHOOD

Age	Virtue Instilled	Psychosocial Crisis	Significant Relationship	Existential Question	Significant Issues
1–3 years	Will	Autonomy vs. Shame and Doubt	Primary Caregivers	Can I be me?	Mobility, Toilet Training, Mastering Skills, Asserting Independence, Learning Limits, Gender Identity

THERE WAS NO way to know we were heading for trouble. Behind us in his car seat, a big, blue-eyed boy sat strapped in and secure, his second birthday just a few days before. As we passed a dilapidated gas station on this rural road, from behind I heard a few sounds I'll never forget: "Tuh . . . eckks . . . aah . . . ckk . . . ohhhhh."

Oh, no! Had little Jon actually read that dented old sign? I sat stunned in the front passenger seat, hoping fervently that nothing had changed while knowing otherwise. Meanwhile, beside me Dad drove on in silence, his eyes locked on the road, seemingly oblivious to what had just happened.

I was undone, boggled—totally unprepared for what I had just learned. My brain huddled around this revelation while I sat still and quiet, eyes focusing straight ahead. No way could I face, much less acknowledge, what just happened or what it meant. Maybe my husband couldn't, either.

For the truth was, Dad and I were both lucky to have finished high school. How could *we* have produced him? The intellectual gulf separating us from him was far greater than a backseat away.

Suddenly, all the problems we'd encountered since his birth began making perfect sense. I had been so worried that he was autistic, crazy, or worse. But now Jon had just made it clear. All this time, he was simply way, way above average.

Already I could look back and see some of the clues I didn't pick up—like the most recent one, right after his birthday party. Early on, our pediatrician had cautioned me not to even think about potty training Jon until he was two years old, or "you'll just be training yourself." Hours after his super-duper second birthday party attended by doting family members on both sides, neighbors, and all their children, I cleaned up the house as I worked up my nerve. After towel-drying my hands, I approached this very big little boy of ours. He looked up with a face still smeared with chocolate cake, vanilla ice cream, and pink Hawaiian punch.

"Jon, you're such a big boy now, you don't have to go potty in your diapers anymore. You can go like Daddy does, in the toilet from now on."

Those searchlight blues connected with my own. After a beat or two of silence, he piped up.

"Oh. Okay," he said.

I didn't realize it, but at that moment Jon was trained. We went to his room, and I took off his diapers and put on training pants, assuring him as much as myself, "Wow. You really are a big boy now!" An hour later, without him saying a word or me offering a single prompt, he walked into the bathroom by himself. When he came out, he glanced over at me, shy but proud—so grown up now, just like Daddy.

And with that, Jon mastered the core, usually prolonged, and potentially traumatic developmental task of every child at this age. Jon was potty trained. There had not been a single slip since then.

Little did I know that a different, lingering wound would be inflicted a few months later.

We had just sold our house on the West Coast and were moving across the country to Texas, overjoyed since Daddy had just gotten hired to his dream job. After seven years of marriage, we had two adorable, sweet, and very much wanted little boys, and together in our old Bel Air station wagon, we were on our way to a beautiful new house, an exciting career for Dad, and a comfortable life for all. Jon was just two, and baby Alan had been born six months before.

We had just the teensiest problem. Little Alan liked nothing better

than to bang his head against the headboard while going to sleep. Thump
—Thump—Thump. When it first began, I brought him in to our pediatrician. Worried, I told the doctor all about it. "There's nothing wrong with
him," the doctor pronounced matter-of-factly. "Some babies just like to do
this. It feels good. All he'll hurt is what he hits."

I was so relieved. So much fretting for nothing! Rocking forward and
back did seem to soothe and settle Alan to sleep.

But ever since the move, Alan did seem to bang harder. Was it insecurity, or was he just bigger and stronger? The crib's hinges were coming
loose and creaking.

Deep in the night I awoke to the sounds of Alan's banging. He'll go
back to sleep, I thought, beginning to doze off.

Not my husband. Apparently he'd awakened too. Naked, he leaped out
of bed and took off down the hall. The determination in those footfalls
woke me. Hazily, I sat up and a moment or two later started after him
while pulling on my robe.

Then the screaming began. I flew down the hall, past our huge sunken
living room with cathedral ceiling and Spanish chandelier. A Texas neighbor had given us an old bullwhip, which I had turned into art by arranging
it decoratively on the wall in a bow to Texas longhorn history.

Daddy must have gone in and ripped it off the wall. Running toward
the door to Alan's room, I watched in horror as my husband reared back
and lashed, once, then again and again, while I heard little Alan scream.
My voice rose above Alan's: "No, no! NO! NOOOOOO!" Through the
doorway, I saw little Alan cowered in a crib, screaming, turtled in his thick
blue blanket sleeper.

For two time-suspended seconds, I hesitated. The man could kill us all.
Just down the hall, his treasured guns lay racked and ready. If I thwarted
his rage by snatching my baby and fleeing, would a gun be his next choice?
Pushing past him as he flicked the whip back for another lash, I ran in.
Scooping up Alan, I pivoted as another crack sounded, feeling my shoul-
der burn. Keeping my back to the whip, I fled past him out the door.

The room next door was Jon's. There, framed in his doorway, two-year-
old Jon stood in his yellow cowboy print pajamas, wide-eyed. Had he seen
everything or just heard the commotion and gotten up? Passing by with

Alan, I huffed, "Go back in your room, Jonnie. Lock the door and go back to bed now!" Scuttling past him into the room next to it, our extra room, I banged shut the door and locked it.

Everything suddenly went horribly still. Terrified, I switched on the ceiling light and, holding my baby tight, listened at the door, ready to wedge a chair or my whole back against it to keep it shut if necessary. Still holding Alan, I glanced over him, looking for wounds.

Alan's big blue eyes stared out of a blanched, pearly little face.

Hearing nothing, seeing nothing, after some minutes I walked shakily to our unmade guest bed and almost collapsed as I sat down. Carefully I laid little Alan out in front of me and clicked on the table lamp. My hands shook as I unsnapped his blanket sleeper. Checking every inch of his body, I found no lacerations or red marks. His sleeper, diapers, the crib rails—all must have helped protect him from the whip, if indeed the whip was aimed at him. Even if it wasn't, what had just happened was insane. Unimaginable. Brutal. My body couldn't stop vibrating while I focused on my baby.

He too was trembling. Snapping him back up to keep warm, I held him close, murmuring my love, saying he was safe, that everything was okay now—though that was a complete lie. A sudden exhaustion swept through me. Weak and shaky, I lay down next to him, face to face, snuggling together. The mattress felt like ice, but it was all we had. We weren't leaving—not for anything. Keeping the lights on, I lay motionless but wide awake while I held, caressed, and nursed him. My blood still pounded.

Alan's wide-eyed look began to droop as he succumbed to the milk and warmth and closeness, and finally he drifted off to sleep. That's when I could let myself go, and I softly cried. Everything seemed raw—surreal and cold. There was no sleep for me, only keening over all that was lost this night.

In shock, overwhelmed from rescuing and now comforting my baby son, I didn't think that the very next room held another solitary, shocked, scared, and confused little boy. Two-year-old Jon's searchlight eyes stayed wide open too, his mind full of this night's terrors. Though in turmoil, he kept still and quiet as he'd been told to, terrified lest he'd be next. He adored his daddy. Is this what daddies do? Jon's worries and feelings whirled around and around his empty room. He had no one to hold him, keep him safe, calm his fears, or answer his questions. When he finally did fall into a fitful sleep, scary nightmares woke him. But Jon couldn't call out or go get comforted like he always could before. Mommy had told him not to, and besides, it was far too scary now.

The sun rose to no warmth or brilliance. I got up, careful not to wake my sleeping baby. Opening the door inch by quiet inch, I listened. Hearing nothing, I carefully padded out and closed the door behind me to look like it was still locked.

A gray, strange world came into focus—a new life. Something in me seemed gone. I felt drained, wary, trusting nothing. What would my husband be like when he awoke? Like the monster of last night or the daddy we knew and loved? What could I trust about him now? About me? About us?

Cat-footing barefoot down the hall into the living room, I saw that the bullwhip had been put back up on the wall. Stripping it off, I carried it out the back door and over to our neighbor's garbage can, lifted the lid, and buried that ugly thing down deep.

Good thing Jon is only two, I thought. Although I didn't know how much he had seen, he and Alan were lucky. They were too young to remember this night. My job was to help them forget it. They needed to love their daddy, not fear him. Nothing like this had ever happened before. Hopefully it never would again. I felt shaky and confused. All I knew was that right now, we just needed to survive. In time, after my brain unfroze and I could think, I hoped to have more perspective to know what to do.

When my husband walked into the kitchen, he acted as if nothing had happened. Of course. From the beginning, his unspoken rule with me was No Problems Allowed. Any hurt feeling, question, or issue I brought up just guaranteed an instant, outsized pushback. There could be nothing to discuss. If I wanted to keep the peace and stay safe, I had to shut up.

For everyone's sake, I did. Besides, who would I call for help? We were new to this city, this neighborhood. I had no idea who to trust or where to start.

In the days to come, when my husband sat down for breakfast or dinner as usual, I couldn't bring myself to look at him or go near. Instead, I stayed at a distance, focusing solely on my sons, gently speaking to them, feeding them, caring for them, cleaning up. In this way we continued on, pretending nothing had happened. With so much at stake, I hoped our family could survive this shocking episode.

Yet for me, nothing could be the same. Though no more violence occurred, I could neither trust him or tolerate him near. Every entreaty of mine to seek counseling he'd scoff at, refuse, or punish. Living suspended in this holding pattern, circling a nightmare moment with no relief or recourse, took its predictable toll. My love was gone, our marriage over the moment my husband grabbed that bullwhip. It would take two more years and another move back to our West Coast hometown before I felt safe and stable enough to separate from him and then, six months later, finalize our divorce.

Eighteen years later, Jon, now twenty, arrived home from university for Christmas vacation. In the kitchen that evening, we talked as we usually did while I prepared dinner. Now towering over six feet, Jon gazed down at me from across the counter. His smile seemed slight and twisted. Through oversize glasses, searchlight blue, knowing eyes looked down at mine.

Lightly he said, "Remember when Dad bullwhipped Alan?"

My breath caught. With one simple question, Jon outed me. The secret I thought I'd protected him and his brother from all those years was not forgotten. He'd known it since he was two!

Yes, he had seen and remembered it all, even to accurately classifying the weapon as a bullwhip.

Hoarsely, I pumped back, "Why do you think I divorced your father!"

We never spoke of it again.

Erikson's Stage 2:
Autonomy vs. Shame and Doubt (1–3 Years)

From one to three years of age is Stage 2 in Erikson's staircase of human development, with its core crisis of autonomy versus shame and doubt. Now a child can walk and talk and has the dexterity to eat, dress, play, and freely move about. All this is heady stuff for one who since birth has been utterly dependent on others for day-to-day survival and well-being.

Finally, children can begin satisfying their own needs for comfort and connection. They begin learning how to negotiate a previously inaccessible world, and as they do, they start to discover who they are and what they can do in it. Stage 2 catapults a child into selfhood or, as Erikson phrased it, "individuation."

In Stage 2 children begin testing limits and rules while exploring a whole universe of options. They try hard at each new challenge, like taking a first step or manipulating a new toy, until they finally succeed. How thrilling it is to become more able—to sit, stand, walk, eat, drink, speak words, help out, and be understood! As long as they are in a safe, bounded environment with parents or caregivers at hand to monitor them, this testing and exploring should be encouraged, for the core crisis of this stage is autonomy: learning to do things for themselves. They begin basic self-care and learn to use the toilet.

Meeting each new challenge, they feel successful and good about themselves. Their core sense of intrinsic worth and goodness grows. Parents and caregivers can support their growing sense of confidence by letting them share small tasks or run in-house errands while marking with sincere appreciation every good effort and small success.

Because at this age children begin to internalize the gender identity of the parent they will grow up to be like, they are unconsciously absorbing what they can from the role model before them. While playing with playmates they may practice the characteristics they see displayed by this parent. The more loving, tolerant, wise, and consistent each parent—especially the same-sex parent—acts toward others, the more seamlessly the child absorbs and reflects those same qualities. The more the same-sex parent reflects negative attributes, the more conflicted children feel about acquiring and mirroring those qualities and the more they will tend to react against them.

Being free and willful in Stage 2 means that children at this age will begin to resist when they encounter barriers to carrying out their will. As any parent knows, this resistance is often long, agonized, and vociferous. Testing limits and throwing tantrums is normal. It is to be expected of someone who has just begun to explore on their own and is finally able to satisfy their own needs. As they pursue their own will, they resist being thwarted, are easily frustrated and begin to say "no," thus beginning the essential lifework of discovering who they uniquely are.

All this testing of limits means that sometimes the child's efforts will succeed and other times not. It takes a lot of trial and error to finally succeed, so making mistakes and experiencing frustration are inevitable.

However, as Erikson noted, the danger of experiencing failure at this stage of development is that it can, if prolonged or if others dwell on a child's failures, feed a child's inner sense of shame and doubt. Shame is that deeply repressed dread that everyone recognizes, the annihilating feeling that "I am bad, defective, ruined, unworthy." Shame is about who I am, stripped naked and revealed as fundamentally flawed, worthless, or contemptible. This, of course, is never, ever true.

Shame stops us in our tracks. When shamed by another, we freeze— our body halts, our chin and eyes drop. Physically, we sag. We don't stand up straight or make eye contact. It's as if we've been exposed as a fraud, found suddenly worthless or unlovable. Continual shame can erode our will to live. It feels intolerable. Left unresolved, shame will lead a child to doubt himself or herself—to sense something deeply wrong in one's core and to think, "I am not worthy of love." The child may even wonder, "Do I deserve to live?" Shame creates depression, inertia, and apathy. Children who suffer it either stop trying or, conversely, act it out by being bad or worthless. Either way, shame creates a self-fulfilling prophecy: I'm no good; I'm bad or worthless.

Yet what is wrong is never the person himself or herself. Though children can certainly feel some level of shame for certain inappropriate actions, it is never true that the child is inherently bad. It is never okay to send out shaming messages, and it is never useful to internalize them. Nothing is "the awful truth about who I am." Buying in to shame only does unwarranted, long-term emotional harm. Children of all ages need support to avoid being vulnerable to shaming messages.

Keep in mind too that at this early stage of life, children's brains are naive and only partly developed. Even though the brain expands to 85 percent of its full size by the age of three to contain all this new knowledge of words, things, and relationships, its ability to process that knowledge is still primitive. Children in Stage 2 think in black-and-white terms. They take words as the literal, forever truth. Things are either always or never, on or off, yes or no, all good or all bad. It takes many years and a lot of experience to rewire the brain to better comprehend the subtlety, emotional complexity, and interrelatedness of life.

Because a child's immature brain is wired to think in extremes of either all right or all wrong, a child in Stage 2 is likely to be overly buoyed by success or utterly devastated by failure. If a child's caretakers or siblings tend to be harsh, critical, or dismissive, such responses are taken literally, which can reinforce and intensify a sense of shame until it is intolerable or even erodes the child's will to live.

That is why children at every age, especially at this one, need to be believed in, loved, and supported through every tantrum and failure. Much better to redirect the child's attention away from some mistake and toward what they learned from it, what they might think or do differently next time, or better yet, what they did do that was right. Take every opportunity to instill inner confidence. Confidence builds resilience and a positive attitude, both of which strengthen a child's ability to overcome adversity and deepen their faith in themselves and in life.

Jon in Stage 2

Jon had successfully grown far beyond his birth issues of pain and trust. Although his body still shied from touch, now at two years old and past the tantrums of six months back, he was a fine, social little boy, truly happy and thriving. For him, toilet training was an effortless step forward in autonomy. With no trauma or error, Jon was handily negotiating the task Dr. Erikson originally defined as this age's primary developmental challenge. Jon was an ever-more inquisitive, able-bodied free agent, busy roaming, learning, and exploring. He was growing into his own power—crawling, standing, walking, running, cooperating with others, and practicing power words such as *no*. Being bright, trusting, responsive, and verbal made it easy for him to follow directions perfectly, which rewarded him with more self-esteem and gained him more autonomy from his parents, who stood nearby witnessing and praising him every step of the way.

Though Erikson focused this second developmental age on the event that most clearly defines a child's movement toward autonomy, toilet training, for Jon that issue was instant and untroubled. Instead, he experienced a different trauma in Stage 2. He witnessed a violent, shocking episode with no one to be there with him, to protect or help him cope.

When he witnessed the bullwhip incident, Jon had to feel as terrified as tiny, screaming Alan and I both felt. But he was left all by himself in his closed bedroom. If I, an adult, was shocked and paralyzed, unable to make sense of the raging Mr. Hyde that the husband and father I loved had suddenly turned into, the problem was compounded for little Jon. He now knew he was a boy like his daddy. Is this what little boys grow up to become? From that moment on, the two adults Jon was supposed to trust and love colluded in pretending that nothing bad had happened when Jon knew perfectly well it had. He was left in shock, holding critical, scary jigsaw pieces that did not fit. He was left with a discontinuity, a tear in the fabric of his known reality. Whom could he trust now? Not Mommy, who shut him away and never ever mentioned it again, or Daddy either, the one he saw turn so scary, the daddy he adored and trusted and would grow up to be like.

Shock immobilizes us. We are left stuck in a moment of danger. Without help, unable to feel safe, some part of Jon remained stuck at this age. From age 2, Jon was stranded with a nightmarish, torture-chamber image of his idolized daddy lashing a bullwhip toward Jon's screaming baby brother. To heal this trauma, Jon needed help, as did the whole family.

It was my responsibility to get that help, since my husband was the one who had acted out of control. But I too was in shock and confused, with no one to talk to. Up to that moment, I had been fully committed to this relationship. But now I didn't know what to think, much less say or do. We had one car. There were guns at hand. If I called the police—twenty miles away—would my husband escalate? He had grabbed a bullwhip. Would a gun be next? In shock, confused and intimidated, I stayed silent. I opted to deescalate and to buy time, hoping nothing like this ever happened again and we might weather this storm.

At the time Child Protective Services was in its inception, and we still lacked a clear definition of abusive behavior, let alone any safe, accepted way of reporting it. Also, divorce in 1970 was much rarer than today. To this day, I cannot know whether doing something different might have worked or made things worse. But I am forever sorry for the choice I made then. I remained silent, and in doing so, I defaulted as a mom. My silence stranded two-year-old Jon and exacerbated all that happened later.

Jon emerged from Stage 2 traumatized, left with a burden of doubt—doubt about whom or what to trust and doubt about what he would grow up to be like and do. As Erikson saw, core crises that resolve in a negative way leave a psychological residue that the child carries forward in life. The doubt and shame that Jon accrued in Stage 2 compounded the traumas that happened later and decreased his chances of navigating those crises successfully. Leftover shame hampered his forward momentum.

Daddy's Own Story from Stage 2

As research shows and trauma experts such as Bessel van der Kolk clarify, those who victimize others are likely reenacting some early but repressed experience of being a helpless victim. A child who is traumatized with no way of healing the trauma stores those raw emotions deep within so that they remain hidden explosives, ready to detonate much later in life. If the person later encounters a situation that triggers those same volatile emotions, the raw, buried feelings explode into the present, and the person will act out that earlier trauma either as victim or, as an adult, more often as the perpetrator. At the time this happened, what no one, not even Daddy, knew was that he had just acted out of his own frozen psyche. He had perpetrated on our six-month-old a trauma similar to one he himself had suffered when he was just a toddler.

Many years later my husband's aunt told me this story. My husband, Cal, was two years old when he met his father for the first time, a tall, hardened soldier returning home from the Pacific killing theater of Guadalcanal.

One morning soon after Dad arrived, Mom noticed two small black, ingrown warts growing on the bottom of little Cal's right foot. She was about to call the doctor when her husband stopped her.

"In Guadalcanal we don't need doctors to take care of little things like this. Go boil a pot of water," he told her. Mom's sister, Sophie, visiting that day, looked on, nonplussed. When the water boiled, Dad took the pot and set it on the kitchen floor in front of his little son.

"Put your foot in that water," Dad commanded. Stunned, the little boy glanced up to find his huge father glaring down at him. Terror mounted, and he began to wail. "You stop crying and do what I say, or I will shove it in there myself!" Dad threatened. Screaming, the boy twisted violently while his dad held him down. "Shut up and do what I say," Dad hissed.

Behind them, his mom wept helplessly. Her sister, horrified, cried, "Frank, no! Stop this!"

Dad took the child's foot and forced it toward the pot. Suddenly the boy's aunt swooped down, grabbed the screaming child, lifted him out of harm's way, ran into the bedroom, and slammed the door, locking the two of them in.

"You bring him back here this minute!" Dad raged through the door. "This is my house and my kid and none of your business!" But Aunt Sophie leaned hard into the door, holding her little nephew tight and murmuring calming words. The house fell silent. Then she heard a car rev to life and tires screech and fade away. They were safe.

But for that little boy, nothing could ever be okay again. His daddy was huge, fierce, terrifying, and in total control. He must do all Daddy said or be boiled alive. Now he knew that Mommy couldn't protect him, so from that moment on he reflexively obeyed his father's orders: Don't cry, don't feel—no matter what—or I will kill you.

That little boy would grow up to be handsome, highly competitive, and charismatic but emotionally callous. He was loyal and laughed well and often, but he showed little concern for others' plights. Unknowingly, his lack of feelings were symptoms that he was one of the walking wounded. Within him lived an explosive set to detonate, and when it did, he would reflexively reenact his childhood trauma, taking the adult role of his father, the role of torturer or persecutor. The trauma of war passed directly from father to son, reenacted the night a young father seized a bullwhip and cracked it toward his baby boy. Unconsciously he kept acting it out in our marriage as well, making me do what he had been forced to do at two: shut up, forget my needs or feelings, and obey.

At the time, I loved my husband deeply, and though I knew something was wrong, I never knew what it was. I also did not know that without help, his wound would only fester. Now, many years later, I am a professional therapist who understands the story of trauma. A wise friend once told me, "All we ever see is love. Whatever doesn't look like love is simply a cry for love." Applying that understanding to this moment, Cal was unconsciously and nonverbally crying for love—in effect, showing "this is what happened to me!" He was reflexively taking his father's role, acting out his father's rage and his own victimization, triggered by our six-month-old baby's head banging.

Yet trauma does not have to travel down from parents to children, generation after generation. Victims of trauma, as well as those who perpetrate a trauma, can find healing for themselves and their families.

Healing Trauma as Soon as It Happens

Traumatic events, like the scene with the boiling water, can leave children (and adults too) deeply affected with feelings of guilt, inadequacy, fear, anxiety, and depression. But we now know that after a child experiences trauma, a caregiver can reduce or prevent long-term damage by giving immediate and knowledgeable care. Research shows that our bodies are ingeniously designed to move us into and out of traumatized states quite rapidly. If we are aware of how the process happens, we can address the trauma right away so that it does not fester.

Our brainstem is in charge of survival, and whenever an event feels life-threatening, the brainstem switches to the "danger" position. This increases the production of stress hormones, providing the adrenaline for fight or flight. When we again feel safe, the brainstem switch flips back to "safety." Flipping the switch back to "safety" is fairly simple to do right after a threatening event, and it is still possible, though more challenging, later in time. However, the intelligence of the brainstem is nonverbal and operates beyond our consciousness, so we need to "talk" to it in ways it understands: through the body.

After imminent danger, it is important to let the whole body discharge the experience by physically shaking out the distress. Animals often shake themselves after some unpleasant or threatening encounter, as anyone who has lived with a dog has seen, and that's how human bodies too release the effects of a scary experience. Taking a few moments to just shake the experience out of the body helps a traumatized child (or adult) release the trauma and reinhabit their own normal body.

Equally important is receiving healing and soothing touch, such as stroking, rocking, and being held close. Mothers and fathers around the world soothe their children in these ways every day. The brainstem associates these experiences with safety and calm and switches off the stress hormones. For instance, because I stayed with Alan, holding and caressing him, nursing him, and verbally soothing him, he never showed any lasting emotional effects from what was, for him, a life-threatening incident.

Healing Post-Traumatic Stress Disorder (PTSD)

If the nervous system is not able to be stabilized immediately, traumatized children and adults can develop PTSD. Yet even the negative effects of PTSD can be minimized and healed. Post-traumatic stress disorder is a long process that typically has four stages: (1) surviving; (2) latency/reenacting; (3) recovering memories; and (4) understanding and healing.

1. Surviving. Typically, right after a trauma we go numb, because this is the perfect prescription for simply surviving. We may purge the traumatic memory from consciousness because the experience is too overwhelming and scary to be comprehended or dealt with—yet. This is not the time for emotional or logical processing. There is no safety yet, no way to know all the information or have the maturity needed to resolve what just occurred.

2. Latency/Reenacting. The second stage of trauma is the reenacting period. Here the raw memories remain latent, tucked deeply away, stuck in the past until some future time when the body finally feels safe—far enough away from the painful events and mature enough to release the memories. Meanwhile, the body retains the memory of what happened and though unaware, the person may act out the trauma. They may damage others' property, disrupt the peace, or violate the rights of others emotionally, sexually, or physically. Or they might "act in" against themselves through depression, drug addiction, anorexia, overeating, cutting or burning the body, compulsivity, criminality, hyperactivity, mental illness, or suicidality. The body itself is communicating, apart from all conscious awareness, that "something terrible happened to me, and I need help."

Hurt people hurt people. This is the stage where the pain is passed forward while its true origin remains unconscious. This reenacting stage is also known as the latency period and can last anywhere from a short time to decades or the rest of one's life. So this is the stage that can be shortened by reading the signals and responding correctly—with love rather than with a diagnosis, punishment, imprisonment, or forced medication. Every reenacting of trauma is a cry for love, and those who recognize the behavior for what it is can treat the enactor with compassion. This is the only way the person can move toward healing—by receiving the love and attention and understanding that were so brutally interrupted when the trauma itself occurred.

In Dr. Zunin's 1897 sourcebook *Contact: The First Four Minutes,* he notes how the Bantu "Bemba" tribe deal with wrongdoers. The whole tribe gathers in a circle around the problem person. Then every person in the perimeter speaks, one after the other, testifying to something they value about the person in the center. They go around and around, reminding the person how good, appreciated, loving, useful, creative, important, powerful and unique she or he really is, until hours have passed and there is no more to say. Then they all celebrate that person back into the tribe. This is communal restorative healing, a cry for love fully responded to with love. This is how a transgressor can be restored back a positive relationship with the self and simultaneously with the whole community.

3. Recovering memories. The third stage of trauma is the beginning of true healing, when split off memories of the trauma return, often in dreams or flashbacks. Each flashback or recovered memory, in order to be healed, requires connecting with others—sharing what is bubbling up, expressing feelings, coming to terms with it all, and integrating these repressed memories into the person's life story. It must take place in a safe climate of compassionate listening and caring, with the clear understanding that this is the beginning of resolving the trauma.

Each traumatized person experiences this stage of recovering memories differently. To some it feels like an ambush. Against their will, clues bubble up—in dreams or nightmares, in intrusive thoughts or images. Often people feel terrified and wonder if they are going crazy. Actually, the truth is the opposite: the body is sensing that it is finally safe and the person is mature enough to remember. The process is one of putting repressed jigsaw pieces back into conscious memory so the bearer can finally know his or her full story and return to sanity—whole, aware, and empowered.

Putting together at least a basic outline of the memories is critical so that the person understands why they have been hurting themselves or others. Up to now, their impulses and hurtful actions seem to be "just who I am." In the third stage of PTSD, people finally begin to realize "that's not who I am. That's just what happened to me." They have been simply acting out a traumatic shock that took place earlier in life. Once this becomes conscious, they can make a choice: whether they will continue reenacting the problem and hurting themselves and others, or whether they will face the original wound in full, grieve what happened, integrate that experience into their life story, and consciously choose to respond from now on to their own benefit and the benefit of others.

4. Understanding and healing. The fourth stage of trauma is where what happened is fully known and understood so that it no longer controls the person's life by being expressed unconsciously. Bringing the painful memories to awareness and feeling the feelings associated with them can avert maladaptive responses. If the behavior does recur, it can be halted quickly or even prevented. Or, if damage is again done, it can be repaired and sincere restitution made. Making trauma fully conscious and grieving any residues of the past allows the person to move quickly toward a more healed future. Knowing what really happened gives the person power to cherish the child they were at the time and appreciate all it took to survive. Then the child can begin to make peace with what occurred in the past. Now the person has the ability to live free from the shackles of the past and consciously choose how to respond in the present, evolving into their best possible self.

The person might take steps to become involved again in life, to engage in physical, personal, and social activities that require being fully present. A few examples of healthy self-empowerment are taking up a new sport, such as yoga, kickboxing, soccer, or rock climbing; taking classes in mindfulness, communication skills, improv, or dance; learning new leadership skills; or volunteering to help others in some similar capacity, for example, aiding the homeless or veterans. The possibilities are endless, and they can be just the beginning.

What Did Our Family Need to Heal the Trauma?

As a family, we could have healed this trauma had we known how. What did we need to know?

We needed to know that all we ever see in this world is love or a cry for it. A traumatized soldier brutalizing his two-year-old son into cutting off all emotion is a cry for love. A dad bullwhipping a six-month-old is a cry for love. Me keeping mum for eighteen years is a cry for love. What does not look like love is a cry for love.

When Jon brought up the bullwhip incident that evening over the kitchen counter, it was proof that though nobody had ever spoken about this episode, the two-year-old Jon was so deeply affected that he'd carried it ever since. That too was a cry for love. He was asking me to help him resolve what had never been acknowledged. But I did not. I let him know that I divorced his father because of that incident, but then I shut up—again.

Please don't make my mistake. Open to that conversation in full. Ask questions, and answer them all.

In the case of our family, the healing process would have included a number of steps: restoring safety; talking about what happened; engaging the whole family in a quest for understanding; acknowledging and apologizing; and finally, grieving together and healing.

1. Restoring safety. Today, I would call the police as soon as I safely could, report the incident to Child Protective Services, take the boys, and leave immediately—to get myself and the boys to safety and to give me the time and space to figure out what to do next. The boys' father would then get the message that he is accountable—that this is too serious of an issue to simply pretend nothing happened. Asking for help can bring about miracles. I encourage anyone in a similar situation to keep asking for help until you find it.

2. *Talking about what happened in a healing environment.* We needed to bring the adults together in a safe professional setting, with a trained psychotherapist mediator and, for Jon (Alan being too little), a play therapist to help him work through what happened that night. Every person in a traumatized family must feel they are in a very safe place, or it remains far too dangerous for them to open up and tell their stories. Each member of the family needs to receive respect, love, and appreciation for doing this hard work of telling the truth about what happened. The truth really does set us free.

3. *Engaging the extended family in a quest to help the perpetrator recall the original trauma being reenacted*—again, with the help of trained therapists and mediators. Problems are usually embedded deep in the family history, and it's likely one or more family members has relevant information. Stories of the past need to be told to shed light on the perpetrator's tendency toward violence.

For example, the aunt who swooped a screaming toddler out of harm's way twenty-some years earlier helped me immensely by telling me her story. It was especially revelatory since the brutal young soldier-father, now my father-in-law, had grown into the wisest and kindest man I'd ever known. Her story showed that war can traumatize and pervert the best of people—but my father-in-law proved that none of that trauma needs to be permanent. Once this soldier was reunited with his loving wife and family, his heart eventually healed, and he grew into a resplendent human being.

To bring out the full story, family members might ask, "Do you recall anything that might have happened early on that may have been painful, shocking, or terrifying?" As the family does this, each person reintegrates the pieces of their own story, and the truth helps connect everyone; it can heal rifts and potentially reintegrate the extended family.

The process of uncovering pieces of family history will likely not be smooth. Talking about what happened is scary; it brings back all the stuff we in some way tried to leave behind. There are often family rules against airing dirty laundry or probing too far into the past. It is of utmost importance that we always recognize and affirm people for being rightfully scared. This is something new, and their fear is natural.

4. *Acknowledging and apologizing.* Once the stories are told, it's important for individual members to acknowledge the part they played and to apologize for actions or inactions that did not lead to healing. When each person knows what happened and why, each can take responsibility for their part.

For our family to heal, I needed to face the dysfunction I experienced in our marriage. By excusing my husband every time he treated me as a child instead of an equal partner, I misread all his cries for love. This choice guaranteed two things: that I and my sons would continue to suffer, and that these cries would likely get worse. And my husband would likely think that he was completely justified in cracking a bullwhip at a baby, with no memory of his own two-year-old trauma motivating this act.

By owning responsibility, family members renew themselves as a community, creating new kinds of relationships and new safe space in the family through their courageous honesty and love.

5. *Grieving and healing.* With the therapist's help, the family can grieve together for the harm that was done, feeling their feelings about the traumatic episodes and learning to hear and trust one another again. This can bring the family back together, reuniting them so they can collaborate in healing.

In this process, Jon could have begun to feel protected. He would have been able to speak his truth, hear the adults take responsibility for their actions, and grieve all that he had lost. In this way, Jon's split reality could have stitched itself back together again. His faith in himself and his own perceptions could have been restored, as well as his belief that the adults in his life could be trusted to act responsibly and keep him safe. The seeds of shame and doubt would not have taken root in his two-year-old self. The truth, once again, could have set him free.

After a family process of healing, tendencies toward violence or reenactment may still manifest, but they will decrease over time with loving attention, compassion, and rigorous honesty. What is vital is to not blame or judge the perpetrator, but to prioritize safety first, then work together to set healthy boundaries and to listen and understand. The person's behavior is a symptom of something else. What is being communicated? What is the true genesis? And then, family members can simply ask: Can we talk about it?

Every reenactment is an opportunity to move into greater understanding, love, and healing. No baby is born bad; no baby is anything less than a miraculous gift full of love, joy, and limitless possibilities. When repressed traumas are healed, a person who has spent a lifetime believing that their wrong behavior is simply "who I am" learns the truth about themselves: That they, too, are perfect miracles, and what behaviorally is going on are repressed early traumas acting out, trying to surface and be healed.

If Healing as a Family Is Not Possible

There may not be an opportunity for a family to experience healing all together. Relationships may be severed because of the trauma, as happened in our family. But Jon's casual remark that evening over the kitchen counter, when he acknowledged that he remembered what happened, provided an opening for healing. Such spontaneous moments do arise, and when family members understand the process of trauma and how to recover from it, healing can take place even years after the original episode.

What could I have done in that moment to restore truth, trust, and wholeness? Instead of answering briefly then dropping the subject, I needed to take Jon's lead and respond fully. "Nobody knew, back then, what to do about these kinds of terrible things that happened to us," I might have said. "We all carried these traumatic experiences within us. We tried to forget them and said nothing. There was no Child Protective

Services to call for backup, and most people didn't go to therapists. But now we do have these services and also know better."

I could have taken responsibility for my part. "I needed to protect you, and I didn't. I was wrong to not bring you with me. I was so busy rescuing Alan that I stranded you, Jon, and for that, I will always be sorry. You needed to feel safe and protected too. I now know I needed to have helped you so much more than I did that night."

It would be important to hear Jon's feelings about that night. I could have asked, "Can you tell me what that entire episode was like for you?" I might have let him talk and talk, and I could have listened. I might have asked what it was like for him when he woke up, what he saw at the door, how he felt then, and how he felt after he obediently went back in. I might have asked what it felt like the next day, watching how we acted and what that meant to him. How did he know the name "bullwhip"? And in the time since—did his feelings and thoughts change or stay the same?

When it was time, I could have offered more: "What your dad did with that bullwhip is never okay. Your dad couldn't remember it, but I now know he was reenacting a trauma that happened to him back when he was about the age you were then. He didn't deserve that terrible experience with his father, just as neither did you or your baby brother deserve what happened. Traumatic events can haunt us for the rest of our lives if we don't get help and do the work of feeling the pain and grieving what happened. The good news is that it is possible to heal traumas, and healing starts by acknowledging what happened. So thank you for bringing this up. It needed to come up a long, long time before. I'm curious to hear what you're feeling about all this, and what you're concerned about right now."

At the end, the most important thing to communicate would have been, "Jon, you did nothing wrong; Alan did nothing wrong. I am the adult and mom who did do something wrong by leaving you alone that night while rescuing only Alan. But something triggered your dad into reenacting a terrible scene something as terrible to him then as what we witnessed him doing to Alan. He does not remember what happened, but his body does."

It was important for us to talk about why neither his father nor I ever spoke of this incident again. "I was wrong to think I should not speak up, Jon. You needed to know, and we all needed to talk about this. I am so very glad you brought it up now so we can begin talking about it. I never for one instant thought you could or would remember, since you were only two when it happened, and I thought keeping quiet about it was the right thing. But you just proved me 100 percent wrong. I am deeply sorry for that mistake, and I know better than to do that from now on."

Resolving the Core Crisis of Stage 2

In Jon's case, severe trauma impeded his forward momentum in Stage 2 and left him haunted with confusion, shame, and doubt. But according to Erikson, the challenge of overcoming shame and doubt is the issue facing every one- to three-year-old, and parents and caregivers can do a lot to help children avoid or resolve self-doubt and instead grow into ever more confident autonomy.

In Chinese Five Element acupuncture, the color green signifies "wood energy"—the impulse of wood to grow unimpeded, straight up into the sunlight. Children ages one to three are full of green wood energy, rising quickly and expanding into their full potential. Cutting off wood energy, for the Chinese, is associated with the feeling of rage—rage at anything limiting a tree's upward impulse toward the light. Toddlers too, when denied their inherent forward imperative, erupt in frustration and rage. But the more children find they can freely rise, acting on their world in interesting and helpful ways, the more they develop the ability to tolerate frustration. They learn self-control and develop the determination to keep trying and to succeed. They keep moving toward autonomy instead of being impeded by rage, helplessness, shame, and doubt.

Parents, help your toddler rise. There are many ways to support toddlers in trying out their new capacities and exploring new territories. The more equitably children at this age are treated, and the more they are given their autonomy within safe limits, the more they learn to tolerate frustration, and the more they claim their independence.

The key is to allow toddlers to feel included in the decision-making process. Parents and caregivers can offer toddlers little choices, which gives them power. In a situation that is not negotiable, just state the requirement clearly, ideally well ahead of time so that the child has time to adjust and be more ready to cooperate. Share what you need from them in calm, simple words. This is far better than simply throwing up limits, which will likely inspire resistance and rage from the young child.

Toddlers can often be distracted from their frustrations and tantrums, not by parents promising some reward for good behavior, but by being creative. Perhaps offer a favorite toy or stuffed animal they have picked out beforehand, or involve them in fun, helpful or kid-friendly activities.

It is never necessary to argue with, punish, shame, or debate a toddler! It won't work, and there are productive ways to turn these moments into opportunities instead of limits. If the child continues to protest a boundary you have set, then without rancor or apology, simply pick them up and follow through while staying calm and matter-of-fact. Redirect their attention to something interesting, fun, or new to see or do. Otherwise, ignore these rants. Pay zero attention to their tantrums; for any attention, negative or positive, rewards the behavior. No coercion, threats, punishment, bargains, gifts, or guilt trips, please!

Then at a later moment, when the child is again able to hear, make sure to notice and verbally express your appreciation for every time they cooperate with you. In this way caregivers are helping the child to grow a tolerance for frustration. Instead of depending on instant gratification, the child builds their own ability to wait and to persevere until they reach the goals they seek. Then, of course, in words they can understand, share about what happened, and tell them why you did as you did, so they can understand and internalize important lessons they then carry forward on their own.

Not every effort the child makes will succeed. And any child who is exploring will hit limits and make mistakes. Mistakes are not bad. They are actually good and even necessary. They simply prove that we are at a new, interesting, and exciting learning edge. Discovering what the limits are or what doesn't work is essential in order to find out what does work and where it is safe to explore. Every day in life, each of us faces those unknown edges, so throughout life we are all inventors and pioneers, trying to reach past former limits and to solve each day's conundrums. Young children need to know that it is okay and normal to take little risks and to make mistakes. Without making mistakes and learning from them, we cannot participate fully in the flow of life—trying, learning, and thereby evolving into our full potential.

When a child makes a mistake, caregivers can prevent shame from taking over by neither punishing nor dramatizing the issue. We never link mistakes in any way to who the child is. Telling a child in Stage 2, who takes words as the literal truth, that "you are bad" or "stupid" or "no good" or "worthless" will only instill shame and doubt into the child, and it is never, ever true.

Any kind of labeling, especially at this stage of the child's life, works against their growing into autonomy. Even labels such as "cute" can infantilize and dismiss a child. Labels such as "bad" or "crazy" can create feelings of inferiority and inner chaos. The child can internalize a lack of worthiness, love, and trust that saps their energy and undermines their forward progress. A caregiver who calls a child crazy or stupid is really sending a message about themselves, beginning with the word I: "I don't understand you." Parents' judgments about their child say more about the parents than they do the child. The perfect label to call a child is simply their name.

Anything but openness to and full acceptance of the child's budding self will only undermine their progress and tarnish your relationship with them. So instead, listen, appreciate, support, and learn from your toddler. Lead to their strengths, accentuate the positive, and keep them safe. Welcome children into your life just as they are! Have fun, laugh, tease, play, share, be curious, and explore the world—together.

In the wild, if a baby is in danger, a mother animal may send messages of alarm from afar to stop their baby in their tracks. In a similar way, parents or caregivers can use alarmed or shaming tones only to stop a child from imminent harm. However, the moment danger is past, it is essential to rejoin the child—to hold and caress the child and wrap them in love and reassurance. Tell them they are perfectly fine and good and loved, and of course share your concern—how you needed them to stop to stay safe. (For more information, see the work of Keith Witt listed in the Resources.)

When a child does make a mistake, simply reassure them or help them remember their own inner sense of right and wrong. Using simple words, parents can even encourage a young child to reflect on what a mistake teaches that is useful, or they can redirect the child's attention to something positive.

In these ways, a child resolves the core crisis of Stage 2 in a positive way. "It's okay to be me!" a child learns in the ages of one to three, as they explore their world and grow into their own fullest potential.

—

Teachings, Airbags, and Safety Nets

- From one to three years of age, toddlers grow more able-bodied, willful, and goal directed. Their inherent core crisis, according to Erikson, is to fulfill this natural impetus toward autonomy.

- The danger of experiencing failure at this stage of development is that it can, if prolonged or if others dwell on a child's failures, feed a child's inner sense of shame and doubt.

- Shame is that deeply repressed dread that everyone recognizes, the annihilating feeling that "I am bad, defective, ruined, unworthy." Shame is about who I am, stripped naked and revealed as fundamentally flawed, worthless, contemptible. This, of course, is never true.

- Because a child's immature brain is wired to think in extremes of either all right or all wrong, children at this age are prone to be overly buoyed by success or utterly devastated by failure.

- Repeated harsh, critical, dismissive, or negating messages can intensify a child's sense of shame until it is intolerable or erodes the child's will to live.

- As long as toddlers are in a safe, bounded environment with parents or caregivers at hand to monitor them, testing and exploring should be encouraged, for this stage is all about autonomy—learning to do things for themselves and feel good about their process within safe boundaries under caregivers' loving supervision.

- Parents and caregivers can support toddlers' growing sense of confidence by letting them share small tasks or run in-house errands while expressing appreciation for every good effort and small success.

- Being free and willful in Stage 2 also means that children at this age will begin to resist or be frustrated when they encounter barriers to carrying out their will. It is normal and to be expected of someone who has just begun to explore on their own.

- Tantrums are often long and vociferous, but the key is to include toddlers as much as possible in the decision-making process. Tell toddlers your plans or expectations ahead of time so they can be ready to cooperate. Then simply remind them of that, and if they protest, pick them up and follow through without drama or debate.

- As needed, parents and others can distract very young children from their frustrations or tantrums not by promising some reward for good behavior but by being creative. Perhaps offer a favorite toy or stuffed animal they have picked out beforehand, or involve them in fun distractions or kid-friendly activities.

- Developing a tolerance for frustration and the ability to delay gratification are the twin keys to perseverance and ultimate success. These are built slowly over time. Parents and caregivers can help children reduce their natural need for instant gratification in favor of long-term successes and rewards.

- The more toddlers are treated equitably, and given their autonomy within safe limits, the more they learn self-control and are able to cooperate.

- Young children, like green wood energy, want to grow unfettered toward the light. Any limit or blockage is intolerable and will provoke rage. This is a normal part of infantile experience to develop through.

- This is the stage where they begin the essential lifework of discovering who they are, while we are also teaching them to tolerate frustration and be able to wait so they can persevere and eventually succeed.

- Believe your child first and always. Stay open. Be clear but kind. Keep your child within safe boundaries, and then let them explore in full, while you support them and withhold judgment.

- Listen to your children more than to experts. Resist labeling your children and treating them as something other than the fully human, miracle beings they are. Anything but openness to and full acceptance of their budding self will only undermine their progress, make them doubt themselves, and tarnish your relationship with them.

- Parents' judgments about their child say more about the parents than the child.

- If a child is in danger, simply stop them or redirect them as you can to something fun, interesting, or new. Once safety and calm are restored, tell them why, and reassure them of their inherent goodness and your unconditional love.

- Children are your teachers. So let them teach you at every opportunity! And express your appreciation in words every time. In every way, let them know they matter and are valued for who they are, just as they are.

- Assigning belittling "cute," "bad," or "crazy" labels can create feelings of inferiority and even craziness. Such labels are "I" statements meaning the same thing: "I don't understand you." So instead, listen, appreciate, support, and learn. The only right label is their name.

- Welcome children into your life just as they are! Have fun, laugh, tease, play, share, be curious, and explore the world—together.

- Teach children how to be safe and how to care for themselves, and they will appreciate you and take it from there.

- All we ever see is love or a cry for love. What does not look like love is a cry for love.

- The burden of pain left over from trauma can be healed and resolved.

- Every past trauma is carried and remembered by the body and will continue to be reenacted until the message is correctly heard, handled appropriately, and finally resolved.

- Victims of trauma tend to show what happened to them in a way that makes them feel powerful, often as the perpetrator. Bad behavior often communicates that "something terrible happened to me."

- In a situation of reenacting, first act to restore safety, get help, and restore calm. Together, in a climate of safety and openness, people can explore what the reenacting behavior is trying to communicate.

- The more trauma is unconsciously acted out, the more damage can be done to self and others.

- The only way to shorten the acting-out stage is to establish a climate of safety, trust, and openness, listening for feelings and needs instead of judging or criticizing.

- When our body feels safe enough to let go, bits of memories begin to bubble to the surface of consciousness. This is the natural time for healing to begin.

- Engage the whole family in a quest to help a loved one to recall the trauma being reenacted. Problems are usually located and embedded deep in the family story.

- Do what the Bemba tribe does: give the person total attention, telling the loving truth about them in a ritualized, nonjudgmental way. Help the one acting out to remember who they truly are by recounting all the specific ways they have been appreciated, helpful, and valued. Then, celebrate that person, back to their true self and to the whole community.

- Take responsibility for your part in a trauma, whether it is something you did or something you did not do. Make a promise not to repeat this behavior, and follow through. If you do repeat it, reflect on it as soon as possible and immediately repair the damage done. Taking responsibility helps everyone else be responsible and proves our trustworthiness to others.

- When addressing trauma in a family, each person openly shares their own perspective on the trauma. Each person describes their experience, feelings, needs, and preferences at each step. Each person shares what this opportunity has taught them.

- The healing process will likely not be smooth. It's scary. Recognize and affirm people for being rightfully afraid; this is something new, and fear is natural.

- Work with professionals whenever possible to heal and resolve trauma. The helpful professional is one who is compassionate and experienced in dealing with trauma and who can establish and maintain an atmosphere of safety and respect for each person involved.

Little, Cheap,
Red, and Plastic

~

STAGE 3A. YOUNG CHILD

Age	Virtue Instilled	Psychosocial Crisis	Significant Relationship	Existential Question	Significant Issues
3-5 years	Purpose	Initiative vs. Guilt	Family and Age-Mates	Can I do, move, and act on my own?	Selfhood in Family, Solo Exploring and Cooperative Play, Toys and Tools, Secret Erotic Feelings, Gender Preference

HE STOPS IN the doorway of his new upstairs bedroom as I am about to dip a brush into a little can of bright yellow paint.

"Yes?"

"Can I go meet new friends?"

Four-year-old Jon asks the question simply, looking up with huge blue eyes. His cheeks are rosy, his fine hair milk-thistle blond.

After two years in Texas, we had just returned to southern California, moving into this fixer-upper a little over a week ago. Jon is ready to explore. His old friends now live thousands of miles away from this sunny tree-lined subdivision. He does need to find new friends.

"Okay," I say then add, "but no farther than three houses away." That way he will stay in view. I've briefly met all the neighbors on either side of our little cul-de-sac, and I know he will be fine with them.

Jon smiles, turns, and disappears. I hear him bounce down the stairs and out the door.

I bend down to paint, glancing now and again out the window to watch him walk up to and knock on one door, then another. Everyone must be out on this bright March morning. The next time I look up, he is gone. Someone must have let him in, but who? Where? As the minutes tick by, my gut quivers with increasing anxiety. I'm such a catastrophist. It's needless, I'm sure.

Finally, finally, there he is! I take a deep breath and heave a sigh of relief. I check my watch. It hasn't even been twenty minutes. I focus again on lengthening a four-inch-wide, bright yellow pinstripe around his new two-toned green bedroom, just as Jon had specified.

Below, I hear our front door open then shut. Up come stair squeaks. I raise a spent paintbrush and twist toward the doorway to greet my little returning explorer.

Edging into the daylight framed by the door comes a face I know but no longer recognize. The smile on my lips freezes. This is not the boy who left!

His face is strangely blank, etched in whitest ivory. His blue eyes are dark as caverns, still as stones. Two small hands numbly clutch a few small items of garish, red cheap plastic—a coin carrier? Key chain? Grown-ups' junk—nothing for kids.

I stiffen. Dread and panic rise within. Holding a forgotten paintbrush, I face the boy I used to know. Suddenly the smell of paint is toxic. My gaze wavers and drops to those perfect little hands full of cheap plastic junk the color of blood.

Trying to sound casual, I pump out, "Where . . . did you . . . get those?"

I hear a dead monotone. "I . . . met a new friend."

"Does this friend have a name?"

". . . Tommy . . ."

"Why did Tommy give you these things?"

Jon looks down between our feet and through the floor.

"I'm . . . not supposed to tell."

Interior knots cinch tighter. Oh, no. Secrets. Inside, I feel paralyzed, but I must respond—swiftly. Jon's whole being, whole life, seems at stake. A roiling fury begins to boil from my depths, drowning out the quivering parts of me. Surging with power, I command Jon.

"Show me where this Tommy lives."

"I . . . don't want to."

Oh, God. He's so scared. That's the same fear that filled me just moments ago. But now boundless rage is ricocheting through me. Laying the brush across the can rim, I try to act calm. I drop to my knees, look into Jon's eyes, and take two cold, passive, cupped hands full of ugly red flags into mine. Together we will face what just happened until the truth is known.

"Jon," I begin softly but firmly, "I'm your mom. I love you. I know something's wrong, and it's about Tommy. Right now, you're going to show me Tommy's house. Tell you what," I say more gently. "We'll just walk along the sidewalk. When you see it, just tell me and we'll come right back home. Promise."

He stands, eyes downcast. Seeing him so still, so frightened, pumps me with even more resolve. Shucking my painting bib, I stand beside him and say encouragingly, "Come, let's go. We'll be back in no time." I take his hand and look down.

Jon stares at the blank wall, unmoving. Limply, he drags as I guide him down each stair and through our squeaky front door. Out on the porch, we stand. Suspiciously, I survey our cul-de-sac, which before seemed so safe and friendly. Somewhere—somewhere very near—is Tommy. Jon's dragging feet increase my resolve.

"Which way?" I ask firmly.

Hesitantly, Jon looks left. We start slowly, taking small, little-boy steps, past the first house, the second, then the third and corner house, continuing left around it until our house is blocked from sight. We have just passed safety, beyond my stated limit, but I don't think of scolding. Seven steps past the corner, Jon falters and stops. His hand pulls me back. I look at him. Jon's gaze seems fixed on something up ahead. Those big terrified eyes say it all.

My eyes follow his gaze. There, sprawled on the fourth house's lawn, is a young guy. He looks about sixteen or seventeen. Spiked hair. Sloppy T-shirt and jeans. Bristling with insolence, he deliberately stares us down. I meet that gaze and hold, instantly ready to tear him to bits without knowing why. Narrow, angry, eyes spit back defiance and hate.

Jon's hand is frantically tugging mine back toward home. I verify the address of the house and burn the young man's picture into memory. Only then do I accede to Jon. Deliberately executing a very slow turn, I begin walking Jon back around the corner toward home, murmuring to him all the way. "Jon, we're okay now, you've done the right thing. I know that was really, really hard and brave, but it was so important."

Back inside the safety of our home, I lock the door and try to relax, try to hold Jon close, but he recoils—from touch, comfort, love, and closeness. I let go. That face, so blank and still, terrifies me. I have no idea what to do.

"Sweetheart, you're safe," I begin tentatively, trying to sound soothing when I feel anything but. "I love you. What would you like? Juice? Food?" He just stands there. "Would you like to rest in my bed?" His room is still a construction zone. After a long moment, he nods with his head down. Upstairs, I gently tuck him in my bed with his stuffed turtle retrieved from his room. He turns with it in his arms and faces away. "Can I sit here with you? Get you some juice?" White-blond hair shakes no two times. "Would you rather nap alone?" Little bob up. I smooth that little silky platinum shock and say, "Okay, go ahead and rest. I'll be downstairs, a whole ten seconds away—if you need anything, I'm right here." I walk off slowly, leave the door ajar, head downstairs to the kitchen, pick up the phone, and dial 9-1-1.

"Something terrible just happened to my four-year-old son," I blurt to a female voice. "We just moved in. My little boy went looking for playmates. He returned not a half hour later, in shock, white as a sheet. . . . He won't say what happened, that he 'promised not to tell.' He just says he met a 'new friend' named Tommy. . . . Yes, I did—Caucasian, maybe sixteen or seventeen, brown spiky hair, oh, perhaps five-ten or -eleven. Four houses away from ours. I believe Tommy has done something terrible to my little boy. . . . No, I can't bear to ask—but I believe Tommy committed a terrible crime. What do I do?"

The dispatcher routes me to a special children's detective. I begin to repeat what happened, but he cuts in. "Just bring him right in to the police department. We'll take care of the rest." He promises to handle Jon sensitively. I hang up and spend a few minutes crying my eyes out. When I can, I wipe them, go upstairs, and look in. Jon is awake facing the other way, holding his green turtle. "Jon," I start apologetically, "I just spoke to the police. They need us to come in right now. They need to know what happened so they can make sure we're all safe and nothing like this happens again." I try to speak as tenderly as possible.

He doesn't move or seem to breathe. I go to the bed's far side so we can see each other. He looks past me. I say, "It's okay, Jon. I'll be with you. We'll take care of this together." This must be the last thing he wants to do, but I can't give him a choice. "If you like, take Mr. Turtle with you." I pull him upright, put his sandals back on, and, my hands in his, coax him to his feet.

We drive in silence—me, stricken and terrified, knowing he feels much worse. In silence we reach police headquarters and slowly walk up cold, wide gray stairs. The officer behind the glass tells us Detective Howe will be right out. She waves toward the backless bench behind us.

I talk to Jon some more. I repeat that it's okay to tell the police the truth. But when Detective Howe walks in, he insists on a private interview with Jon. I know Jon shouldn't face this man alone. I try to protest.

"Sorry, ma'am, this is procedure. Once we finish, I will bring him back. Then he stays and you come in, and I debrief you."

I am trapped. We can't get up and leave, nor should Jon be left alone again. How do I support my little boy through another trauma? "It's okay, Jon," I tell him. "I'll be right here. It's okay to go with him. He's exactly who you need to tell about what happened. I love you, sweetheart, and will be right here waiting until you get back."

The detective takes Jon's hand and leads him through the door. I watch Jon walk helplessly off as the heavy door shuts behind him. Every second drags on forever. Like a stone, I sit while my inside chews itself up. When the door finally reopens, my heart flies to a little boy who looks suddenly old—desolate and solitary. My God, he's barely four!

A female officer comes to sit down beside Jon. The detective faces Jon. "You did a great job just now, Jon. Thank you for all your help," he says while shaking Jon's little hand, then turns to me. "Come with me."

"Jon, I'll be back soon and we'll go home," I fling behind me as I numbly follow the detective through that door. He ushers me into a long, tiled room, empty but for a long wooden bench in the middle. Jon must have sat here before me. It's so cold, formal, and alien. He sits at one end. I sit in the middle.

"I am required by law to tell you the exact words and story your son told me," he begins officially.

Chilled, I stiffen. "I—I'm not sure I can do this."

"Sorry, ma'am, this debriefing is required," he says, then proceeds. The words spill out, one after another, like bullets from a machine gun.

"He brought Jon to his room and locked him in. He had a big, mean dog—"

I quail, twist, cry, "No! No!"

"—Jon was crying, kept saying, 'No. I don't want to.' . . . Tommy sits him in a chair in front of him and unzips his fly. He takes Jon's head in his hands. Jon tells me, 'I can't move. . . .' "

I crumple, cry, whisper, "Please stop—stop."

" . . . 'Do it or he tears you apart.' . . ."

My body twists off the bench. I hit the hard, cold tile and double up, choking. "Noooooo, nooooo, noooooo. . . ."

"Ma'am," he coolly continues after a short pause, "what I can tell you is that what your son told me is solid evidence that can and will be used against his perpetrator in a court of law, should you decide to press charges. Your son will not need to appear in court. I am convinced that Jon told the truth. His taped testimony is all the proof we need. It's enough to convict. We know this guy. He already has a long record of petty crime. If you press charges, I have no doubt he won't be around to bother anyone for a very long time."

Between sobs, I gasp, "I . . . definitely . . . want to press . . . charges. . . . How?"

"Jon's statement is enough. Just sign here. I'll fill out the report and arrest warrant later. You can take your son home now."

I walk back through the door, shattered. Jon sits on the bench with the detective. He looks up with relief and desperation.

"We've done the right thing Jon," I say shakily. "The police will take it from here. Let's go home."

Side by side, we walk out those ominous doors into bright sunlight. I strap him into his car seat and begin the drive home. "Jon," I start, trying to focus on the road through leaking eyes, "Tommy is very sick. Today, he tried to make you as sick as he is. But you're a fine and very good boy, and nobody—not he or anyone—can ever change that. I know who you are, and I love you. We all can choose to be either good or bad—that's always our own choice. Most people are just wonderful, but people as sick as Tommy is have to go away. They have to be kept far away from people so we can be safe and they can get the help they need to get better. And that's what you just helped the police do. Because of what happened today and because you told the truth—which I know had to be so very hard, but such a brave, important thing to do—telling the truth will now help everyone keep safe. We won't have to worry about Tommy scaring us and making children do awful things nobody wants to do, and Tommy will be taken to a safe place where he can get better."

At home we go to the kitchen, where I persuade Jon to drink some juice and eat a few bites of toasted peanut butter and jelly. Exhausted, Jon just wants to go to bed. Again, I gently tuck him into our king-size bed. How small and forlorn he looks! I caress that little head, murmur my love, then quietly leave the door open and head downstairs.

Now, only in the aftermath, I realize that I haven't called my husband, Jon's father. How can I ever erase what Tommy forced on my four-year-old boy? Every bit of this is my fault.

Tears rise, and everything blurs.

When breath returns and my eyes see again, I approach the phone. My fingers shake as I dial.

"Hallo," I hear him say genially.

"Hi, it's me. Something terrible has happened," I begin. Admitting it out loud is excruciating. Words come in halting bits between choked sobs, "Jon's . . . been . . . molested. . . ."

"I'll be there shortly," he snaps and hangs up. I gag, wipe my eyes, and try to breathe. Returning the phone to its hook, I surrender to the emotional tides as they rise and crash, rise and crash. Suddenly my husband bangs through the door.

"Where is he?"

"Upstairs, in our bed. Please stay down here. Let him sleep. He's been through such total hell. He needs to rest so bad."

Everything seems disembodied, eerie. Who am I? Who are we? How can we even go on?

Eyes pick up movement. Jon is making his way down the stairs.

"Hi, Jon," his father says. He gets up and in silence follows Jon into the dining room. Instead of giving comfort or a hug to his son, Dad says instead, "So, Jon, now you're going to become a homosexual?"

My eyes snap up at my husband, disbelieving. Jon glances up at his father, then back at me with kind of a dazed question. Jon does not understand the word *homosexual,* but he sure knows what Tommy forced him to do. Is Daddy saying now that he's going to be like that and do that to little boys when he grows up too?

Furious, I spit back, "No, of course not! Are you kidding? Not at all!" Bending down, I take Jon's little hands in mine.

"Jon, it's been a really tough day. Did you sleep a little?"

He nods, but his eyes don't want to meet mine.

"Good, honey. We love you so much. We're all together, home again and safe, and now it's time to eat."

Like an automaton, I put water on to boil, shake a little salt in it, then go fish a bag of spaghetti and jar of spaghetti sauce out of the pantry.

The days that follow feel forced and unreal. The unthinkable happened. I utterly failed to protect my little boy. My vibrant, four-year-old son came back dead, ruined.

"He'll snap out of it," is all my husband says every time I tell him Jon needs professional help. I am clear any argument is futile and sure to be punished. What can I do? I don't know, except to be there for my son, give him my full approval, show him how nothing on earth can touch or change the good, perfectly wonderful boy I know he is. I try to let him know how much I love him and believe in him, how dearly I hold him as precious.

But my own agony is growing. I begin staying up late at night cleaning up, watching TV, and sipping wine. Then I switch off the TV, curl up on the couch with a blanket, and pass out. I can't bring myself to go upstairs to bed, can't bear my husband's touch.

Dad acts like nothing is wrong.

Two weeks later I hear a knock on the door. I open it to see a young matron. "Hi, I'm Marielle, your neighbor in that house." She gestures down the street to a house facing our cul-de-sac. "My son David just met Jon, and we enjoy having him over," she begins. "They play so well together." Then her voice lowers. "Jon told us something bad happened with Tommy."

Surprised, I think, *Well, I never told him not to talk about it.*

Marielle looks at me imploringly. "The whole neighborhood has been terribly worried about Tommy. He's always been scary, a menace—a really scary kid. Please do something. So many of us here have young children, and we'd be so grateful to you. "

I stand there, thunderstruck. The neighbors knew about Tommy all along? So my child gets molested because nobody bothers to tell me about a known menace living only four doors away? Now these same good neighbors, who never warned me or did a single thing themselves about a real danger they all worried about, now want me to do what they didn't?

I want to wring her neck—all their necks. Instead, I look her straight in the eyes and speak low and deliberately. "Don't worry. Jon and I definitely have taken care of it. Tommy has been arrested, and the police assure me he won't be around for a very long time."

"Oh, thank you, thank you so much," she gushes. "We've all been so worried. . . ."

"No problem," I say, trying hard to keep the fury out of my voice, and slowly close the door in her face.

A month later a call comes from Detective Howe.

"Mrs. Raymond? Just called to inform you that Tommy was sentenced today—to three years in state prison. Jon's taped testimony was key in his successful prosecution. Please give Jon my appreciation and sincere congratulations again for being so courageous and telling the truth. I know how terribly difficult that was. But because he did, now a really bad guy won't be around to trouble him or anyone for a long time."

I thank him and say goodbye. I feel great relief, but no peace or comfort. Tommy did horrible damage—damage I don't know how to deal with. Jon has to live with these horrific and debasing memories. Tommy may be in the state penitentiary, but Jon is just as imprisoned by what Tommy did to him, and I am too.

Erickson's Stage 3:
Initiative vs. Guilt (3-5 Years)

It can happen just like this: the end of life as known and trusted. This devastating encounter occurred when Jon had just turned four, well into Erikson's Stage 3. During this stage, between the ages of three and five, children are curious and social beings, busy discovering who they are and what life holds for them during playtime and beyond. With new abilities and now new responsibilities, they are ready and eager to take initiative, testing their newfound autonomy and growing their intelligence and good sense in a slightly larger world than before.

Children's challenge at this stage is to think independently, decide on a course of action, and then take the initiative to venture forth on their own or with playmates to meet their own needs. The core questions needing answers are: Who am I out in the world? What can I think and do? Can I meet my own needs, make choices, and act in ways that help me succeed? Can I trust the world to be a good and safe place to grow into and discover more of who I am and what is possible, or do I learn it is not and must retreat instead? The more these questions can be answered in the affirmative, the freer and more resourceful the child grows, eager to meet others, interact, and pursue their goals.

The good news at this stage, Erikson pointed out, is that children are more ready to learn and grow than at any other stage. They possess a new moral sense and more mastery over their bodies and behavior, and together it all adds up to a strong sense of deep purpose: to learn and grow on their own. They take more initiative to fulfill their own needs at home and to begin moving out into a larger world. Naturally curious, they test their wings through playing out adult roles. They forever wonder and ask "why" to expand their understanding and push the limits set for them by their parents and caregivers.

But not all initiatives end well. And here is where the core challenge of

Stage 3 becomes clear. Erikson pointed out that the key danger to avoid in this stage is feeling overwhelming or chronic guilt about some situation that ended badly.

To be clear, not all guilt is unhelpful. A three- to five-year-old child becomes able for the first time to feel responsible for his or her actions, and guilt can be an internal corrective helping them do so. When we feel some guilt, it proves that we realize our thoughts and actions have consequences and that we care about how we affect others. Guilt can help teach us how to treat ourselves and others. It also teaches us what not to do, thus helping us learn how to cooperate, cultivate a welcome presence, and contribute to society.

The people who feel no guilt at all are most likely to be dissociated, disconnected from others' feelings and their own. This makes them more likely to become ego-driven and self-justified. The less empathy, guilt, or conscience, of course, the greater the likelihood of causing real harm to both self and others.

But when children instead feel overwhelming or chronic guilt, it can become excruciating. Or, if left unaddressed and then repressed, guilt can continue to flay and depress children from within. Even if guilt is unconscious, it lives on at a visceral level, as raw and crucifying as it was back at the moment it took root.

Guilt at this stage is subtly different from the shame that a child might have felt in the previous stage. In Stage 2, failing at or being prevented from becoming more independent feeds an inner sense of shame and doubt about "who I am." In part this takes place because when we are very small, with brains still undeveloped, we hold the naive, childish illusion that "I am the center of the world and the reason for everything." Failure at that stage leaves us feeling as though we are all bad, ruined, or fundamentally flawed.

Guilt, by contrast, is a slightly more discriminating feeling. At ages three to five, we know we are able to choose what to do or not do and that we have choices about how to act toward others. More and more, we realize we are not quite the center of the world, and so things that go wrong at this stage become not about *me* but about my *behavior*: what I did or didn't do that was bad or wrong or that did damage or hurt someone.

It is possible for a child to experience guilt in this stage added onto unresolved shame from the previous stage of growth. If this happens, the child can feel both fundamentally bad or unworthy and also guilty for having done something bad. When this happens, the child's sense of self can become extremely fragile, and the child may become confused or depressed, perhaps freezing in their forward development or acting out their "badness" in ways that harm others or isolate, hurt, or sabotage themselves.

Guilt can enter their experience also because in Stage 3, according to Erikson, children's genitals are "now energetically erotized." It means that between the ages of three and five, children discover their genitals and begin to explore them. Children may feel new and unfamiliar urges; they may experience naive erotic fantasies about their friends or siblings or parents. These are all normal things that a child usually keeps hidden and private, and their discoveries may be mixed with shame, guilt, and the terror of adult discovery and reprisal. At this age, a child usually has no concepts or words for any of this, and typically their parents are just as mute. So at this pivotal moment children are most often left to their own devices to navigate alone the first surging tides of immature and innocent genital sexuality.

Jon in Stage 3

By the age of four, Jon had made it through some very tough experiences and was just beginning to really flourish. He was bright, honest, curious, sweet, social, trusting, playful, and, as far as I was concerned, good as gold. He treated his baby brother well. He was doing everything right, becoming more independent, and feeling great. In our previous home, Jon and his little brother had hosted one or more of the neighborhood children almost every day, playing and creating magic moments together. Now in this new neighborhood, gregarious young Jon was lonely and needed new friends. He took initiative and asked for and received my permission to go out and seek them.

But in life everything carries some degree of risk, whether it's seeking new friends or doing nothing at all. In a new neighborhood, the risks rise. From the window I could monitor Jon's progress in the cul-de-sac with the neighbors I'd briefly met. I had never known Jon to disobey, and had I seen him head for the corner, I would have called him back or run after him. I have never forgiven myself for letting him out of my sight that day, for as a four-year-old child, he was entirely my responsibility.

All Jon did that day was walk one house too far and knock on a door. He went on his first foray out on his own a trusting, social, curious boy. That boy never returned.

If Jon carried any unresolved shame from his earlier experiences, he may have already lacked a solid sense of intrinsic worth. From here on, he could also feel shame and crucifying guilt about how he had been forced by Tommy to act in ways that exacerbated all doubts about his worth as a person.

Because his parents didn't seek help and could neither help themselves nor help Jon heal emotionally from this trauma, little four-year-old Jon was left completely alone to deal with his newly opening sexuality and the horrific shock of being sexually terrorized and violated. For a child in Stage 3, words are taken literally: either black or white, good or bad, right or wrong. When Tommy said, "Do it or my mean dog tears you apart," Jon was paralyzed. His child's mind believed every word. Then, after returning home in shock, devastated by what he had been forced to do, he did not receive compassion or reassurance from his father. Instead, Jon heard a confusing rejection. To survive as a good, worthy son, little Jon would utterly disown his body and renounce his emerging erotic nature. Jon's blossoming and very normal erotic urges simply shut down.

From then on, Jon fled from his body into his head. He stayed remote from physical contact, as he had avoided in the beginning of his life with the colic. From then on Jon's body seemed to grow awkwardly, more like a jigsaw puzzle out of whack—distorted, not integrated or whole. He gave the impression of being uncomfortable and stranded in his own body. Jon never did embrace his physicality, never went out for sports more than absolutely required, never acknowledged, relished, or owned his own body. When he reached young adulthood, his sexuality to some degree remained frozen and disowned.

And there was one more thing I always noticed but disregarded until many years after his death. A residual symptom of his molestation remained where he was violated, in his mouth. After those unendurable minutes with Tommy, his lips seemed to be permanently open, pulled apart by a slight sag, where before his little chin had been sure and forthright. In every picture from then on, that sag is there.

But things could have been different. Healing is possible, even from horrific, long-term abuse. With time, with caring and sensitive assistance from his family, therapists, and other professionals, Jon could definitely have overcome and resolved this profound wounding. He could have moved on to inherit his healthy and satisfying, full self.

What did Jon and his family need to heal from this horror?

Healing from Early Sexual Trauma: Helping the Child

A child who experiences such terrifying and devastating abuse needs to feel safe again, to have his or her fears calmed. To do that, the parents first need to calm down. It's the principle of putting on your own oxygen mask first.

One way to help everyone calm down is to get the child medical attention to assess and treat any damage. It is important to make sure that the child's compromised body survived unhurt and is safe. Knowing the child is physically all right helps both child and parents to mentally calm and restabilize.

A doctor could have reassured Jon that he was okay and could have emphasized to us, his parents, how critical therapy was at this point for both Jon and us. A doctor could have referred us to reliable psychological professionals. We could have rallied around our little son with the help of experts who knew what to do in this—to us—unknown and shocking territory.

This did not happen with Jon. In the moment of crisis, I reacted as Mama Bear protecting her cub by setting out to learn what happened, identify Jon's perpetrator, and protect my son from this menace. Removing a clear and present danger from the community certainly does help the victim feel cared for, protected, and safe again to move freely about their neighborhood.

But my actions were far more helpful to me as Jon's parent than to my small and traumatized son. I forced him to show me Tommy's house, where he unexpectedly faced his now-furious molester, seeing that Jon had betrayed him. Not a half hour later, I drove Jon to the office of another total stranger, a detective, to tell the entire, unspeakable humiliation he had promised Tommy not to tell. After Jon had just escaped a devastating trauma, my reflexive actions on his behalf traumatized him again—but I had no alternative. My little boy could never be safe otherwise.

Healing Sexual Trauma in Stage 3

Because children in Stage 3 face the core challenge of guilt, they are prone to believe that what happened was all their fault. They are afraid they are now all bad and that you will blame and reject them for what happened. Children may fear you will stop loving them and will abandon them. Any child who has been abused, but especially children three to five years old, need to hear, over and over, that what happened was not their fault.

We could have told Jon, "You haven't done anything wrong. Tommy forced you to do what he wanted you to do. You are not to blame. Only Tommy is. Yes, what happened was just awful, but none of it is your fault. In fact, whatever you did worked! You got away from a terrible person and came back home to us safe. We're just so happy you're back home! That's what matters, and that's all we care about."

Jon needed to be reassured that going out to meet new friends was a perfectly fine thing for him to do. Of course he needed friends! And he was taking responsibility for it too—such a grown-up thing to do!

And he needed to hear the truth: that nothing Tommy could do to him would change who Jon was. We might have said, "You will always be our fine, smart, and good little boy. What happened today has nothing to do with you. It is all Tommy's fault. He is much bigger and older and much, much stronger than you are, and he knows better. But Tommy is very sick. Mean or sick people can sometimes make us do things we don't want to do. What matters is that you succeeded in getting away and getting home to safety!"

Rape and molestation are crimes of violence. The victim's life is in jeopardy. Many rapists and some child molesters don't leave their victims alive to later identify, convict, and send them to prison, so whatever a survivor does to remain alive is exactly the right thing to do. Jon did all he could to resist, and he succeeded in getting away with his life. He was smart and also lucky. In many instances, any kind of resistance or efforts to escape will be met with rage and retaliation, including murder.

Jon (like any child surviving something similar) needed to hear that all that matters is that he did what he had to in order to get away and return home alive. Parents and all significant others need to rally around, welcoming the person home and wrapping their survivor in love, joy, and the empowering truth—that whatever they did to stay alive through such a shocking, horrible experience worked!

We might have said, "Jon, you're our hero! You faced a really dangerous young man who trapped you and threatened you with his dog—and you were a little boy all by yourself. Whatever it took for you to get away and come home safe worked. To do that takes courage and intelligence. And then you told the truth to the police. Because of what you did, the neighborhood will be safer. You are our hero!"

So we might have talked to Jon in words he could understand, emphasizing that he did nothing wrong and everything right. This would have given him the best chance of resolving the guilt that follows after such devastation, especially for a child in Stage 3. Assuring him, over and over, of our complete love, joy, and pride in what he had managed to do would have helped empower him as a survivor. Our words could have helped him know in his heart that all he did to survive was courageous and exactly right.

Jon needed still more. He needed a child psychologist specializing in trauma and molestation to help him heal. Because children in Stage 3 who are traumatized may shut down and lose their energy for taking initiative, Jon especially needed healing so he would be able to keep exploring in life. A therapist could have helped Jon release the trauma from his body—the necessary first step to preventing post-traumatic stress disorder. The therapist also could have helped Jon, over time, learn to trust himself and others again. The effects of this trauma on his developing sexual and emotional self could have been neutralized as Jon learned to process the trauma with the therapist's help. (See the Resources section to find help after trauma.)

A child therapist might have engaged Jon in play or art therapy. Playing with toys often brings out the child's hidden feelings about what happened. For example, if the child has nightmares of a huge bear towering over the bed, the child might pick up a toy bear in the therapist's office and act fearful of it. The therapist then has a clue about how to address the leftover trauma, perhaps first by helping the child release the frozen reactions that were needed then but never acted on. The therapist can encourage the child to yell "No!" and physically run away, for example—just one of many trauma-releasing techniques.

The therapist can then work gently to help the child correct unhelpful thinking about what happened and about themselves. Working with the therapist helps the child desensitize from the horror of the event. The child regains trust in themselves and in their own ability to take initiative, and then they can let go of the past and move forward.

We as Jon's parents also needed to talk with him about how to work together to help him remain safe when he went out on his own. We might have asked him, "What can we do to make sure you will be safe? Should I go with you from now on to meet new people? What else can we all do to make sure we all stay safe?" Parents might tell children that most people are wonderful, but there are always a few sick and scary people out in the world. They might talk about how to recognize such people—what to do if they approach, how to run for help, get to safety, or use a cellphone to call 9-1-1.

The more the child is an integral part of recovering a feeling of safety, the more they can also recover their lost sense of empowerment. The family can collaborate in making a safety list, writing down every guideline together and discussing or modifying it as needed. Involving the child in these plans helps a child in Stage 3 resolve the core challenge of guilt in favor of taking initiative and continuing to seek new experiences in life.

Healing the Family

After such devastation, Jon and his parents needed therapy. Neither parent was qualified to counsel Jon, nor should we have tried. Instead, we needed to realize that what Tommy perpetrated on Jon actually happened to all of us. Each of us needed professional help, individually and together.

We, his parents, needed therapy to come to terms with how we had failed to protect our child. I had made a mistake that I would never forgive myself for—not protecting my son in a new neighborhood. I needed to voice and work through those feelings with the help of a trained therapist. Jon's dad needed to learn that his first words to Jon after the trauma had nothing to do with Jon; more likely Dad was just reflexively voicing his own fears, and they came out in the form of hurtful words that blamed the victim. Jon's dad needed to put on his own oxygen mask first by taking time—before he drove home and saw his son—to calm down and think about how he could best love and soothe his little boy. Both of us needed to be educated about what our son was experiencing and feeling at this age and how we might best support and reassure him. We needed to calm ourselves down first so we could focus on what Jon needed and how best to support him and express understanding and empathy to him. Each of us needed healing so we could integrate this experience.

All of us needed to process this terrible violation much like mourning a death, in this case, the death of trust and innocence, plus the sexual violation. Many years ago Dr. Elisabeth Kübler-Ross outlined the stages of grief, noting that people go through the same sequence in the event of any loss, even something as seemingly trivial as losing their contact lenses. These stages are: denial, anger, bargaining, depression, and finally acceptance. Today we know that the stages do not always follow such an orderly progression but can switch places and sometimes occur simultaneously in an individual's experience.

A family that has experienced trauma to one of their children can use this situation to gather their support behind their child, to bond more deeply, and to work together to heal. In this process they can recommit to one another. The parents can take parenting classes together and collaborate on homework. The children and parents can feel safer and more transparent with one another, more able to talk about their feelings and needs and to ask one another for support. The children and the parents can continue to learn from each other. They can plan creative events and play times for the whole family and can include their friends or relatives. Cooking or baking together, playing games or backyard sports, going on family outings or picnics, or hiking, swimming, and all things physical can help heal the residual effects of sexual trauma and help a child know, care for, and trust his or her own body again. Such a terrible experience can become the catalyst drawing a family into a deeper, more loving, and committed reunion. The terrible wound they all suffered can be used to bring about new life if they recommit themselves to turning what happened to everyone's benefit—working toward greater safety and awareness, more fulfilling communication, and ever-deeper love.

Our family also needed to get to know the surrounding community. Neighbors are potential friends and playmates. They can also be essential resources. Besides the occasional cup of sugar, neighbors can provide information, expertise, and a long-term perspective. Mom and Dad needed to get to know the neighbors as much as Jon did. Jon was taking the initiative to meet them on his own, which in this new context was inappropriate. This is far too risky a business for one so young and unprotected. That's why he should never have left home unaccompanied. Instead, all three of us could have gone out to meet our neighbors together. We, like Jon, had social needs, and it was important for all of us to get acquainted with the people on our street. Exploring together could have brought us closer as a family. Our more united front would have discouraged the kind of victimization that Jon (and all of us) suffered.

Healing the Community

The neighborhood community too needed healing. Communities of any size must step up to welcome new members and alert them to any possible dangers either to self or others. Too often, neighbors keep mum about problems. Secrets, like the kind Tommy tried to make Jon keep, are big red flags. Secrets split us from ourselves and from one another. They erode trust and corrode confidence.

Neighborhoods can inadvertently collude in keeping secrets through a process of inertia. It's easier and seems safer to stay uninvolved and keep your mouth shut than to take action and speak up. Certainly there are costs either way, but if we are to err, it is better to err on the conservative side—on the side of conserving life. This we can do by building neighborhood relationships through get-togethers, online neighborhood forums, and outreach efforts. Disconnection and silence marginalize. Today more than ever we need to promote safe and healthy connections.

Years ago when I was little, my mom and I would sometimes hear our neighbors fight at night. Things would crash and the wife would scream. I'd tell Mom, "We need to call the police. He's going to kill her." She would look at me sternly and say, "No. We are not getting involved." Every time she said it, I was shocked. We were involved by simply hearing. What we do or not do can have serious consequences.

After this trauma, Jon without knowing it acted according to the solution—doing the right thing by openly sharing with the neighbors what had happened to him. Jon's ability to take initiative in this way and tell the truth is what brought Marielle to my door to meet me for the first time. She had the same need I had and every parent has—to protect our children from harm. Though it was a simple matter to reassure her that we had acted in everyone's best interest, I wish she could have taken action on what she knew before my son was harmed. But I too had a responsibility to do my own due diligence on behalf of my children's safety.

The bottom line is that all of us could have used this devastating experience to become stronger as individuals, as a family, and as a community. Ignoring a trauma only acts to split us from our own feelings about it and from one another. By doing nothing, we ensure that nothing will change, making what happened more likely to recur. If instead we work through our feelings and thoughts in an open and sincere way with others and with an expert mediator as needed, the results can be transformative. We can redress wrongs and reinstate safety. Within our wounded selves, healing is possible, even from the most horrific trauma. This moment could have become a catalyst for healing, deepening our love and connections with Jon, one another, and with our neighborhood.

Helping Children Take Initiative

The key in Stage 3, according to Erikson, is for the child to learn to take initiative and most of the time meet with success. Always keeping the children within safe limits, parents and other caregivers can coach children toward age-appropriate opportunities, where the child can experiment with new activities and grow into new and larger roles.

During this stage, once parents have set a safe perimeter, they help the most by encouraging each new initiative their child takes. They make sure to notice every inch of the child's progress and to verbally acknowledge and sincerely appreciate each effort.

Parents of children in Stage 3 can use encouraging words with their young child. Instead of blaming a child or saying "You're wrong," they can say, "Good try!" Parents can ask young children if they would like help or would prefer to figure things out on their own. Then, of course, they can follow the child's preference. Taking initiative, for a child aged three to five, means being more of a sovereign self. From this age on, sovereignty means being able, more and more, to choose what we need or want and to act on our own to satisfy it. Whether we succeed or not, we learn from the experience, and we can correct our actions as needed.

Parents best support their three- to five-year-olds by being flexible and allowing them the freedom to push out their edges on their own. Instead of telling them what to do, parents might ask questions such as, "What do you think? What just happened? Did that work the way you hoped? Why or why not? What did you learn? What do you suppose would be better? How would you feel if that happened to you? What would you prefer if it were you?"

Asking questions like these will help young children grow in their ability to make good choices, and it will also help them minimize feelings of guilt or shame. When parents ask questions, they send a positive underlying message: "You are capable, you are intelligent, and I believe in you.

I know you are able to figure things out as you go along and to make safe and healthy choices." This message gives young children the ground they need to believe in themselves, to go forth and overcome adversity, and to eventually succeed. As long as parents maintain a safe perimeter, children's ability to grow into independence begins right here, at this stage. Parents and caregivers can support their child's taking initiative instead of being the know-it-all, the boss, or the critical voice. Encourage young children to develop their own good sense and inner compass. Know that mistakes are essential in discovering what does work and that every effort the child makes is good, for it teaches something useful. If that learning continues without end, successes all along the way are guaranteed.

To encourage a child, praise and appreciate only their effort, not the outcome. The quantity and quality of their effort is the only thing they have control over. Parents might appreciate the result of a child's effort, but do not praise that result, no matter how successful. Praising outcomes instead of efforts can lead children to feel responsible for the outcome. Then, if efforts do not work out as hoped, children can feel guilty about the results. Praising outcomes instead of effort also works over time to discourage greater efforts.

Be unfailing with your unconditional love and trust, especially if children make a choice that does not lead to success. To keep putting forth effort and taking initiative, children need to feel parents' solid support, especially in their hard times. When children know their parents believe in them no matter what, children learn that they matter and there is hope beyond every trauma.

In the family setting, Erikson suggested that children at this age need parents who invite them to share in the activities of making a home, such as baking, caring for pets or younger siblings, helping with simple repairs, or tidying up the home or yard. This is also the stage to take children exploring in the wider world and to give them opportunities to try new activities. With the support of loving adults, children in Stage 3 can succeed and feel empowered as they begin to flex their wings.

—

TEACHINGS, AIRBAGS, AND SAFETY NETS

- The core issue for children in Stage 3, according to Erikson, is to take initiative in small, healthy, and empowering ways and to be seen, supported, and encouraged in these attempts. They are busy growing their ability to become independent as they take their first steps out into the world beyond the family.

- The danger to avoid at this stage is guilt—unresolved bad feelings about mistakes they made or things they did that were not successful.

- Guilt at this stage is different from the shame that a child might have felt in Stage 2. Shame is feeling bad about "who I am." Guilt, by contrast, is feeling bad about "what I did or didn't do" that was wrong or that hurt someone.

- Though some guilt is helpful because it teaches children how to treat others, overwhelming guilt needs to be avoided or else healed. This may be crushing guilt from traumatic experiences such as Jon's or guilt that adults instill in a child through criticizing or blaming the child instead of encouraging and supporting them.

- With children ages three to five, parents and others must still be protective, but within safe boundaries they can allow children to interact with others on their own and explore age-appropriate opportunities.

- Instead of blaming a child or saying "You're wrong," parents can say, "Good try!" Parents can ask young children if they would like help or would prefer to figure things out on their own. Then, of course, they can follow the child's preference.

- Instead of telling them what to do, parents might ask questions such as, "What do you think? What just happened? Did that work the way you hoped? Why or why not?" Asking questions like these will help young children grow in their ability to make good choices as they learn to take initiative, and it will also help them minimize any feelings of guilt or shame.

- When parents ask questions, they send a positive underlying message: "You are capable, you are intelligent and I believe in you. I know you can figure things out as you go along." This message gives young children the ground they need to believe in themselves, to go forth and overcome adversity, and to eventually succeed.

- To encourage a child, praise and appreciate only their effort. Appreciate but do not praise the result or outcome of their efforts, no matter how successful. Their attempt is the only thing they have control over. Praising outcomes instead of efforts works over time to discourage greater efforts.

- Stand by a child with unconditional love and trust, especially in their hard times. When children know their parents believe in them no matter what, children learn that they matter and there is hope beyond every trauma.

- Respect children's bodies, and ask permission before touching. This teaches them that they have the right to say no to uncomfortable or unwanted touch. Kids who understand this are much more able to stay safe in the world. Check the Resources section for books and other resources for talking with kids about safety.

- Read your young children books that help them recognize "good" and "bad" touch, and talk with them about it and encourage their questions as you do. Excellent titles include *It's MY Body,* by Lory Freeman and Carol Deach; *Your Body Belongs to You,* by Cornelia Maude Spelman; *Do You Have a Secret? (Let's Talk About It!),* by Jennifer Moore-Mallinos; and *My Body Is Private,* by Linda Walvoord Girard.

- When moving to a new neighborhood, support your young child in taking initiative to meet new friends by going with them to explore and make acquaintances. Bake cookies to share, knock on doors, and introduce yourselves. Ask your neighbors about age-mates, child safety, problem areas, or people to steer clear of and why. Your neighbors can provide the scoop on schools and other neighborhood resources.

- A trauma caused by physical violation is best handled by professionals who specialize in children and trauma. Parents, who have also been traumatized in the process of their child's violation, can never therapeutically treat their own victimized child. They are too destabilized and wounded themselves, and they need therapy independently of their child. Healing deep-seated wounds is a trained skill that must be done by someone other than parents, even if the parents are trained.

- Following a trauma (or any other problem), parents or trusted adults should never project their worst-case concern onto an already shocked young child (or anyone else). Children internalize their parents' doubts about them, and at this stage of their lives that doubt will form a residue of guilt. A few words from a trusted loved one can become a self-fulfilling prophecy—for good and also, more powerfully, for ill.

- Over time, watch for acting out, withdrawal, or other dramatic changes in a child's personality or behavior that could indicate they need additional help dealing with a past trauma, and find professional help.

Divorce

~

Age	Virtue Instilled	Psychosocial Crisis	Significant Relationship	Existential Question	Significant Issues
3-5 years	Purpose	Initiative vs. Guilt	Family and Age-Mates	Can I do, move, and act on my own?	Selfhood in Family, Solo Exploring and Cooperative Play, Toys and Tools, Secret Erotic Feelings, Gender Preference

AFTER JON'S DEVASTATING molestation, Dad refused all mention of it, including any possibility of therapy. It was only a matter of months until I took steps to divorce. Never being allowed to speak of—or be able to discuss and together correct any problem—meant that none of my own or our sons' concerns could find resolution or healing.

The bullwhip incident two years earlier had put me on high alert. The love and trust for my husband that had once burned so full within me were simply extinguished, never to be rekindled. Wary since then, especially for my sons' sakes, I took seriously the things I used to chalk up to just immaturity. The hard way, I learned that behind his million-dollar smile lurked a different, troubling side—one he never showed our two wonderful extended families. Today we have words for this kind of relationship: domestic abuse. But back in 1971, without any labels, I struggled to make sense of it.

Dad's reaction to Jon's horrible violation helped to seal a decision only growing clearer over time. I had to divorce their father.

My husband and I made an appointment to meet with a lawyer—the one lawyer he insisted must represent us both. The night before this meeting, he forced me into giving up my half of our property, which was guaranteed to me by law. Handing me a pen and a sheaf of papers, he demanded, "Sign off on all these, or forget about the lawyer or any divorce." In my hand were signature forms to sign off on every asset— stocks, bonds, our beautiful out-of-state second home, joint checking and savings—everything we had built over ten years together. After our marriage but before having children I had continued working full-time, and all five years' worth of my personal salary, less the $35 per month personal allowance he cut me, had gone into our "untouchable" savings account. That account too I was to sign away.

For the children's sakes and my own, I wanted nothing more than a good divorce. Thinking, *Well, I never married him for his money, and if this will produce a good divorce . . . ,* I took another sip of wine, took the pen he held out, and signed off on everything. I agreed to no alimony, a modicum of child support, and about five hundred dollars in the bank to cover that year's property taxes. I kept the house we were in, all responsibility for paying its mortgage, insurance, taxes, and maintenance, plus primary custody of our boys. He kept the out-of-state home we owned and all our assets.

Over time it would become clear that nothing I ever did could have given me a "good" divorce from one so wounded. My cooperation merely landed my boys and me in immediate and perpetual poverty. Signing away my rightful assets put me in a powerless, one-down position with him that continuously disadvantaged our sons. For the eleven and a half months a year that our sons lived with me, we were lucky to cover the bare necessities and make do with the little we had. For a few weeks every year, my boys could enjoy their father's lavish lifestyle. Though this rags-versus-riches split may have been more or less okay with me at the time, it was incredibly shortsighted on my part and was still illegal. Not only was it unfair to me but, more to the point—and what I didn't consider at the time—it was terribly unfair to our children. They were now forced to cycle between two homes with vastly differing values, lifestyles, resources, and possibilities. Only later would I learn the toll this kind of extreme disparity takes on children's psyches, creating doubts in their minds, dividing their loyalties, and even splitting their young, forming identity into two—one for Dad, another for Mom.

The day Daddy moved out was absolutely the worst day in four-year-old Jon's life. As his daddy carried his final things down the stairs and out the door, Jon's crying turned incoherent. In abject agony, he slid under his bed and stayed there all afternoon, sobbing harder and faster than it seemed possible. The few times he spoke between sobs he kept vomiting out a desolate "I'm too bad a boy. . . . I'm too bad a boy. . . . "

I knelt on the floor next to the bed while he emptied out his heart. Over and over, I repeated the truth, that Jon was a great and fine boy, the best boy ever. That Daddy's leaving had nothing to do with him. That Daddy loved him and would always be in his life as his very own and wonderful daddy.

When, around twilight, I could finally draw Jon out, he just threw himself across his bed facedown and kept on sobbing into his pillow. I sat next to him, caressing him and earnestly repeating that Daddy would never leave him. That Daddy loved him just the same and always would, that they would still be together, have fun, and do things always. That because of things wrong between Daddy and Mommy, he just had to live somewhere else.

Jon didn't, wouldn't, couldn't buy it.

I don't remember how many hours this went on. It seemed like forever. I stayed as close to Jon as I could without him flinching away and crying even harder. I had to believe he would be reachable, that in time he would calm down and be okay. That he'd reconnect with his daddy and his father's wonderful family. I also had Alan, his two-and-a-half-year-old brother, to worry about, who thankfully had no such reaction. Clearly too young to comprehend the gravity of Daddy's leaving, little Alan remained pretty stable.

Determined not to cause my sons more pain, I tried my best to keep an even, neutral keel. One way of doing that, I thought, was to never share one negative word about their father. Children need that secure family balance of both father and mother to lean on, especially in troubled times. Why confuse and undermine my sons by badmouthing or otherwise depriving them of one of the two adult supports they needed to trust for their very survival? Neither my problems nor those of his father were the proper business of a child. What Jon and little Alan needed to do was to love their father and enjoy a good relationship with him. My job was to aid that process.

I'd learned by experience what not to do. From the time I was little, I'd heard "what your dad did to me" stories from my otherwise phenomenal mom. Believing every word, I grew up dismissing, even hating, my dad. Finally one day when I was sixteen, he showed up for his ten-minute weekly visit, and I threw it all in his face. While I raged on, he stood quietly facing me and heard me out. Some forty minutes later, exhausted and out of breath, I stopped. After a respectful moment, he asked evenly, "Are you done?" I gasped out, "I . . . think . . . so." "Good," he said, turned, and left. The dad I was so sure I knew could never have stood his ground or calmly listened while I raged. He would have either fled out the door or slapped me down. He had just proved himself not the man I hated. Having to discover who he truly was gave me, in time, the real father I could value and cherish as my own.

Never would I poison my sons like Mom had innocently done with me. But beyond staying neutral about their dad and our divorce, I had no idea of what to say. From then on, whenever Jon pressed me, I simply admitted to "problems" between the two of us that made us have to live apart, problems between Daddy and Mommy that had nothing to do with him or his brother. I repeated that no matter where either of us lived or how far apart we were, his dad and I would always have Jon and his brother in our lives and would love and support them forever with all our hearts.

But that was not nearly enough. Jon was left stranded, in perpetual agony, missing critical information. He desperately needed professional help not only to heal from being molested but also to learn how to not blame himself for the divorce. He needed a neutral expert to help him understand and reconcile at his four-year-old level what was taking place at home. Given what had happened to him just months before, and Daddy's first reaction to it, little Jon didn't believe my vague answers. He was sure he was the reason his daddy had left. At four years old, he remained convinced, with his child's literal, self-centric brain, that what had occurred was his fault. Nothing I could say—with passion, humor, logic, or quiet conviction—could change my sweet little son's mind or touch the depth of his suffering. His adored daddy left because he was too bad a boy.

Heartbreak showed in his body language. That blond little head bowed, eyes downcast. Every photo from that time shows a disconsolate, lost, and grieving child. Instead of seeking to talk or play with others, his bright smile shining, Jon turned inward and stayed in his room, morose and withdrawn. Nothing excited him or lifted his sorrow. Even in Disneyland, Jon's small shoulders sagged under the weight of his heavy, sundered world. His pain projected onto all of us, and in that happiest of places, we all had a perfectly awful time.

I had no idea what to do. With only a high school diploma and unemployed for over five years with no savings but now all the responsibility for a home and two little sons, I had gotten myself out of a marriage right into a wringer. Still, I was determined to stay in our house so that my boys would keep their home, their friends, and their friends' families in this neighborhood—as much of their familiar and trusted world as possible. Though Jon was in desperate need of help and I knew it, I was a brand-new head of household with primary custody, no money, and no job. My first focus had to be finding work and making ends meet.

Broke and scared, I could only hope—desperately hope—that love and time would heal Jon. Someday all the pieces would be revealed. He would put them together himself and finally understand. In the meantime, I would do all I could to love Jon and help him and his brother stay healthy and stable at home and keep connected in good ways to their dad.

While I focused on finding a job, Jon was in such unrelieved agony that for the first time he began to torment his little brother. Downstairs cooking, circling the classifieds, or cleaning, I'd hear some fracas and fly up the steps to find little Alan sitting on his bed wide-eyed and red-faced, lips tightly pursed, looking ready to explode. I would first plead then lose patience and finally demand to know what happened, but Alan kept it all inside. Time after time, he never told. With no dad to back me up, I had no leverage. Stuffed and silent as Buddha, little Alan seethed with the same helpless rage and pain that riddled Jon. Though I would harangue Jon every single time, he of course kept mute, and without knowing any more, I didn't know how or exactly what to punish. My ultimate threat to Jon before walking out in frustration was always, "When Alan gets bigger, boy, are you going to be sorry!"

Meanwhile, Alan learned to cope by shutting up and tuning out. Too little to fight back or compete in kind with his highly verbal older brother, Alan kept from being his brother's target by simply limiting his talking. He remained quiet and entertained himself in his room or visited neighborhood friends' homes. When he spoke at home, it was usually only to me; around his brother and relatives, he kept quiet or listened. I understood him perfectly, so when he entered school I was shocked to find that he was diagnosed with speech impediments and learning disabilities and placed in special education. With the help of speech and other therapists, little Alan worked hard, quickly improved, and soon tested out of special ed. He would go on to prove himself just as able to earn straight A's as Jon—and that's when I finally understood that Alan's early, supposed disabilities were simply how he had coped with Jon's own cries for love. Jon had projected his own agonies about the molestation and divorce onto his helpless little brother, and Alan had reacted by shutting down, which made him appear incapacitated when he in fact was anything but.

What more could I do to help Jon and his little brother through our divorce? I would be asking that question for years to come.

Erikson and Divorce in Stage 3: Initiative vs. Guilt (3-5 Years)

As we have seen, Erikson pointed out that in this third stage of development children are now autonomous, verbal, and physically adept. Able to take care of many of their own needs, they are now ready and eager to move out into the neighborhood, play with others, and actively help out in their family as their own person. They want to be of value. They love to learn and are eager to matter and fulfill a purpose larger than themselves.

Erikson also noted that at this stage most children are now quite clear on their gender. Identifying as a boy or girl, children tend to bond with and idolize their parental gender preference or find their gender model among other children's parents in the neighborhood or community. It is natural to yearn to be like that godlike role model, knowing that one day they might grow up to be like them. Children between the ages of three and five are continually observing gender models and seeking out adults who model the gender they feel the most affinity for and slowly evolve into.

At the same time, Erikson observed that the child at this age is uniquely poised and ready to engage as a more independent self with extended family members and to play cooperatively with siblings, cousins, or neighborhood age-mates. Children in this stage become autonomous for the first time. They are able to exercise their power to fulfill their own goals and needs, and they are usually excited to cooperate in following the rules and being helpful.

Knowing just these three key developmental issues common to children ages three to five can be an enormous help if families must move through a painful transition such as divorce. The more that parents and other adults know about these stage-based possibilities and perils, the better able we can be to attune to and address the child's needs. We can read problem behavior for what it truly is, a terrible cry for love. Instead of blaming and punishing a child already in pain, we can respond with compassion for their inner suffering. By offering understanding, we can help them feel known and normal instead of bad or abnormal, which only induces a terrible inner guilt. We can redirect them to some creative or helpful pursuit and praise them for doing so. We can believe in and trust our child's good soul and so help them navigate this core challenge of ages three to five: moving beyond guilt to feel they are of value to their family and friends.

Jon and Divorce

Had I known about a child's stages of development, I might have chosen to postpone the final divorce to some point in the next developmental stage when Jon would be in school, one step farther removed from the home, more invested in befriending schoolmates and taking his first steps into the wider world. Had I understood more about why little Jon was feeling so devastated, I could have spoken to his unnamed fears, shame, and feelings of guilt, and he might have calmed down and felt more cared for.

Because children at this age benefit from being emotionally prepared before a big event, I could have helped ready Jon for the shock of his father's leaving by, for example, reading him children's books about divorce and responding to any questions those stories raised. At that time there were few such books, but today there are many excellent options (see the Resources list for some suggestions). While reading, I could have asked Jon for his own ideas about what he might need if he were going through what the book's main character was experiencing. Soliciting Jon's ideas would have spoken to the need that children in Stage 3 have to collaborate with their caregivers and have their initiative valued. Together Jon and I could have imagined a new future beyond the immediate crisis—how he would have a stable new life with a second happy home to enjoy in a different locale with more friends, relatives, and special things to do.

Certainly Jon's father and I should have shared responsibility for what was happening by together helping our sons adjust. Before separating, my husband and I should have sat down with Jon and his little brother and together talked about what we were going to do. In words the children could understand, we could have gone over what it would mean for them. Each of us could have assured them of our forever support and could have answered all the questions Jon had. In our case, when Dad walked out with no explanation, that severely traumatized his bright and sensitive four-year-old son and filled him with the alarming certainty that he was to blame.

When Jon sobbed inconsolably under the bed, sure that he was worthless and responsible for this shocking event, I could have responded in somewhat different ways. First, I needed to calm myself down and put myself in a more peaceful place before kneeling to talk to him under his bed. Then, to connect my nervous system to his, I could have begun by simply syncing my breathing rate to his, which could have helped him begin to feel more peaceful too.

Next, I could have begun connecting with him through words, acknowledging what he was likely thinking and feeling and asking him to add to or correct anything, if possible. Trying to engage with him and to reflect his truth back to him might have helped him know that he was valuable and that I wanted to understand.

I could have gradually slowed down my breath at the same time, giving his breathing time to slow with mine and helping to further calm his nervous system. While breathing slowly and easily, I might have kept calmly reassuring him that I understood and cared about how he felt. I could have brought Jon a favorite toy or stuffed animal to help soothe him.

I might have gone on to say things like, "Though this must feel really horrible right now, knowing only what you as a little boy can know, parents are way older and all grown up. And when big adults need to separate, it's never what either parent wanted or thought would ever happen. And it's never, ever about their children. It's about two adults not getting along or meeting each other's needs. After parents have tried and tried all they can, then their only choice left is to separate. But no matter what, both parents will always love their children and be there for them all their lives." I would have known that Jon was beginning to relax when I saw him yawn or heard deep sighs or noticed him trembling or shaking.

Keeping ourselves calm and balanced, especially through difficult and traumatic times, is our most powerful inner resource for keeping ourselves safe during a trauma. The same holds true for our children. Slowing down our breath and rate of speech, listening deeply, and reflecting children's feelings and words back to them all help to create more peace and connectedness in the midst of drama. This helps children weather the storm and come out on the other side feeling like a whole person.

When Jon acted his own pain out on his brother, I could have supported his burgeoning independence by asking for his help in solving current dilemmas. I could have given him more opportunities to be the "good guy" instead of simply reacting in a way that consigned him to a "bad guy" role at a time when he was already miserable. I could have found low-cost help for him, even while in a financial vise myself, perhaps through enlisting the help of family members and sharing how he was projecting his internal pain onto his brother. Of course, in these situations, it's always a good idea to enlist a child trauma expert to help a child make a positive transition, and it is well worth whatever the cost to keep a child from being traumatized.

Let's take a closer look at how these strategies can work for families going through divorce.

Taking Care of Young Children
Through Divorce

Divorce is a family rupture that is bound to be traumatic for children at this stage, even if family life has been dysfunctional or chaotic. The only home that the children know and depend on for shelter and life itself is sundered, putting everything and especially them in sudden jeopardy with no idea of what lies ahead. For children of any age, but particularly this one, divorce is a devastating, global shock. What can they know, trust, or believe? Who is really there for them? If the exiting parent represents their adult gender model, as was true for Jon, their personal loss at this stage will likely be even more excruciating. But because they love and need both parents, divorce, of course, raises the natural and most terrifying question: If one parent can go, will the remaining parent leave, too?

During any fraught times but especially during divorce, pay extra attention to your children, especially if the children are ages three to five. Spend time with them doing quiet, calming things like reading to them. Or help children in Stage 3 exercise their creativity by engaging them in fun activities, such as simple arts and crafts. Or work together making easy treats, or have them invite playmates over for playdates or picnics in the backyard or at a park. Ask them to help out in small, fun ways so they can feel valuable, then praise each instance of help or cooperation, whether it's bringing out snacks, feeding the dog, fetching the newspaper, or contributing in any way. And as you do, stay available for their questions, and do your best to answer all of them.

Children of any age need solid ground beneath them, but this is especially true for children in Stage 3 because this is when they begin to bloom on their own. Something as devastating as divorce can cut them off at their roots if parents and caregivers don't consciously work to support this initial, tender bloom. When children at this age receive special attention during a crisis and are appreciated for taking positive initiative on their own, they will feel they matter, can contribute, and are valued. They will then have a better chance of resolving the core crisis of Stage 3 in favor of taking initiative and fulfilling their own goals instead of staying passive—either not initiating or else giving up—and falling prey to guilt.

Place the Children's Welfare First

Divorcing parents remain forever joined in the higher, equal purpose of raising their children and serving the children's best interests. When divorcing parents weigh each decision in terms of what will serve their child's welfare, they discover something quite marvelous: What is good for the child is good for the parents as well, and for everyone else too. If we focus on our children and do right by their needs at every stage, we are being good, responsible adult models whom they can trust and emulate, and we then find that our own needs are taken care of as well. Putting the children's best interest first buoys everyone over troubled waters, helping to heal the parents as well and keeping each person resilient, connected to others, and safe.

If either Jon's mother or father—or both of us—could have focused on the best interests of our children instead of what was going on between us, we would have made better and more equitable choices from the start of the divorce process. And as we did, we might have been able to calm down, take personal responsibility, and commit to make any needed changes. If there was any chance for reconciliation—or at least a respectful, separate-but-equal dissolution of our marriage that placed our children on the best possible footing—this was a moment for rigorous honesty and doing that work.

Divide the Assets Evenly

The number-one way to take care of children through divorce is to insist on an equitable divorce settlement, where assets are shared equally. Parents must remain on equal footing in divorce so the children will not be faced with the chaos that ensues with permanent economic and social inequality. Divorce presents enough challenges for young children without forcing them to negotiate a sudden, permanent imbalance between their parents.

Sometimes women are easily convinced that they are worth less than their husbands or are bullied into getting less than an equitable distribution. That is never okay, it is against the law, and it always works against the children's best interests. If there is inequality between the parents, the one who is well off can carry unfair weight and can exert more control over the other.

Children need to feel parity between their parents' two homes, for that is the solid ground they depend on to grow. Having to straddle two very different playing fields can, as time goes on, force a child into divided loyalties. It can even sunder a child's emerging identity into two disconnected selves—one loyal to Dad at his place, the other to Mom at hers. The child splits, with one half forced to be always "bad"—disloyal to the absent parent, whichever one that happens to be. In Stage 3, feeling "bad" can prevent a child from moving forward into taking more initiative.

Treat Your Ex with Respect, and
Insist on Being Treated with Respect

No matter how divorcing parents feel about their ex, it is crucial for the sake of the children that parents remain adults and show each other the same consideration and respect they would show others. Children in Stage 3 especially will become confused when their parents disrespect each other. They will act out or feel depressed or scared because the ground beneath their feet has turned shaky. They need to obey and trust their parents, but which one?

If a child senses they are being subtly (or overtly) lobbied to love one parent more than the other, the child will feel both destabilized and demoralized. The more they must take sides, the more guilt grows, because they know that favoring one parent actively disrespects and hurts the other one—whom they also love. Being pressured to take sides raises conflicting emotions in children, for they love and need both parents to feel okay so they can continue to trust them and feel safe enough to survive and grow.

When young children feel unsafe, their attention suffers, learning becomes compromised, and normal developmental growth slows. Children may freeze in place, or their social or emotional growth suffers while they try to avoid falling into the deep emotional cracks that keep opening up around them. To be fully able to learn and grow, children need to feel safe in a known, stable, and coherent home base.

In cases where divorce is more amicable, it becomes possible to continue acting as a family unit in activities such as hiking or having all the relatives over for dinner. Seeing their parents cooperate and treat each other with respect helps to calm young children and buoy them up during troubled times. It gives them a sense of continuity and helps to instill in young children a sense of trust in life—that after bad things happen, all is not lost.

To help children in Stage 3 move forward with taking initiative and not sink into crippling guilt, divorcing parents need to do whatever they can to involve the children in planning fun activities. Parents of children aged three to five might solicit the children's help in inviting the relatives over, or they might find other creative ways to support the children's need to exercise their creativity. Feeling that they matter and are of value to each parent helps children to more readily and calmly accept their new living arrangements. And helping to plan fun outings reassures them that life can move forward in new and fun directions, even though it might look different than it did before divorce.

In cases where a divorce is not amicable, it is especially crucial to protect young children by treating the ex with respect and insisting on being treated in the same way. Exes might be required to sign a written agreement outlining the specifics of what constitutes fair and equitable spousal treatment, not only to certify safe passage for one another but also to unite and guarantee safe passage for their children.

How to Talk with Young Children About Divorce

Every divorcing parent knows how difficult it is to break the news to children. This is especially true for young children, because their whole lives up to now have been lived inside this home where both parents are their everything. Young children love their parents intensely and depend on them entirely. They cannot imagine how they will survive if this secure home base changes in any way. And worst of all at this age, they will be prone to blame themselves and suffer intense guilt. To them, they are the center of their universe, which means that whatever happens in that universe is all their fault.

If you and your spouse have decided to live apart, it's best to talk with the children together. Tell them the truth about how you feel about this decision and what it means for each person in the family, but do not go into detail about your adult problems. No child—but especially no child from the ages of three to five—can imagine or comprehend the complexities of adult relationships, nor should they be put in that position. Children need to love and trust both of their parents and be loyal to each of them. Children in Stage 3, whose young brains are wired to believe themselves responsible for the family breakup, need to be assured by each of you, whether alone or together, that none of this is their fault. Not burdening them with adult complexities helps to keep them free of residual guilt so they can calm down, learn, and grow.

So what can you tell young children about the divorce? When you do speak with them about it, keep the words simple and neutral and the message short but hopeful. Be factual, clear, and calm. Never pretend that all is fine when it isn't or give the children false hope that you might come back together. Divorce is an adult decision of last resort after a long process of exhausting all other options. The truth is that both of you tried your best (even if that doesn't feel quite accurate in the moment), and you still could not get along and be happy.

Use inclusive "we" or "us" words, not "he or she did this" or "your daddy or your mommy is . . ." No pointing fingers or calling the ex a bad guy; no shaming or blaming the ex. For example, you might say, "We have been disagreeing and fighting together too much, and despite all we tried, it has just gotten worse. And that's not good for us or for you. It is time for us to face this truth and live apart, in separate homes. Neither of us ever expected this to happen, but this is the only way the two of us can be happy again."

Assure them of your continuing love: "Always remember that nothing on earth can ever change how much each of us loves you. Each of us will always take care of you. What is wrong is just between Mommy and Daddy, and it's time to do what's right for us both—and for you too. Though it will be different at first, in time it will get much more comfortable and even be fun. You will have two homes, two families and sets of friends, and different fun things to do in each place." Reassure them at every opportunity that both of you will always love them and always be part of their lives and that that will never ever change.

With children in Stage 3, you might read picture books that tell stories of families dealing with divorce. You can pause at each page to share feelings and answer questions. This is a great way to renew the parent-child bond during this confusing time, which can help children feel loved and included so they become able to integrate these scary developments in a more peaceful way. Touching or sitting close to your children helps them feel aligned with you and instills the hope that together you and they will create an okay new reality.

For example, with Jon, who was four, we could have explained our divorce with both of us together holding him and his little brother and talking about how things would be different. We could have made sure they knew we were doing this because we had both tried our best but were too different to be happy and stay together. We could have said, "Everyone deserves a home where everyone is happy." Above all, we needed to say, "Both of us will always love and be there for you and for your brother. Nothing will ever change that." I could have talked about how the boys would stay with me in our own home, in their own rooms, and how they would continue to have their neighborhood pals to play with and soon go to school with. Dad could have talked about taking them places, doing fun things together, and having another home to come to and enjoy with their grandma and their aunt and uncle. He could have shared how they would go sailing on the ocean together and learn to swim. I could have said we would go to the beach or mountains, and they would be able to bring their friends and explore together. Children need to understand that they may experience benefits from a situation that at first feels painful but in time can feel normal and perhaps even great.

No Secrets

Do not ask children of any age to keep secrets from your ex. Secrets are about hiding things that aren't okay—or they wouldn't be secrets. Secrets are destructive, just like gossip, and no child should be required by a parent to keep a secret from, or, conversely, to gossip about, the other parent. When children need both parents to survive, keeping secrets strands children in the middle between their parents.

Especially for small children, having to keep secrets from one or both parents confuses them and undermines their natural development. It compromises them and fosters feelings of disloyalty, shame, and guilt, which can adversely affect their self-concept and create distortions in both their behavior and relationships. Over time, keeping secrets simply teaches children to deal with problems by being secretive and manipulative—to lie or withhold information instead of being honest and solving problems actively and creatively.

Tell your children, "It's fine to share where you went and the things you did with your other parent." When the parents are open and transparent, children will learn that their parents are honest with each other and can be trusted.

If something bad or uncomfortable does happen, the caretaking parent needs to alert and include the other parent in full in the moment. And for children, speaking about it is of paramount importance, for the truth is freeing and enables them to receive the support and protection that keep children feeling loved, in balance, and open to life.

Respect Your Children's Feelings, and Teach Them to Respect Their Own Feelings

One of the things about divorce that is so powerfully traumatizing for children is the fact that their world is breaking up and they feel helpless, having no voice in this volatile process. Because children in Stage 3 are learning for the first time to express their own voice, you can use this knowledge to help them express their feelings in age-appropriate ways. Create room for your children to make their feelings known about what is taking place.

Children of any age, but especially children ages three to five years old, cycle through normal but erroneous self-blaming emotions and other dysfunctional reactions to divorce. They may at one moment or another feel relief, insecurity, guilt, self-loathing, grief, and anger. They may act out their pain by persecuting siblings, as Jon did, by defying the parent or damaging property or possessions. They may turn their pain inward against themselves by becoming isolated or preoccupied or going into a deep depression. They may develop personality, emotional, or behavioral changes or may experience fears and nightmares—fears that the parents are untrustworthy and fears that they themselves will be betrayed and abandoned.

These are all desperate cries for love and understanding. Their immature brains are processing an impossible conundrum in their lives, and it's upsetting and scary because it's outside their control. They need their parents' unswerving belief in their goodness and normalcy; they do not need blame, anger, distrust, or punishment.

Of course, if children are hurting themselves or others or are damaging property or defying their parents, they first must be stopped, but then they need to be calmed and reassured that the real feelings motivating these actions are normal and understood. They need to be believed in and helped over this devastating moment so they can calm down and hold hope for the future. They feel awful, and that's what they're showing you; they are somehow sure they are bad and are acting out their own inner chaos.

Give children room to express their feelings. Hold them, reassure them, and love them. Keep everyone safe and understood through every defiant, upset, angry, devastated, or terrified upheaval. Children—but especially young children—in the midst of divorce need frequent, solid contact and communication with both parents. They need to know you will be there for them even when they feel awful about themselves and about what is happening.

Especially encourage children to let you know when something you are doing feels wrong or off base to them. Young children in Stage 3 enjoy being able to help others, so enlist their help with this. You might say, "Mommy and Daddy are both human beings and not perfect. We are going to try our best, but we need your help. Your feelings and needs are very important to us. If one of us says something about your other parent that makes you feel bad or confused, it's okay to speak up, and say, 'Please stop saying those things to me.' It's really important that you help us by letting us know when things bother you, and we promise to listen. And you know what? We both will appreciate you more for being so honest!" In this way both parents empower the children to express their feelings and protect themselves.

Whenever children do let you know that something feels wrong, take time to praise them, and then follow through on what they shared. No questions asked, no "yes, but," and no bargaining. At the same time, never make your child a promise—or a consequence—you aren't 100 percent sure you can keep or carry out. Retain their trust by listening, being realistic, and following through consistently.

Children love both parents and desperately want the family to be together like before. It is normal for them to want this, and it can be expressed many ways. Whatever a child does to lobby for bringing Mommy and Daddy together again, it's important for parents to first validate the child's feelings. You might say something like, "Of course you want us back together, but we already tried really hard to stay together and failed, and there was no choice but to separate. Neither one of us wants to go through that again. So please do not expect that or even hope for it. But we are always your parents, and we can still work together to be great parents, even if we're apart, and we can still respect each other too." Don't crush them, but speak truthfully. The sooner children realize that reconciliation isn't possible, the more quickly they can accept it and move forward in their lives.

Give Young Children Small Choices to Make

One way to help children—especially children in Stage 3—remain stable in the midst of chaos is to give them every opportunity to make their own choices about the many things they can control. They can make choices about their room, their clothes, their free time, which fruit or snack to eat, who to play with and when, how to exercise, where to take naps, what crafts or toys to play with, which books they'd like to have read to them, which shows to watch or movies to see, and more. Be creative, be flexible, and look for opportunities to give them even more choices. Start a list of free choice possibilities, and keep adding to it. Let them participate with ideas of their own. The benefit to children in Stage 3, who are moving into autonomy in this painful, stressed time, can be invaluable.

⁓

TEACHINGS, AIRBAGS, AND SAFETY NETS

- In this third stage of development, children are now autonomous, verbal, and physically adept. They are eager to move out into the neighborhood, play with others, and actively help and be of value to their family as their own person.

- Children in Stage 3 become aware of gender identity, noticing and reacting to gender models in the family and the neighborhood. Identifying as a boy or girl, children tend to idolize caregivers or other adults of their same sex.

- Especially in painful family transitions, parents need to read problem behavior correctly—as a cry for love. Stop negative behavior, but instead of blaming or punishing a child already in pain, help them feel understood. Ask about the fears behind their behavior, for example, "You're not bad. You are upset, sad, and scared. This is really hard." Believe in and trust your children. Give them little opportunities to be the "good guy or gal" whenever possible. Notice and praise instances of goodwill and cooperation.

- Because parents and home are a young child's entire world, consider postponing painful transitions to a later stage, when children are moving beyond the nuclear family and are more mature and independent, bonding more with age-mates.

- Pay extra attention to your children during fraught times. Help young children through troubled times by reading picture books with them about issues like divorce, such as *Dinosaurs Divorce* by Laurene Krasny Brown and Marc Brown; *It's Not Your Fault, Koko Bear* by Vicki Lansky; and appropriate selections from the Berenstain Bears series.

- Parents' highest priority, in divorce and always, is to do their children no harm and, to the best of their ability, always serve the best interests of their children.

- Prior to a divorce, parents should sit down together with their children and talk with them in words they can understand about what is going to happen. Of course, it is vital that both parents assure the children of their forever support and answer all their questions.

- In a crisis, keeping calm and in balance is our most powerful inner resource for ourselves and also our children. Slowing down our breath and rate of speech and listening deeply will help to create peace in the midst of drama. This helps their nervous systems relax and be restored to sanity.

- None of the negative feelings or issues between adults are to be shared with children, especially young children.

- Children after divorce are confused, grieving, and depressed. Children ages three to five especially may feel at fault or unworthy. They need a calm, safe environment and expert guidance to safely work through their loss.

- Continually reassure your children of your love and ongoing presence in their lives, and let them know that in time all will settle down. Give them solid hope that life can and will become even better for them.

- To keep your children on an even keel, do not agree to anything but an equal divorce settlement. The law calls for an equal division of resources, and this is in the best interests of the children.

- Give them choices between alternatives at every opportunity. Be creative in helping to empower them with positive coping skills, especially in situations where they feel confused, helpless, and in despair.

- No secrets allowed. Secrets are about hiding things that aren't okay or they wouldn't be secrets. Empower young children in divorce by letting them know it's okay to say no to keeping secrets or to telling on the other parent.

- No describing the terms of the divorce to the children except to say it's fair and equal for both parents (and make sure it is).

- When speaking about the divorce to the children, use nondivisive language. For example, always use inclusive terms, such as we. Do not personalize or blame using pointed words such as *she, he, your mother,* or *your father.*

- No putting the children in between. Splitting children's loyalties endangers their mental health, fosters guilt, and deprives them of the full parental support they most need during divorce.

When All Is Lost

STAGE 4. CHILDHOOD

Age	Virtue Instilled	Psychosocial Crisis	Significant Relationship	Existential Question	Significant Issues
5-12 years	Competence	Industry vs. Inferiority	Neighborhood and School	Can I befriend, cooperate, study, organize, play, and learn?	Individuation, Sense of Humor and Self-Control, Building Skills, Developing Work Ethic

FIVE-YEAR-OLD JON needed help. Shortly after he was molested at four, his father left our home forever as we divorced. In deep grief, feeling forsaken and "ruined" and blaming himself, Jon became seriously depressed.

I was thirty, a new, suddenly broke single parent who had been unemployed for seven years. I was determined to keep our home life as stable as possible and remain in the house to allow Jon and Alan to keep their familiar bedrooms and friends. I took a personnel job on the nearby university campus and then, to cover the costs my new small salary did not, put out an ad for a roommate.

Still, my top priority remained finding Jon someone to talk to. I had no idea what to say or do that would help Jon ease or heal the anguish of seeing his father leave him because he was sure Daddy thought him "too bad a boy." After some discouraging attempts with local nonprofits and low-cost counseling, it was clear Jon needed more expert help.

So despite the cost, I found an expensive, newly licensed, bright, and youthful male psychologist who offered to see Jon individually. I took Jon in, introduced the two, and left as the psychologist instructed me to. Then, to my surprise, before that first hour was up, the psychologist called to say

Jon was ready to be picked up. I arrived to find the psychologist seated behind his desk. Without rising to greet me, he summed up his evaluation of Jon in a few brief words: "Your son is fine. Jon needs no further psychological help." Overwhelmed with relief, I scribbled a check for his fee of one hundred dollars, a serious slice out of my new monthly salary, thanked him with all my heart, and left with Jon in hand.

On the drive home my head began popping with questions I must not ask about this private session. Keeping my eyes on traffic, I tentatively ventured, "So, how was it?"

"Fine."

"What did you do?"

"Nothing."

I got it: Butt out, Mom, none of your business.

Yet from then on, to my surprise, Jon did seem to brighten. Though I couldn't quite believe it, maybe the psychologist was right. Maybe Mom was just catastrophizing. Perhaps time and growth would heal Jon.

My attention turned to finding a renter and babysitters.

Twenty-one-year-old Kay, with black eyes sparkling, rented our playroom with her truly scruffy dog, Scruffy, and moved directly into our hearts. A straight-A organic chemistry major, Kay adored all growing things, including kids and plants. With her supervising, we grew a vast vegetable garden that provided everything from pumpkins and corn to lettuce and zucchini. Sunday afternoons the four of us spent at the beach line-dancing to live ethnic music, Kay and I holding the boys up between us so they hung along in perfect step. When Jon broke a finger, we all trooped to ER, where Kay made Jon laugh through his pain by blowing up surgical gloves into blimp-like hands and twisting the fingers into highly irreverent poses.

Two years later Kay finished college with honors and waved us a sad goodbye. One afternoon before she left, Jon came into the kitchen where Kay and I were cooking. He looked up shyly at her and piped, "Kay, can I marry you when I'm twenty-one and you're thirty-six?"

Kay threw back her black ringlets to laugh heartily then knelt to face Jon at his level. With sparkling eyes, she grinned, "Jon, you won't want me then!"

Seven-year-old Jon had done the math correctly—and in that moment I knew he now had hope for the future. Jon was beginning to heal.

The boys also needed the very best babysitters. Starting when she was fourteen, our neighbor Tracy became the boys' babysitter, confidant, and private chef. She called me her surrogate mom, and I felt blessed to have this adorable and zany surrogate daughter. I would return from work and open the door, and the first whiff told me I needed another dozen eggs because Tracy had baked the boys her zillionth sponge cake.

While I made dinner, Trace would kibitz sitting on the kitchen counter, sharing a day's worth of teen angst, study topics, and life problems. After dinner, often with the boys chiming in, we might have fun rocking out dancing or loudly singing along to Elton John, Joan Baez, or Cat Stevens. Or we'd hold creative cook-offs with top ramen, mac and cheese, or omelets.

Before long, Tracy brought in a gaggle of other young and equally dear teens. Fixing dinner, I would find myself surrounded by young people sitting on the counter or standing around with sodas. Together, they turned my home into the set of a free and fabulous teen sitcom, where all topics were fair game. The kitchen bubbled over with bright ideas, goofy tidbits, laughter, deep questions, and passionate opinions. Sometimes Jon or Alan would come in to listen and join in; other times they would stay in the living room a few feet away to watch TV or hang out with their own pals.

For years our house stayed alive with these freewheeling teens. Jon and Alan could interact with so many cool, bright big brothers and sisters, who showed my sons what they might expect to deal with as they grew up. Without my trying to make it that way, our house became a happy refuge, a rich experience in an otherwise impoverished situation. Jon and his younger brother could take what they liked from this often-delectable stew and know how to recreate it anywhere. Though I had failed to find Jon expert help, all this liveliness at home was a great gift for him, and it all happened effortlessly.

About the time Kay arrived, Jon entered school and discovered something wonderful—that all the terrible things that had happened to him in earlier years could simply be left behind. Every weekday morning he could enter a whole new world, where none of that existed. No one knew. Here he could work hard and prove himself someone worth loving and believing in. At school he could discover he had superior abilities and could apply himself and achieve.

Teachers loved him. Jon was present, curious, and highly verbal. He was quick and questioning. He observed people closely, and over time he developed a droll sense of humor attuned to the absurd. In school Jon had a second chance to prove to himself and to Dad that he was a good, fine, and worthy son. That motivation helped him embrace every assignment and do his best. From the start of his school experience, he excelled in math, English, spelling, reading, writing—everything. Without telling me he had entered them, year after year he came home a finalist in countywide spelling bees and math contests.

In school Jon could leave behind that "ruined," devastated little self and find a new identity. It was a safe new world with good-shepherd teachers and new peers to befriend, full of brand-new possibilities. In school Jon was learning he was okay, that he was good, fun, capable, and worthy. He learned that he mattered, and by simply doing his best every moment, life was worth living.

In kindergarten Jon met Paul, a slight, bright, black-haired boy. Soon the two were inseparable, friends for life. At Paul's house Jon found a welcoming, happy family of five with both parents who spent plenty of time with their children. They all loved to play games around the dining table, laughing and teasing one another. Just as Tracy found a home in our house, quickly Jon became one of their own. Starved for the intact family life he had lost through divorce, Jon thrived on the banter and the games. After school, he would typically walk home with Paul and stay until dinnertime. As the sun dipped below the horizon, he would show up at home full of homemade fudge and yet another story of their aging and slightly notorious dog, Mindy the Beagle. In her honor, Jon's favorite final word on any subject became an emphatic and resounding "Beagle!"

Paul was the first of other brilliant friends Jon would meet at school and keep throughout his life. From school, from his friends, and from all their families, Jon received the validation he so desperately needed and he was blossoming into an astute and highly social boy. He was full of fun and apt to comment with quick wit on whatever was going on.

While beyond our home his life kept brightening, when Jon finally had to return home, he would open the door and—sometimes despite all the liveliness—reenter a painful past he wanted to forget. My having a job stranded him even more. Though we had some daily time together every morning, evening, and before bedtime, finding quality time to have fun together was more difficult. Often Jon would just go upstairs to his room, close the door, and look out the window to the mountains above and the city below and breathe until he was ready, then pour himself into his homework. For Jon, life existed beyond the home, and there his future deeply beckoned.

Though in the evenings our house was awash with young people, Sunday mornings were always family time. That's when I took Jon and his brother out to breakfast, where just the three of us could talk. Everyone could order what they wanted, and I had the luxury of no cooking or work to do so I could fully engage with my two amazing boys—just being with them and enjoying the fascinating person each was becoming.

Yet I didn't realize how much Jon needed more—more of my dedicated attention during the week as well.

Late one night when Jon was eight, after I had put the boys to bed, Tracy and I were talking as usual sitting on the kitchen counter on either side of the sink. Suddenly we heard crying upstairs. Neither of my boys ever cried. Tracy and I ran for the stairs. At the top we found Jon on his bed, sobbing uncontrollably into his pillow.

We sat on his bed on both sides of him. "Jon, Jon, what's wrong? We're here, we love you. Are you all right? What's going on?" I stroked his little blond head, trying to soothe and understand. "Please talk to us. What's wrong?" He just kept crying.

Finally, he gasped out, "I . . . love . . . what you . . . do . . ."

I couldn't figure out what he meant. "Jon, that's so sweet, and I love you too—but why are you crying?"

He never answered. Slowly, while I continued to stroke and reassure him, he stopped crying and eventually drifted to sleep.

Trace and I tiptoed out the door. On our way downstairs she said, "He loves what you do? Why does that make him cry?"

I had no idea.

Only many years after Jon's suicide did I remember this moment and finally understand that Jon had given me exactly half the message. The full message was, "I love what you do . . . with everyone but me." Jon desperately needed the full attention he heard me freely giving to Tracy.

One way he expressed his inner pain was by being hard on his brother and highly questioning and critical of me as a mom. Just as my mother had with me, I never dismissed him, pulled rank, or told him to shut up and obey. Instead, I listened and did my level best to answer his every challenge. As a parent, I was accountable, and Jon deserved honest answers. He mattered and had a right to know. Though some topics were off limits—none of a child's business—I always tried to respond as honestly as I could and take nothing personally.

However, Jon had to face a different kind of parenting during the two weeks a year he visited his dad out of state. One evening when my boys were at their dad's I was surprised by a phone call.

I picked up and heard their father say, "We have to send Jon to military school."

Stunned, I asked, "Why?"

"He's questioning me."

"Right. But why does he need to go to military school?"

"I just told you. He's questioning me."

"I know. But what is he doing wrong?"

"Don't you understand English? I told you, he's questioning me!"

As my ruff rose, I took a big breath and switched tactics. "Is he doing drugs?"

"No."

"Is he failing in school?"

"No."

"Doing anything illegal?"

An exasperated "No."

After another big breath, I said with some edge, "Then why would you send a perfectly good boy to military school?"

Dad roared back, *"How many times do I have to tell you! Because he's questioning me!"*

Now furious, I filled my lungs and yelled right back, *"So . . . just . . . answer . . . the questions!"* and slammed down the phone. I understood Dad's frustration—I had to deal with Jon's challenges fifty weeks out of the year—but the truth was, Jon was simply doing what any smart, normal, and inquiring young student should. He was questioning everything, including authority figures like Mom and Dad.

As Jon and his brother grew, it became ever more obvious that my superbright boys would soon intellectually supersede me. At eight years old Jon could adroitly debate me for forty-five minutes on little issues like making his bed—and win! Though I'd been a mediocre student in high school with no desire to go further, now there was no choice. To keep up, I had to return to school and get smart—quick.

I entered the local community college and signed up for two night classes. After work, after class, after cooking or cleaning, in the evenings on one side of our couch I slaved over homework while Jon coolly completed his on the other.

After my first semester's finals, I returned home astounded by my grades. I opened the door to find Jon facing me.

"Jon, you won't believe what I got!" I burst.

"What did you get?" he asked dryly.

In both awe and pride, I announced, "I got an A+ and a B+!"

Jon looked at me as if I had just died. After a beat or two of total silence, in a voice dripping with contempt, he asked, "You? Got a . . . B?"

Suddenly mortified, I realized, *Oh, my, that's right! Jon never got a B!*

Next thing I knew, Jon was dancing around the coffee table singing, "Mom is a *Beeeeee,* Mom is a *Beeeeee,*" while I curled on the couch in the fetal position and moaned back, "I'm not a Beeee, not a Beeeee. . . ."

To remain this kid's mom and to never suffer another humiliation like that, I had to never again get another B. I didn't—and wound up graduating with highest honors, all due to Jon.

Meanwhile, by the age of nine or ten, buoyed by all his successes both in school and with great friends and their families, Jon had grown more upbeat and connected to life and even to me, though he never forgave me for divorcing his dad. He invented endearing nicknames for me, like Bozley and Mazzie. One Mother's Day morning, the boys made me stay in bed while downstairs they took over the kitchen and then brought up breakfast in bed, a glass of orange juice and a plate with two perfectly done crepes filled with vanilla ice cream.

On my birthday Jon, knowing I liked to sew, presented me with a thoughtful gift, a sewing pattern for pants, a zipper, navy thread, and three yards of deep blue cotton. "You need some new pants, Mom," Jon observed. He was right. That same hot July afternoon, I cut out and sewed up those pants and proudly wore them for years—and still have them.

Buoyed by lively times and relationships both inside and beyond our family, Jon seemed to be slowly healing. The devastations he had experienced in his early life no longer seemed to determine his identity. Astute, super bright, highly verbal, and filled with curiosity, Jon was beginning to make his way in the world.

Erikson on Stage 4:
Industry vs. Inferiority (5-12 Years)

At the age of five or six, Erikson observed, suddenly babyhood is over. Each of its core issues—to trust or not, to be autonomous or be ashamed, and to initiate or feel guilt—has been resolved for better or worse. A taller, stronger, increasingly adept and independent child now begins the solo journey into the world beyond the family.

In Stage 4, the child takes that giant step out into school. From this point on, Erikson noted that the child's main relationship is with school, peers, and neighborhood. Though home and parents remain vitally important to a child, they become less central over time. Erikson suggested that, little by little, children face the fact that their real future—the work of developing their own self and their own story—lies beyond the family. Stage 4 marks their leap from the nest into the rest of their life as independent, freer agents.

For Erikson, the core issue of Stage 4 is industry versus inferiority. Erikson's term industry means the ability to apply oneself and to feel that one matters. In this stage the child learns to feel either effective or inadequate. Feeling capable or successful is the key that unlocks their growing curiosity. From age five or six until puberty begins, children are busy discovering, both in and out of school, that through hard work they can succeed. Or, if those efforts continue to fail, are punished, or are denied, children become demoralized and feel inferior.

To the extent that children feel safe and know that they matter, they will feel free to investigate their world and be who they are. To the extent that children are treated as good and capable people worth believing in, they will venture forth and take the risks to learn and grow. Being taken seriously, being treated with respect, and getting validated by others all strengthen a child's inner character and build the solid foundation for an enduring work ethic.

Erikson pointed out that at no other stage is a child more eager to learn and contribute. Long years have they waited to grow up enough to finally be a real person on their own terms. At this stage of life they yearn to be able to join in, to be who they are, and to help out. They want to have a voice that is taken seriously and responded to honestly. Instead of being shut down by an authority figure saying, "You're wrong!" or "Don't talk back to me!" they need to feel respected, heard, and appreciated. They need to be encouraged and supported in growing more adept and independent. At this stage they begin to think more critically and question everything. When caring adults encourage their questioning, then they know that being curious and working things through on their own matters and that what they say will be taken at face value and responded to with honesty.

At this age, Erikson said, children need to know that who they are is important. They need to be treated, spoken to, and talked about in ways that help them know that they are worthy and authentic human beings. Busy trying new things and having new thoughts, children need to know that others appreciate their ideas and notice their efforts. They want these attempts to be taken seriously and responded to but never criticized or judged. Being able to trust that their experiments will be welcomed as special and not simply judged as right or wrong sets young minds free to think and express themselves. In this way they begin to learn independently and to take full ownership of their choices. Their minds enliven, and their trust in their own internal compass grows.

As babyhood ends, earlier libidinal feelings and fantasies seem to subside. That is why Freud termed this stage the latency period, for from the age of five or six until puberty, the sexual impulse appears to go dormant. However, Erikson noticed that when children leave home behind and enter school, that same creative, reproductive energy is not dormant. Instead, it is transformed into intellectual, playful, and social "intercourse." That budding creative drive is what helps the child in Stage 4 rise to the challenge of school, work industriously, master skills, connect and play with peers, and grow in knowledge, competence, and self-esteem.

Jon in Stage 4

For Jon, life itself began to provide experiences for him to feel successful. From the age of five or six on, he began to be surrounded by friendships full of love and trust, which allowed him to grow into an independent young person who could move forward with confidence. A vibrant home life and successful school life with new friends and their welcoming families helped give Jon the foundation he needed to believe in himself—moving toward what Erikson called industry and away from inferiority.

Though Jon never received the therapeutic help he needed, he began to receive exactly what Erikson said a child at this stage needs. Sparkling new life in our house helped to fill some of the hole left by his daddy. Welcoming these young people into our family helped Jon and his brother take the first of those momentous steps that Erikson said a child takes at this stage of life—growing up with the help of people outside the immediate family.

Even more powerful healing, however, happened once Jon entered school and found only success and validation. His new friends' families welcomed him in and filled him with renewed meaning and positive identity. Here he mattered; here he could have fun and discover himself in full. His trust in himself and life accelerated. He formed lifelong friendships and found the homes away from home that Erikson said a healthy child at this stage needs.

Jon was in fifth or sixth grade when, one day finally cleaning under my bed, I discovered a dusty packet of his earlier schoolwork. Sitting on the floor intrigued, I leafed through an assortment of multicolored assignments topped by A's, then discovered, in large, childish cursive, a short essay from when he was six, with the assigned topic written at the top in faded blue mimeo: "What I Did on My Summer Vacation." Underneath, Jon had titled it, "My Trip to the Psychologist" and wrote that his mother took him to a psychologist who had him cover his eyes with a pillow and then do everything the psychologist said.

> He told me to walk, then stop. I did. Then he told me to feel a step with my foot. When I felt it, he told me to step down. I did. Then he told me to walk straight ahead. I did, and turned when he said to. At one place he said to stop and reach down and feel some water in a pool. I did. Then he took me back to the office, put the pillow over his eyes, and told me to now take him for a walk and I did. I told him when to step down, when to walk straight, and when to turn. When we came to the pool I told him to stop but he didn't hear me and fell in. When he got out he was all wet. He didn't believe me when I told him I said to stop. We went back to his office. He called my Mom and told her to come, that I was fine and needed no help. I had fun at the beach all summer with my friends and was glad I never had to go back to the psychologist.

The story behind that long-ago visit to the psychologist lay finally revealed. Because Jon seemed okay now, so far removed from those horrendous first few years, I laughed and laughed, rereading that short paragraph written in a little boy's careful round hand, imagining the psychologist falling in and rising from the fountain completely soaked in his suit and shoes. Now I knew why the session ended early, why the psychologist stayed seated behind his desk when I arrived, and why he called early and said Jon was fine. And why Jon shared nothing afterward.

Only after Jon's suicide and after I became a therapist myself did I realize the shocking violation of professional ethics this psychologist committed. I entrusted him with my hurting son and paid him to assess Jon's mental health. He pronounced Jon fine when he could not know, after one bungled trust-building exercise, if Jon was fine or not. If he was upset and didn't want to work with Jon, he owed it to both Jon and to me to say so and simply refer us to someone else. Instead, he invented a fraudulent verdict on Jon's mental health. And because I trusted his word, I defaulted on getting Jon the help he needed to heal the painful traumas afflicting him.

Of course, after that visit Jon refused all further professional help. He had watched a real psychologist cover up and not be honest with me, when Jon knew exactly what had happened. That psychologist failed Jon and me as well, first by not believing him, and then by closing the door to Jon receiving further help.

I knew without a doubt that Jon would never have betrayed the psychologist's trust by not saying "stop." If that psychologist had told the truth about what had happened so that Jon could respect him, and if I had gotten the necessary referral so that Jon had received the psychological support he desperately needed, perhaps his inner conflicts and pain could have been healed and not left to simmer unrecognized for so many years until some crisis took him to suicide.

Meanwhile, during that same time period—and again unknown to me—Jon really did try to hang himself on the tree by our front walk but was rescued just in time. It shows that early on, Jon not only thought up a plan to kill himself but actually followed through. What little Jon did constituted a terrible cry for love that was never heard, not by me or any of the professionals I brought him to.

Yet despite all these betrayals and missteps, Jon slowly did seem to improve. Though the toxic residue of the past still simmered within him, success at school and in building enduring friendships plus our bevy of bumptious teenagers at home all helped to provide the foundation Jon needed to begin trusting his ability to make his way in a wider world. On the cusp of adolescence, Jon, though still wounded, appeared to be starting to thrive.

Setting the Foundation for Success

Give your children the keys to success. Support them as they move toward industry—toward applying themselves and being curious about the world outside the home. Give them permission to explore and investigate free of judgments and imposed constraints. Shower them with recognition for every good effort they put out, every movement toward some goal. When we as adults appreciate them for saying yes to projects and for liking to communicate their ideas and experiment, it reinforces the fun that children can find in their own efforts—in being industrious.

For children ages five to twelve, parents, teachers, and others can make industry feel either like work and drudgery or like play—full of fun, surprise, success, mystery, and adventure. When learning itself is fun, then every journey becomes an exciting, even revelatory growth experience. Investigating the world around them without being judged for their actions increases children's curiosity and their trust that life will continue to open up in vibrant ways. Young people experience success when they are encouraged to stay open and keep trying, for all accomplishments and exciting discoveries start with simple, sustained effort and the freedom and curiosity to ask good questions.

In contrast, the gates to inferiority are oiled by adults criticizing, belittling, or just ignoring children's efforts. Also, lessons that are boring, repetitive, or tedious smother eager young minds. When children are punished for asking questions or for "questioning authority," or when children are demeaned, overly corrected, or treated as inferior by parents or teachers, they can over time develop traits such as timidity, anxiety, procrastination, and self-doubt. They can become withdrawn or overly obedient, depressed, anxious, or rebellious.

If children don't try, of course, they will feel inferior and unworthy and express that in some form of negative behavior. Putting forth a serious, sustained effort is what matters. To be industrious, we simply apply ourselves and do our best.

Sometimes effort will result in mistakes or failures. Mistakes are never bad in themselves, for every mistake that isn't fatal helps to redirect us toward solutions. So believe in children, and acknowledge and reassure them through every failure, but don't dwell on failures or punish children for mistakes. Instead, praise them for trying! Eventually, effort leads to answers. Simply correct them if their actions violate safe rules or do not respect the rights of others. True selfhood is won by those who are encouraged to believe in themselves, who always give their best effort, and who never give up. If we simply keep doing that, we can only succeed.

Praising every sincere effort that children make helps them believe in themselves. Encouraging them to enjoy the process of learning, to think for themselves, and to relish every new discovery or "aha!" moment supports them in seeking rewards that mean something. Through this process children grow more resourceful and can become ever more creative and productive over time.

Showing Children They Matter

The more a child senses that "I matter; I am worthy, good, and able," the more the child feels empowered to succeed. But the more a child experiences the opposite sense that "I don't matter" or "I am bad, cannot succeed, or am unworthy," the more despair, anxiety, or negative behaviors will take over instead. An otherwise fine child begins to feel inferior and incompetent and more readily falls prey to acting out their pain or giving up.

How can parents and other caregivers show children that they matter? Whether we know it or not, adults are doing it in each and every moment. Children are adept at reading all the signals adults send. From the body language—a look, particular tone of voice, gesture, or physical shift—children receive the answers to fundamental questions such as, Am I wanted? Good? Safe? Am I loved just as I am? Am I worthy? Intelligent? Capable? Believed in and trusted? And, can I trust myself to succeed?

Listening to Your Children

To show your children they matter, perhaps the most important thing you can do is simply listen to them and take their thoughts seriously. Listening is such a simple activity, and yet it sends children a critical signal: "You are important and matter in my life. You matter so much that I will take time to listen to what you are saying." Jon clearly needed this that evening he lay weeping on his bed, and it crucifies me to know that only too late did I understand his cry for love.

I now know how vital it is for parents to practice deep listening with each of their children. If I had practiced it with Jon, I am certain that over time his morose attitude at home would have lifted. Though he still needed professional help, he would have been receiving from me the best that a parent can give.

Listening to your children involves two steps: listening deeply and then responding with respect.

Listening Deeply

Here are suggestions for practicing deep listening with your children.

Consciously clear your mind of internal chatter. Before any conversation, take a moment to breathe. Keep breathing as you listen. If other pressures intrude in your mind, continue to let them go. Focus instead on your child.

Let go of any need to control, judge, or fix your child—ingredients that muddy the purity of your attention. Simply listen. That alone conveys to children that you care, that they matter, and that they are safe to be who they are.

Hear your children out without interrupting. Simply listen to what they are saying. Let them pause in between their thoughts. The biggest revelations often come after long pauses.

Listen from your heart to hear the feelings and needs underneath their words. That way, when it is your turn to speak, you can reflect their feelings back so they can feel understood instead of alone. This helps them to calm. With Jon, had I been more empathic about what he was hearing and feeling at that time, I might have asked, "Are you feeling sad because you need more time and attention with me?"

Listen from your mind so you can put a name to their emotion, and ask if that is what they are feeling. Connecting words to their emotions helps to diminish internal chaos and helps children feel known and understood.

If you mislabel their feeling, they can correct you: "No, that's not it, it's
_____." This can build their own sense of personal power and help them
clarify their feelings to themselves as well as to you.

Listen from your mind so you can remember their exact words. Using
some of their words as you respond to them reassures them that you truly
heard them.

When your children speak, believe them. To know they matter, children
must be believed. Let that belief radiate from your eyes to theirs.

Expect your children to tell the truth. Children learn to be trustworthy
by being treated as such. They don't lie if they don't have to. Lying really
says, "I'm scared." When I was seven my mother told me, "I have to go
to work from now on. While I'm gone, I must trust you. You are a very
good and smart girl. I am going to give you your freedom. You can do
whatever you like on one condition, that when I come home, you tell me
everything that happened. I promise that no matter how bad you were or
what terrible thing happened, as long as you tell the truth, I will never,
ever punish you. But I must warn you, the moment I find out you lied I
will know I can't trust you, and that is when you lose all your freedom."
Mom kept her side of the bargain, which I discovered at sixteen the very
first time I lied to her. She found out, and I had to sign over my first car to
her—and there went my freedom.

Adjust your body language to match theirs. This is reassuring and says
nonverbally, "We are the same."

Meet them at their level. You might bend down, kneel, or sit facing
them. Or you might sit side by side so you can hear and respond in parallel. Meeting children at their level tells them they matter. If they have to
look up at you while you look down on them, they will take away a different message.

Make eye contact. Looking fully into their eyes shows children that they
are the most important thing in the world to you at this moment.

When you look into their eyes, see only goodness. How you look at your
children communicates volumes. See the miracle they are, and they will
begin to believe in and discover the miraculous in themselves.

Wait for them to finish before you speak. This conveys respect and appreciation. Interrupting puts speakers down by cutting them off. It says, "You and your message don't matter as much as who I am and what I have to say." With children, parents have a duty to empower them by hearing them out fully before responding.

Responding with Respect

After you have listened deeply to your child, it will be your turn to speak. How you speak tells your children who they are to you—whether you trust them, consider them worthy, and regard them as capable and smart equals who can understand and learn anything they want if given the opportunity.

Express appreciation. Don't launch right into your response. Pause to thank them for speaking and for trusting you with this important information. Appreciation builds their confidence and tells them they matter.

Repeat back to them what you heard them say. Only then do children know that you in fact paid sincere attention and truly heard them. Hearing their words in your mouth tells them that they are important and worth paying close attention to. You can also rephrase what they said, and check back: "Do I have it right or not?" Let them correct you until you do. Be patient, as this will help them clarify what they are trying to say.

Clarify feelings and needs. Ask for more clarification if needed. Children (and adults) who have not been taught to express their feelings and needs have a hard time articulating them. For example, when Jon was crying, I could have started by confirming what I did see—that Jon was deeply distressed. I could have asked, "Are you feeling sad?" And if he said yes, I could have made some guesses as to why: "Are you feeling sad about something that happened at school? Are you feeling sad about something at home? Are you feeling sad that I am talking to Tracy right now?" I also could have made guesses about what he needed: "Do you want to spend time with me like Tracy and I spend time together? Do you want more of my attention?" And so forth. Asking questions shows you care and acknowledges that children too are experts—on themselves. It promotes relationships based in equality.

Probe for what your children are feeling and needing. For example, you might ask, "When you say _____, are you feeling _____ because you are needing _____?" Again, let them correct you. Questions like these build a partnership in bringing out the truth. They help both parents and children develop skills in identifying what is truly amiss. See reference to Marshall Rosenberg in the Resources section for a more thorough presentation on this vital topic.

Speak from the heart. In this way we show children the purity of our attention and offer them our empathy. It is possible to speak from other parts of the body as well. When we speak from the head, we can be logical and pragmatic, or we might be talking down to children, judging or criticizing them, or blaming them. When we speak from the gut, we are communicating raw emotions such as fear, anger, or intimidation, perhaps by growling at our children, warning them, or being queasy and fearful. Children can sense, even if they can never say, what part of your body you are speaking from. Their own bodies will respond in kind. Speak from your heart rather than your head or your gut, and your child will respond from the heart as well.

Tell the truth. Telling children fictions undermines and confuses them. Children are always learning if they can trust you. Not only is that their core issue at birth, it's the question on which every relationship in their life hinges. Without trust, there is no relationship. When adults fib, children eventually find out, and the fibber loses their trust and respect. If children can trust you to be authentic, they can trust themselves to be the same. You don't need to tell them more than they are capable of understanding, but you do need to be authentic. (This is separate from their ability to cope with adult subject matter. Do not burden children with adult business.)

Use warm, authentic, and natural tones. Our tone of voice conveys our feelings, both pleasant and unpleasant. A warm and vibrant tone of voice communicates that we love them and are available for them. Children, especially younger children, take everything very personally. Let them hear open and warm tones, and they will be reassured that they are valued and are okay.

Use normal words. Children know when they are being talked down to. Trite baby names, little pretenses, or the use of singsong or coos all tend to disempower children, to infantilize or insult them. Don't try to fake them out or dumb them down! Bring them up instead. Speak simply, kindly, and honestly. They need to believe you and be treated honorably.

Notice what you say. Is what you say all about you—your self or your own interests, needs, or rules and how they should be obeyed? Is what you say full of gossip, adult preoccupations, or trivia? If it is, children hear that they don't matter. Instead, respond to what your children say. This tells them that they matter enough to be heard.

Speak to an equal. Do you expect to be the sovereign or expert in your relationship with your child, or do you expect to be worthy equals? Here's the truth: you can't be both. Whichever one you choose will tell children volumes about who you think they are. Speak with your children, not at them.

Respect children's body space. Mind their body language to sense if touch would be welcome or not. Without asking first and getting their permission, never impulsively reach out to touch, pat them on the head, or straighten their clothes as you interact. Respect children as you would a best friend. As you approach, if you notice any hesitancy or discomfort, stop and give them more space. Only give what they are comfortable with, and when in doubt, check in with them.

Appreciating What Children Do

To motivate your child's success, notice and express appreciation for every effort the child makes. As long as a child's attempt falls within safe boundaries and does not violate the needs or rights of others—both of which do need your intervention—the school of life is often a child's best corrective. Give feedback only if they ask you for it or you check in first: "Would you appreciate some feedback?" And respond accordingly.

When Jon's younger brother was small, he would come up with the most creative but wrong ideas of how things work. I would simply say, "What a good idea!" and never "You're wrong!" For why would I want to dismiss or undermine such a lively mind? I knew this little scientist would soon figure out what works. As he grew, Alan retained this inventive, magical faculty and continued to trust his ability to think things through on his own, and eventually he succeeded beyond measure.

Parents can support the learning process by staying open and patient and holding a long vision. Mistakes are how we learn. They show we are at a growing edge. Like Socrates, adults only need to ask good questions. Unless some danger or crisis is in the offing, this is usually the most helpful thing to do.

By appreciating the hard work our industrious students put into every effort, we encourage them to keep trying and keep working. Take note of and verbally or nonverbally acknowledge each action your children take that is good, kind, loving, fun, beautiful, interesting, curious, or exploratory.

As I did with my younger son, parents might say, "Wow, you thought of that on your own? What a good idea!" Ideas do not need to be right to be good ideas. They emerge when children feel safe rather than criticized or evaluated. When children's ideas are appreciated but not judged as good or bad, right or wrong, children can feel safe to brainstorm and will grow in thinking, trying, and sharing openly. When they have the creative space to explore, they learn that exercising their ideas and imagination can be both fun and rewarding, and they learn to follow through.

Children are most enthusiastic at this age. Take advantage of it! They have an expanded imagination free of society's regimentation. Help them master knowledge by trusting them to do so and by offering them your unflagging support and encouragement.

Evaluation and Grades

Parents can support their children's progress by praising children's efforts and not focusing on their grades, whether to praise or to punish them. Grades are a flawed measure of ability. Not only that, but over time grades become an increasingly punishing system of rewards. Slogging up that steep hill of learning just for the payoff of a grade only to find ourselves back at the beginning needing to do it all over again can become an exhausting and punishing cycle. Over time it actually discourages children, who can begin to feel trapped, as if they are running on an endless hamster wheel.

Success is never measured by a grade. Grades reflect conditions far beyond academic performance. Grades say as much about the health of the student's body, home life, or their social, economic, and political network as they do the school environment. Grades may also be a function of the teacher's biases as well as the teacher's teaching ability.

However, children tend to think in black and white, so they take grades very personally—as proof of their success or failure. Unfortunately, all too often so do their parents and schools. Children come home with bad grades, and parents and teachers blame the child instead of looking at the teacher's skills or asking what in the child's environment needs improving, such as better nutrition, a healthier home or friendships, or a different educational setting. Focusing on a child's grades tends to equate their entire worth with a grade. Children can identify with A's and come to believe that anything less means total failure. Or they can identify with D's and never try. Also, grades are the result of a onetime performance. The more we can disentangle a child from identifying with a particular grade, the better.

Children should be rewarded for the effort they put out, not the grade they get. As Thomas Edison reportedly said while working on the light bulb, "I have not failed. I've just found ten thousand ways that won't work." Persevering and learning from every error takes us to success. What is important is to enjoy the process of discovery—finding something new to savor and be curious about in every moment.

Grades are especially problematic because most schools choose to grade "on the curve." This means dividing a class into percentages of A's, B's, and so forth to form a standardized bell curve or "normal distribution." No matter what the class or test, 20 percent of the students receive the top scores, or A's; the next 30 percent receive B's; 30 to 40 percent (the center of the curve) earn C's; and 10 to 20 percent receive D's or F's. Grading on a curve pits students against one another, as one student's success comes at the expense of another's. If one student gains, another loses. It is an evaluation system based on outcompeting peers rather than rewarding all industry and real learning. In this zero-sum game, students lose. It fosters competitiveness instead of community and breeds feelings of inferiority in students who might be putting out wonderful effort but who never achieve top scores. Grading on the curve is too often divisive and demoralizing.

Schools could measure students' work another way. In "criterion referenced testing," students' grades are calculated not by comparison to their classmates but on the basis of how well they are mastering the course content. In this system, it is possible that all students receive top scores. This is a fairer and more egalitarian way to grade, and it encourages all students to do their best because they will be rewarded for their own work rather than for how they compare to their classmates.

Supporting Your Child's Success at Home

While school holds a child's gateway to the future, the family and home remain the child's personal refuge. Parents can support their child's successes at school by making the home an extension of the best aspects of school.

Children are nourished by a home environment that is freewheeling, happy, insightful, and real, where problems are acknowledged but having fun is just as important. They thrive in a home full of healthy food, camaraderie, trust, safety, creativity, spontaneity, fun, seriousness, and equality.

At home, *create a climate of safety,* open to all, accepting, understanding, tolerant, and warm. A safe environment means not judging or evaluating your children, simply extending unconditional love. Seek to bring out in them what is beautiful, good, and true within safe and clear limits. For example, to provide a climate of safety and interaction at home, parents can rule certain things off limits, such as illegal drugs or social media at certain times. Be here now with your children, fully present and real.

A climate of safety means a home that is free of emotional and physical violence and where conflict is acknowledged and resolved with equanimity. Drama may happen occasionally, but it is not constant. Children cannot focus on their studies when there is ongoing conflict at home. Chaos or drama of any kind stimulates their bodies to produce adrenaline and cortisol to fuel their survival, thereby shutting down the higher brain functions of thinking and reasoning. Chaos at home saps children's focus and energy and undermines their performance. It is deeply threatening to young children, dissolving their solid ground.

To support your child in school, *be a trustworthy adult.* Maintain an atmosphere in the home that is supportive, open, and truthful. Being trustworthy means being consistent with your children and available for them when they need you. It means being positive, warm, and open-hearted. It means playing with them, being real with them, and interacting with them at their level—and leaving them alone when they need privacy or time with their friends. Being trustworthy means influencing your children by example, not by control. No judging, shaming, or criticizing allowed, for being treated like this prevents children from flourishing and causes them either to plummet into despair or to mentally fly off like pigeons, never to return.

Respect your children's lively, creative imaginations. Parenting is the ultimate improv lesson. It requires a mind-set of being facile and present, open to whatever pops up. When children feel respected, they know they are heard. They feel included, not shut down. Refrain from criticizing or judging, and most of all, administer no punishment. Everyone is legitimate here, okay and equal. Establish healthy and safe boundaries. No meanness or cruelty allowed.

Respect your child's industry. When children are working on some task, avoid any urge to kibitz, judge, insert yourself, or take over. Be of help without distracting—perhaps bringing them a snack or drink or quieting any outside distractions. If time is limited, let them know this beforehand so they can be prepared. Then they can budget their work and not be surprised or cut short when time is up. Help only when asked, and remember that less help is more. Ask questions, which helps them learn to think independently instead of expecting you to solve their problems for them.

Expect children to test the rules. Be prepared for it when they do. An important part of development is discovering what's true for themselves and finding out if you mean what you say and will follow through. When you set a clear boundary, let them know what the consequences will be for violating it. Then, without drama, simply follow through each time.

Have fun with your kids! Have as much fun with your child as you do with other adults. Parenting is a once-in-a-lifetime opportunity to relish your children, and these years are too soon over. Seek out fun activities with your children, which will bring out their joyful spirits. Taking time to have fun with your children at every age shows them that they matter and supports them in doing their best work in the rest of life.

When Children Make Poor Choices

Of course, as they are testing what is possible, children will sometimes make poor choices. When they do, never punish them, which reinforces the wrong thing and tends to shut children down. Alternatives to punishment are available that will support them instead.

When faced with negative behavior from your child, speak to the child calmly about what they did. Gently probe the child for the feelings or needs that helped to generate that behavior. Take the time to listen to your child's experience. Then empathize in full. In other words, imagine what it would feel like to be in their shoes.

It's always a good idea to share a similar story from when you were their age, to talk with them about it, and to share how that situation resolved. Hearing your story will help your children absorb your history into theirs; it will deepen their connection to you and correct innocent misconceptions. You might ask for their reactions or other ideas, and together you might come to new insights and solutions. The more you tell your stories to them, the more you become a real human being to them instead of just a role.

Furthermore, telling your stories to your children helps give them insights beyond their age level that they can use to their own benefit. Jon would bring his young friends home, and at some point I'd hear him call out, "Mom, tell them the stories!" I had told my boys many parables of my own youth, and by asking me to share some of these, Jon was acknowledging that he found them not only enjoyable but also somehow worth sharing. Of course, I was just doing what my mother had done with me. As a kid, I had adored hearing her tell stories of her life at the turn of the century, a life that always sounded exotic to me.

If your child makes a bad choice, probe for the feelings that motivated that choice. Feelings are never right or wrong; they are just feelings. Likewise, the needs that generated those feeling are never wrong either. We all share the same basic and sometimes contradictory needs (for example, security, love, adventure, sovereignty, intimacy, community, independence, self-worth, and self-expression).

But problems may arise with how we choose to meet those needs. We can meet a need for expressing frustration, for instance, by inverting a box of popcorn over someone else's head. Or we can meet it by pounding a pillow or asking a counselor or friend, "I'm so frustrated that I failed this test. Can you help me figure out some of these answers?" When, instead of punishing your child for bad behavior, you instead help your child understand their confusing feelings and needs, you are giving them skills that will last a lifetime. Through recognizing their feelings and needs, they become able to explore alternative ways of meeting those needs.

With negative behavior, as with failures, do not dwell on a child's poor choice. Simply correct them if their action violated safe rules or did not respect others' rights. You might offer simple and doable alternatives, and you might also ask them for their own ideas. You might request them to tell the truth about any lapse and promise that if they do, you will never punish them. Then provide fair warning for the consequences of lying about this or anything else, and be fully willing and able to follow through. Always reward a child for telling you the truth. When we do something wrong and admit it, that is punishment enough and simultaneously reinforces being responsible. Truth is freeing. Lies constrict. Being fully responsible returns us to full power, which sets us free to grow into our full potential. We all want to be respected as authentic; we all want to feel connected, understood, and worthy.

The Power of Love

Just one stable, clear, kind, available, and authentic person can give a child the safe harbor that helps them learn to trust others as well as the resources inside themselves—and life itself. That one relationship may come from the extended family, from the neighborhood, or from the school. Whoever that person is, they will love and encourage the child and support their being themselves. They will see only beauty, courage, and genius in the young person, and thus the young person will learn to see those things in themselves.

From the age of five on, Jon was blessed with many such relationships, and so, despite his tough beginnings, he began to thrive. Even without the benefit of expert help, Jon was healing. I could only hope it would be enough to see him through adolescence.

———

TEACHINGS, AIRBAGS, AND SAFETY NETS

- In Stage 4, the core issue for children is industry versus inferiority. Working hard and feeling successful continue to motivate their growing curiosity and ability to learn. But the more their efforts fail or are punished or denied altogether, the more children become demoralized and feel inferior.

- Erikson noted that children's main relationship in this stage is with school, peers, and neighborhood. Although the home and their parents remain vitally important, they become less central over time.

- Children between the ages of five and twelve are more eager to learn, work, and contribute than at any other time. So when children sincerely wish to join in, say yes! By helping, they learn to feel good about themselves as they build competence.

- Adults can make industry feel either like work and drudgery or like play. When learning itself is fun, every idea or effort becomes an exciting stepping-stone to explore and discover new things.

- Tell your children how much you appreciate their every effort at trying, learning, and growing. Praise their effort, not the end result. Every successful step leads to a successful result.

- Mistakes are fine, normal, and to be expected. They only prove we are at a new, exciting edge. Learning what doesn't work is as necessary as discovering what does.

- Acknowledge and reassure children through every failure, but don't dwell on or punish them, except to correct them if their actions violate safe rules or do not respect others' rights.

- When children ask you for help, give it to them with respect and trust; then let them take it from there.

- When children are working on some task, avoid any urge to insert yourself or take over. Be of help without distracting them, and remember that less help is more.

- Be truthful. Speak to children as respected, good, and worthy equals.

- Children need to know they matter. Show them how important they are to you in your thoughts, your words, your tone of voice, your eyes, your smile and touch and body language.

- Use deep listening techniques with your children. When your children speak, give them your full, pure attention. Listen with your heart, mind, ears, eyes, and whole body to help them feel understood and valued. Repeat back their words to help confirm that you understand them and care for them.

- Guide children by asking good questions and being their collaborator, not their boss.

- Have fun with your child as much as you do with other adults. This no-miss, once-in-a-lifetime opportunity is too soon over.

- Grades are flawed measures that report on far more than mere student performance. They grade a teacher's teaching; they report on how well testing works; and they show the effects of a student's energy, health, nutrition, friendships, or problems at home. Teach children that grades say nothing about who we are or what we can be or achieve. What matters is trying, for the more we try, the better we get, and success becomes inevitable.

- Encourage your child's school to move away from grading "on the curve" and toward a more egalitarian system such as "criterion referenced learning." Grading "on the curve" artificially promotes competitiveness in classes, possibly exacerbating the problem of bullying and negative comparisons. By contrast, "criterion referenced learning" treats students as unique, independent individuals; it is more democratic and promotes community.

- To support your child in school, be a trustworthy adult for them at home.

- The best thing you can give your child is a home climate of clear boundaries. Within those boundaries, give them total safety and the freedom to be who they are with your unconditional love and respect.

- Feelings of doubt, insecurity, confusion, fear, or distrust deeply undermine children's ability to focus and learn. To pursue their personal growth, children need a climate of trust and safety.

- Believe in your children at all times. Even if they are wrong or get demoralized, show them you trust their intelligence and heart. Encourage them in their journey of discovery.

- Even when children are speaking critically to you, don't shut them down; listen for their feelings and their needs, and connect first there.

- Never punish a child for telling the truth. Instead, reward the truth every time. That way more authenticity and trust can keep building between you. Punish lying, but let them know in advance what the consequences will be—and be sure they are fair and easily implemented. Then simply follow through as promised every time. Show them how to make better choices instead.

- Support your children's friendships with others. Welcome their friends in your home, and take your children and their friends out and about (with their parents' approval, of course).

- Expect children to test the rules, and be prepared for it when they do. An important part of development is discovering what's true for themselves and finding out if you mean what you say and will follow through.

- Just one stable, kind, and authentic person can give a child the safe harbor that helps them learn to trust the resources inside themselves.

Hitting Hyperdrive

~

STAGE 5. ADOLESCENCE

Age	Virtue Instilled	Psychosocial Crisis	Significant Relationship	Existential Question	Significant Issues
12-18 years	Fidelity	Identity vs. Role Confusion	Peers and Role Models	Who am I? Where and with whom do I belong?	Finding Unique Identity, Fitting in Peer Group, Exploring Sexuality, Testing Career Paths

JON WAS HALFWAY through his first year in junior high when I got a call from the school's counselor. Had Jon done something wrong?

"Mrs. Raymond, I have a problem. I have no idea what to do with Jon and wondered if you could help. Jon's IQ does not qualify him for the mentally gifted classes..."

"Okay..." I'd never been told about Jon's IQ so what else could I say?

"But he keeps outperforming all the students in his classes. I am at a loss as to what we should do. Do you have any suggestions?"

That was the world's easiest question to answer. "Well," I began, "why don't you put him in one of the classes anyway and see how he does?"

"Oh, what a great idea! We'll do that. I am so relieved. It's been weighing on me for quite some time now. Thank you, Mrs. Raymond."

From day one in the Gifted and Talented Education Program (GATE), Jon thrived. He met and made more lifelong friends, such as lanky, dark-haired Todd, an inquisitive and superbright boy who quickly became a forever friend. And another classmate, Dean, who graduated from junior high and headed straight for Stanford and a PhD. In GATE, Jon found he could learn alongside these new peers.

At his junior high graduation Jon was surprised to find himself class valedictorian. He had deeply appreciated this rare opportunity and done his best in it as a result, and he had a lot to say about what he had observed in his GATE classes. He thought that too many GATE students took this privileged education for granted and didn't really try. They just coasted along, and their work was generally mediocre. On his own and unknown to me at the time, Jon wrote a many-paged letter that he hand-delivered to the school administration with his observations and point-by-point suggestions for improvement.

By his freshman year of high school, Jon was the very picture of a gawky adolescent. At puberty his shock of fine and straight blond hair thickened, turned beige, and formed permanent and very uncool-at-the-time marcelled waves. He wore braces and horn-rimmed glasses, and his voice turned reedy. Self-conscious and uncomfortable, Jon was a brainy boy morphing into an adult in a body ratcheting ever taller. Before there was the label, Jon embodied a perfect geek.

As a GATE freshman in high school, Jon began sailing through a full high school course load, including advanced placement electives. But he was soon bored with high school and, still fourteen at the end of his freshman year, cast about for more challenge. On his own he discovered that his GPA qualified him for early admission into the local state university to take one course there per quarter, and he signed up without telling me. He would get entry-level college courses out of the way while finishing high school. Out of the blue one evening, Jon ambushed me with a completed, officially signed university acceptance form, flipped to the back page, pointed to a line under his signature, and said, "You get to sign here." I first hesitated but then signed off, unable to deny him this opportunity. I then reeled when Jon chose, of all subjects, a whole year of one of the most dreaded courses on campus: the calculus sequence. Two hundred fifty smart, much older, and supercompetitive STEM majors took this required course every quarter. All this in addition to his daily six classes in high school? What a setup to fail! But as usual, Jon worked really hard.

At the end of his first quarter in calculus, Jon earned the top score in the final exam and his first A on a real university transcript. Though floored, I was the world's proudest mom. Then, surprisingly, he whined and backpedaled. He couldn't go on, he said; it was just too hard. I agreed it sure was, but because he had just done the impossible, I encouraged him to try anyway and just take one step at a time. He could drop anytime—he already had four university units at an unbelievable 4.0. Reluctantly, Jon reenrolled. At the second quarter's end, once again he was the class's top scorer, earning himself yet another A, and this time had even invented a few new proofs. His professor was ecstatic.

Yet again, Jon wanted out. Surprised and baffled, I again suggested he face his fears but take it day by day, slowly, and opt out anytime. Jon made it through a full year of calculus with straight A's, always first in his class of two hundred fifty, but always wanting to quit between quarters.

And he did this while maintaining a 4.0 in high school.

What was really going on in that class? Jon never let on, at least to me.

In his sophomore year in high school, Jon began tutoring calculus to a few bright and curious peers. One of his students was dear, sweet Laurel, who liked this young man and turned to him now and then for support in difficult moments. In between calculus sessions they went on a few casual dates. When we got a new puppy, Jon brought her over to see it. I watched them stand by each other in our backyard, gazing with delight at the puppy's antics. It was hard not to notice how much of a pair they looked.

But in spite of being on a fast academic track and having friends he enjoyed and hung out with, Jon seemed miserable much of the time. At home his unhappiness was palpable. When he was thirteen I remarried, and my new husband and I took our combined three sons on a summer camping trip in "Moby Truck," our old white truck and camper shell. On the road, Jon sat in the back with a book in front of his face, refusing to speak or even look out the window. He hated being forced to leave his room and his friends to go on this trip. His silence made for a long, uncomfortable journey. While the rest of us pointed out sights and stopped to explore, Jon stayed in the truck, unmoved. Was this normal teenage sullenness, or was something else going on?

His high school pictures from that time show a desperately unhappy young man. At fifteen he sits facing the camera, looking lost. His face is slack, his huge blue eyes, as if from far away, hollowly boring a hole through the lens. Broadening shoulders sag. His lips are parted as if stunned. The face is a mix of sorrow, dismay, and reproach—looking directly at you the viewer.

When Jon brought home this picture I sighed, exasperated. Such a brilliant, fine boy—composing himself to look so pathetically miserable! I thought he was manipulating us. "Oh, really?" I challenged. "Can you make yourself look even worse?"

Only after his death did I find Jon's high school yearbook, a little leather journal signed by other students the last day of each school year. My heart broke as I read his peers' own words testifying to what he continually faced from them—the envy, cruelty, and ridicule that adolescents who are different in any way face. Then I had to face how I too had judged him, stranding him to face this treatment on his own.

But many of these same entries ended with apologies. A boy wrote, "Jon, I'm really sorry for being so cruel to you for such a long time. I now know that you're a great guy. I hope we have a lot of classes together next year." More of the truth came out with another boy's message: "Jon, You're the SMARTEST person I know. I don't know why they tease you. Maybe they're jealous? I'm sorry if I ever did." Jon's retro wavy hair was also a target: "Sorry about persecuting you so much in German—I was jealous of your 'mod' hairdo. . . . Well, continue in excellence and party down this summer."

But some apologies also held a clue about how effectively Jon handled these cuts: "Jon—For a freshman you're not that bad, besides being too smart. For all my hassling you, here is an apology. Hey, thanks for all the help in math. Take it easy this summer." Or, "Jon, you're a very, very smart person and you used to make me sick, but now I admire you for taking two math classes this year and still getting straight A's. See you later, Love, R." Others appreciated his wry, quick wit: "Jon Dear, You're so hilarious! You truly made Mr. C's class worth coming to every day! You've got such a fun personality! Lots of love, A." Or, "Jon, Thanks for brightening up my days with your friendly Hellos!! You're one of the nicest and most sincere freshmen around. Love, B."

Of course, Jon didn't tell me any of this. He was a teenager, learning to separate from me and take full responsibility for himself, so he kept it all private. I understand. If he had shared about the teasing and harassment,

I surely would have gone to the school administration swinging. And I am sure—and Jon knew—that my actions would only have damaged his standing among his peers.

Then at 7:00 a.m. one lovely spring Saturday, sixteen-year-old Jon announced that he was due an hour and a half away for a three-hour test, and I was to be his chauffeur. Once again, unknown to me, he had signed up for something—this time, to take the General Education Diploma (GED) test to get out of school early.

I knew Jon wanted to leave school early. But I didn't know two things: first, that he—as usual and behind my back—had meticulously done his college application homework. Official requirements? Check. Scholastic Aptitude Test? Check. Back came impressive results, especially in math. In hand was all the right stuff to earn entrance to some good university.

And second, he never mentioned that he had already surveyed the nation's universities, selected three, and sent out applications to MIT, Princeton, and Carnegie Mellon. He knew better than to tell me. He was too young to leave home for a university far away—especially some elite school I couldn't afford. Without a word, he waited for the results. Finally, the admissions office replies began arriving. MIT rejected him; Princeton put him on a waiting list. Then Carnegie's big brown manila envelope arrived. Though only sixteen, Jon had been accepted.

That's when, with CMU's congratulatory letter in hand, Jon chose to fill me and my husband in on what he had planned. He was floating on air.

Carnegie Mellon might as well have been on the moon. There was no way we could afford it. Not to mention an elite school all the way back east, its culture so different from that of California. Then, to top it off, being two years too young? I was thrilled for him yet terrified. Everything in me said, Don't let him go! But could I really refuse him an opportunity he had wrought of his own hard work?

Overnight Jon changed. Suddenly he seemed truly happy. His school picture that year shows a playful and quite assured young man, his face tilted forward and his lips pulled into a self-confident grin so broad that two impish dimples I had never noticed appeared. Here is a self-made survivor, a winner ready to tackle any challenge.

For Jon, going to Carnegie Mellon was a given. Despite every legitimate misgiving, I could not deny him. This was his well-earned entry to a fabulous life. After all the awful things Jon had experienced early on, it was time the scale rebalanced. So we rallied around and supported his plan.

All too soon, the day of his departure arrived. Jon stowed his baggage in the car and said goodbye to his brother, and my husband and I drove him to the airport.

I kept my head straight ahead so he couldn't see the tears leaking out my eyes.

"I'm going to miss you. . . ." My voice broke before I could finish the sentence.

"I'll call and send letters. Besides, you're busy."

"Sure, but there's only one Jon Raymond, and that's you, and there's no replacement."

"You're being silly, Mom. I'll be as far away as a phone or the mail. You don't have to act like I'm dying or something."

"Okay, sorry." I tried not to sob.

"You should be happy to see me moving on!"

"I am, but I can't bear that you'll really be gone, okay?"

"Beagle."

Summarily dismissed, I stared ahead, tearing up and sniffing, then reached out to hold his hand, but it eased away. He never could stand being touched. At the airport he waved us off and disappeared through the Passengers Only door. We saw the plane taxi away, as I wept next to my husband and continued all the way back to the car.

In September of 1985 Jon, who had just turned seventeen, became a new freshman, one of the youngest on this elite campus.

After he arrived, he took a few weeks to settle in while I waited for news. Finally, my phone rang. What a thrill to hear my son's buoyant, still reedy voice, talking as if simply continuing yesterday's conversation! As usual, he was withholding a lot, as I would learn from others later on.

Like the nightmare of his arrival on campus. He wrote his Great-Aunt Amelia that "he was ten times disgusted" to get to his assigned dorm room, open the door, and find "the rug had residents," the bare brick walls had "holes to blow in cold and see the view through, and the toilet—CENSORED." Then he joked, "Of course, I felt right at home and started to unpack—just kidding." Apparently, he threatened the head of the housing department that he would leave college if he didn't get something better, then bivouacked in a dorm lounge until they assigned him a slightly better room.

In that same letter to his great-aunt, he added dryly, "The people here are very different. They don't respond to any of my passing greetings, but when I ask them questions, they are very explicit about how I can solve my problems."

But that day, in his first call home, I heard none of that. He just cut to the chase.

"Hi, Mom. . . . I've got good news and bad news. Which do you want to hear first?"

"Oh, geez. Give me the worst first."

"The bad news is, I'm staying here."

"Ohhh. . . ." We both knew the price of a Carnegie Mellon education was astronomical. "Okay, so what could possibly be the good news?"

"The good news is, you're paying for my graduate education."

"Huh?"

He had just attended a "by invitation only" new program orientation with thirty-two handpicked other freshmen. This accelerated program in theoretical mathematics condensed six years of study into four. In the first two years he would complete all requirements for the bachelor of science degree. The next two years would be devoted to completing his master's. At graduation, a stellar career would be assured. The impossible price tag of his education would be truly an efficient investment. By the age of twenty-one, Jon would have a graduate degree in theoretical math—Einstein's field!

Who could refuse such an offer?

Little did we know the full extent of the academic gauntlet he just signed up for or the hazing Jon would have to endure from his "very different" peers.

One morning, asleep in his dorm, Jon woke to a knock on the door and a voice outside saying, "Hey, Bro, come on out!"

Here he was, a gawky, barely seventeen-year-old geek from California with horn-rimmed glasses and still-reedy voice—tall and still uncomfortable about it.

The banging continued.

"Come on out, Bro, you've gotta see this. You're famous, dude."

Jon dressed and stepped out of his room as a few new "buddies" trooped him down the hall and out across the commons, pointing to a fence in the snow. Slathered over it in large, dripping red letters was the word GOOBER. That, they told him, was his new name, and what an honor it was to be so officially recognized in writing on this fence.

Jon wrote the family all about it later in one of his newsy letters, telling the whole tale with gawky, self-conscious humor.

All he left out were his feelings.

Back home, I was enraged, aching for him. Who needs that kind of ridicule? What a cruel and heartless bunch! I tried to get him to talk about it, but every attempt got ducked or stonewalled. He was busy taking it in stride like a man, proving his mettle.

Only after Jon's suicide would his younger brother finally share that Jon wrote him from Carnegie Mellon, saying he had become so deeply depressed after entering school that he began going to a campus psychotherapist. Again, Jon was doing his best to field every challenge on his own, while at home his loyal younger brother kept his secret.

But as time went on, with psychological support Jon did restabilize. Meanwhile, he once again made long-term friends. One Christmas he was invited to stay in Paris with a CMU friend's family over the break. In their three-story walkup lived five other families, each one from a different part of the world. Each day a different family hosted the whole building's occupants to a traditional, five-course feast over lively conversations covering the globe. When dinner finally ended in the wee hours, the young people were let out to play in Paris. Jon came home saying, "You don't know how to live!"

In the dorms Jon didn't party or drink or go after girls. Instead, he watched with great tongue-in-cheek humor as everyone else around him did. He worked hard, wrote the family long, fascinating, very funny group letters of the goings-on around him, and slowly made friends. Jon seemed genuinely ready to help out struggling students with school or anything else that was bothering them. The same spirit for helping others that he had shown toward his high school peers finally turned into a paid role in his last two years in a dorm as residence hall supervisor. As a freshman dorm mate wrote us after hearing of his death, "[Jon's] experience and expertise was much appreciated in our largely freshman hall. Jon gave freely of himself, asking nothing in return. He was kind, warm, sincere, and truly funny. He was also one of the most brilliant thinkers I have ever met, even here, at a university widely known for the intellectual acumen of its student body. . . ."

All the while Jon kept succeeding in his studies and moving toward graduation.

Jon apparently had two brief girlfriends early on, though I found out about them only from others. At the end of a long letter to his Great-Aunt Amelia: "Well I knew you would just have a fit if I never mentioned girls, so to fill you in, I met this girl named Lori—she's absolutely beautiful—she majors in creative writing—or 'word engineering' as she calls it—so scientific!—and she takes voice lessons and sings in the choir, which I have definitely decided I like listening to. The rest of the story falls under the category strictly confidential."

During the summers he returned home and got a job. One summer he worked for a foundation that organized travel plans and secured host families for international students. Jon was such a quick study that over three months he was promoted three times to end up their assistant manager. He became famous for his quick comebacks. Once an angry student demanded to speak to his superior, and Jon shut him down with, "I have no superior." At his farewell party, the entire office surprised him with a cake with the words *I Have No Superior* written across the top, and made him eat his words.

Exploring the world on his own, Jon was coming into his own. The grueling program could not stop him; as he moved forward in it, his clarity of purpose grew. He was beginning to forge his own identity and his own path forward.

Erikson on Stage 5:
Identity vs. Role Confusion (12-18 Years)

Erikson saw that each adolescent's core issue is to form their identity. Somehow a young person must consolidate a more independent adult identity that builds on their earlier childhood self and integrates a new-found sexuality into all this complexity. At the same time, they are busy exploring who they are and where they belong in relation to new peers, schools, advanced coursework, and the looming world of work.

"Who am I in the eyes of others?" becomes the pressing question. Young people are now busy bonding with their peer cohort, for this is the generation they belong to and will be interacting with for the rest of their lives. The opinions of others become central, for it is in others' power to say yea or nay, to include or exclude. With the need to belong comes an outsized emphasis on appearance, for each young person's body is changing beyond all their control.

From the inside out, all is in flux. Erikson noted that at puberty, much of the identity a child forged and took for granted as "me" is thrown up into the air. All that they were and thought they knew about themselves no longer fits. A physiological reformation is occurring while each youth is assailed both by strange internal forces and new external challenges.

Internally, sex hormones are differentiating male from female and preparing them for the reproductive capabilities of full adulthood. The changes in their own bodies are enormous and embarrassingly visible. Bones elongate, faces pop with eczema, hair grows where it never did before. New libidinal feelings and sexual fantasies flood the senses and the mind. Young people have no idea exactly how to cope with all this. They will not know for years exactly what their adult self will look or feel like. Who can they be? Or befriend? Or love? All are but elusive question marks. They have high hopes and dreams yet little idea of their true personal potential.

Neither do young people know how they will earn their living as adults. During their teenage years they can only speculate about what their long-term career might be. Meanwhile, in and out of class, they can be callow and cruel as they vie with one another across social, romantic, academic, sports, and vocational forums.

Since the results of this multifaceted growth experiment cannot be fully known for years, each adolescent experiences the same anxiety. Who am I? Who are you? Am I okay? Who am I sexually? Attractive? Desired? Where do I fit? Who am I like? Not like? What is possible for me in love? In work? In life?

And just at this moment when youth are insecure yet must still navigate many tides, they find little support from the broader community. Modern society offers few rites of passage or structured mentoring relationships to usher young people into their unique, sexually mature, adult identities. Youth must rely for the most part on peers for community. Among their peers, youth seek a safe harbor of allies where they can express themselves and give and receive validation for the newly mature self each is becoming.

Learning to be independent means that youth no longer freely share with parents. The closer they were to their parents as children, the harder they as teens often attack and drive their parents away. The same is often true with friends or relatives of their age group. As Erikson pointed out, "Adolescents have to refight many of the battles of earlier years . . . [by] appointing perfectly well-meaning people to play the roles of adversaries" (Erikson, *Childhood and Society*, 261). As much as they need to connect with an intimate few to help one another move through this scary and mysterious process and explore their new identity as sexual beings, youth also must protect that intimate, safe circle by aggressively excluding all others.

Young people at this age are, as Erikson saw, highly clannish, intolerant, volatile, and fickle. They may even be cruel in excluding others who are deemed disloyal or are rivals or simply different. Though their intolerance is often devoid of insight or compassion, it is important, Erikson noted, to understand that this is a still-forming ego's defense against identity confusion when they really don't know who they are. With their still-immature brains perceiving the world in black-and-white terms, they regard peers as either ideal friends or ideal enemies.

Erikson described the adolescent mind as "essentially a mind of the *moratorium,* a psychosocial stage between childhood and adulthood," and between "the morality learned by the child and the ethics to be developed by the adult" (*Childhood and Society,* 262–63). Feelings of embarrassment, being overwhelmed, elation, anger, envy, shock, chagrin, despair, and humiliation are typical and intense and can change moment by moment.

As Erikson pointed out, the core danger at this stage is role confusion. He defined role confusion as serious doubt about one's sexual identity or occupational identity or even a complete loss of identity caused by temporarily overidentifying with clique or group heroes. Erikson noted that youth holding serious doubts about their identity are at risk of acting out on others and against themselves. (It's never one or the other; if you are a danger to yourself, others around you are equally at risk.)

Though Erikson cited delinquency (acting out against self and others) and psychosis (acting in against the self) as the most common responses to role confusion, other responses are certainly possible. For instance, if someone experiences role confusion regarding sexuality, they may deny their sexuality altogether or, at the other end of the spectrum, may become flagrantly sexual or promiscuous. Troubled adolescents may act out role confusion by controlling food intake through anorexia or bulimia. They may show role confusion through taking drugs, self-mutilating, or contemplating or attempting suicide. These are all cries for love saying, "I don't know, trust, or value who I really am." Such symptoms may equally be indicative of post-traumatic stress disorder (PTSD) linked to early childhood wounds such as those Jon suffered early on. All these symptoms need understanding and caring professional attention to help the person through each stage and rebuild a coherent sense of identity.

Erikson felt that the most prevalent kind of role confusion for adolescents involves the world of work. After grammar school, education becomes increasingly competitive. Suddenly young people find themselves ranked in tiers, and competition for grades or status becomes fierce. How do they negotiate, out of their former skills and identities, some new identity out in the real world of jobs and the pecking order of careers and power? There is no road map.

What a confusing time! Teens are transforming *socially*, moving from a primary bond with parents to peer affiliations they can trust as they learn to know themselves apart from their parents. They are transforming *physiologically*, moving from an innocent, benign latency period to a suddenly confusing, charged, scary, and potent sexuality. And they are transforming *emotionally*, moving away from dependency on their parents and toward an independent, stable identity that is uniquely their own. Their challenge at this stage is to find out who they are.

Jon in Stage 5

The adolescent Jon got a fresh start in the process of finding out who he was once he gained entry to the accelerated GATE program. There he discovered new friends and bright peers and, together with them, relished learning their more challenging coursework—and this experience taught him that he didn't have to settle. His junior high counselor had given him a wormhole to a new universe; if this one existed, there might be others. From then on Jon took matters into his own hands and worked steadily, always open to other, greater options and achievements. As a result, he never wavered in forging his identity at a far younger age than most of his peers.

But like many high achievers, Jon was the geeky kid, and being different, he faced social challenges from other students. As Erikson saw, insecure adolescents inevitably cast their peers in one of two roles: either in-group or out-group. Hazing or bullying is more likely at this stage. In order to share deeply and intimately with a trusted few, they fiercely protect these intimacies by cruelly excluding others. Jon suffered such hazing not only in early high school but all over again at a whole new level when he entered university.

But Jon found his own ways of coping with the teasing. For in reading his peers' entries, I was surprised to see a Jon I didn't quite recognize. At school he was apparently always available to help his peers with their studies, even students who gave him a hard time. But at home Jon was busy distancing himself from me, independently forging a unique identity while bonding with his peers. So at home he was much more likely to be in my face, calling into question anything I said. By the time he was an adolescent, Jon's verbal skills were truly formidable, and if he found a chink in my argument, he took full advantage.

As a therapist looking back at this difference between Jon's public persona and his private one at home, I see now that it makes perfect sense. At home he was safe to let go and unload some of his pent-up feelings by being our daily in-house critic. In this way, he was separating from me and asserting his own individuality, which he needed to do.

As was true in his younger years, I never pulled rank and said, "Shut up and do what I say." Being a mom meant I was responsible for the reasons behind my words. He deserved the best answer I could give so that he could understand, grow, and make more informed and independent choices for himself.

His challenging me forced me to grow too—into more independence and a new career. As we studied on opposite ends of the couch or crammed for and commiserated over tests, Jon enjoyed being the logical, knowledgeable one, learning in tandem with his parent. Today I know that spending time in parallel activities with teens is one of the best things that parents can do—acting as equals in doing either required or fun, active, mutually interesting, and positive things to learn and grow.

But Jon's sexuality, the other main form of identity that Erikson said is forged at this time, remained underdeveloped. Though he might have had brief relationships with girlfriends, in college he lacked the experiences of pairing off that usually take place during this time. Though it is normal during adolescence to feel awkward and disjointed, Jon didn't seem to inhabit his body or feel a bit comfortable in it. It seemed to embarrass him, and he stayed remote from it, from sports, from nature, and from other opportunities to be physical.

Jon's silent refusal to participate in the family vacation when he was thirteen certainly shows the teenage Jon individuating—choosing to do his own thing regardless of the family's wishes. But more was going on. Clearly, in retrospect, Jon also needed professional help to deal with his feelings and needs in his new blended family, especially in regard to his identity and sexuality and his past traumas. When we returned from vacation that summer, Jon should have gone to a therapist, but it didn't happen. Back home, Jon returned to embrace school, homework, and hanging out in his room or at his friends' houses.

Adolescents and Intelligence

Once Jon landed in the GATE program, I wondered why he hadn't been placed in accelerated programs all along. He had apparently tested "normal" on an IQ test in first grade, and I had never been informed about it. A child who could read at age two is not likely to have a merely normal IQ. Had Jon been put with similar peers from first grade on, could that have improved his whole school experience? By the time he reached adolescence, would he have felt less like an awkward, outsider geek?

Today we know that emotional intelligence (emotional quotient, or EQ) is more closely associated with success in life than is IQ. Someone who has high EQ can recognize and navigate their own emotional states as well as those of others. They are self-aware and might adjust their responses according to what is needed emotionally in the moment. By contrast, a high IQ indicates ability in understanding information, logical reasoning, or facility with words or numbers rather than emotional savvy.

Few schools devote regular class time to teaching EQ, assuming emotional skills will be taught at home. But parents were typically never taught them either. Lack of attention to emotional intelligence may be setting up youth for needless failure or even tragedy. In Jon's case, school—especially after he entered the accelerated program—took his intellectual development past all expectations, but he was never formally taught emotional intelligence to balance and ground that intellect. He lacked any training in how to stay emotionally stable, how to remain resilient in crisis, how to successfully relate with others, how to develop perspective, or how to thrive and be happy. As a result he was vulnerable in those areas, a vulnerability that grew as he rose ever higher to leave adolescence and enter adulthood. And Jon was far from alone.

What does teaching EQ look like?

It means teaching skills such as listening—not just hearing someone's words but listening with one's whole being ("active listening"). It involves teaching empathy—how to perceive and manage one's own feelings and needs and how to sense and respond to those of other people. It means teaching how to express and receive emotionally charged material—messages that communicate deep and intense feelings. It means enabling young people to speak in authentic voices able to make a difference. It means helping young people learn to manage difficult emotions, to grieve, to survive, and to overcome the inevitable disappointments that arise in life. Practices such as meditation, yoga, mindfulness, and self-calming can be taught to help youth address anxiety and deal with any panic that arises. All these skills and more create inner resilience and should be educational priorities—taught formally in age-appropriate ways and modeled and practiced throughout school in tandem with intellectual pursuits.

Sharing the Pain of Adolescence

As an adolescent, Jon never told me in words that he was hurting. Only in retrospect was it obvious how he clearly kept communicating that hurt in his behaviors and body language. Poring over his school photos after he died ripped me apart—so poignant and raw! I never asked the obvious—why he looked that forlorn. Instead, I judged him.

I missed his pain in part because I saw in his pictures a version of my own miserable teen self, and I couldn't bear to face her. I had done everything I could to leave her far behind, and my success in doing so stranded her back there in adolescence. So, unable to see Jon clearly, I stranded him in adolescence too. Jon was revealing his misery while Mom thought he was doing this for effect.

I wish that I had been more curious, caring, and transparent. I wish that I had acknowledged what I was seeing. I could have said, "When I see this photo, I recognize the huge pain in your eyes. I don't understand why it is there, but I know it is real. Though you have been very brave trying to deal with this on your own, no one should have to face pain like this all by themselves. We all feel lost in the wilderness at times, and we all need help. I am here with you, and together we can find ways to help you. I am willing to do whatever it takes or costs, because this is not okay and you need and deserve relief. I am open to whatever you are. Sometimes parents aren't the right person to talk to, and that's okay too. We can find someone else if needed."

I could have taken the initiative by telling Jon about the miserable adolescent girl I was and how she helped me become who I am today. "I was a weirdo who loved horses and did none of the things other girls did. No one wanted to have anything to do with me. They called me names and laughed at me. I thought myself ugly and felt so bad, I kept my head down when I walked so nobody could see my face. In high school the only boy who asked me out called the next day and took it back. And you know what? He was no prize, either!" I could have added, "But all those horrible feelings were not wasted. Looking back, I see they ended up teaching and motivating me to go much further than those lucky few who never know such awful times."

He might have resisted, being convinced, as all young people are, that no adult can ever understand what they are going through. And of course, they are right, for they live at a different time than their parents. But what connects the generations is our brain's limbic system—the human emotions, which are the same throughout the centuries.

I could have responded with something like this: "Of course I cannot possibly know what you are going through because you are a different person, and you are a boy living in a different world than I ever lived in. But what we do share are the feelings. I can empathize with how painful it is. I have lived through some terrible moments myself, and I want to help you do the same."

I could have reassured him that he wasn't alone. "We all think we're alone, but the truth is, we never really are. You have fine friends, me, your dad, and great relatives like Great-Aunt Amelia, who care for and love you to pieces and have gone through things like this and can really help if you just ask. I am here for you. I may not always know what to do, but I will stand by your side. The idea that we have to tough it out alone is an illusion. Life is collaborative, and love connects everyone. We all need help at different times in our lives." Had I shared all that, I do not think Jon would have felt so alone.

Youth need to know that even in our darkest times, light will eventually appear. They need to know that things have a way of working out over time, that solutions will show up if we just stay open and keep seeking them. Being there for our adolescents in their confused and hopeless moments means being willing to talk with them openly about ourselves and modeling in every way the hope that life gets better over time.

Even if teens don't want to confide in their parents, we can still tell them our stories and be open about sharing our feelings. We can show them goodwill and empathy. We can pay attention to them and be genuine. Even though kids at this age can't use their parents' experience as solutions, they can still take from adults' stories of their own challenges a sense of hope, as long as parents do this in the spirit of simply sharing as equals rather than telling their teenagers what to do.

Adolescents and Bullying

If your child is looking as lost as Jon was, bullying might be the reason. A 2016 national study of 4,500 students ages twelve to seventeen by the Cyberbullying Research Center found that a whopping 73 percent of respondents reported being bullied at school, while 34 percent of them reported being cyberbullied, with a significant number reporting both. While intolerance and clannishness are common in young people, as Erikson saw, hazing, threats, cruelty, degradation, and bullying are never okay. They destroy any sense of safety and put an adolescent's well-being in danger. Neurologically, sensing danger limits cortical functions like focused thinking and activates our survival system, releasing stress chemicals like cortisol and adrenaline. Studying is out while our midbrain gets ready to fight, flee, or freeze.

When adolescents are facing bullying, it is not enough to "let kids work it out on their own." When we refuse to act, parents and schools are shirking their responsibility to protect our young people and give them an equal chance to succeed in school. By doing nothing or by being hesitant and ineffective in our response, we are in fact reinforcing cruel and antisocial behavior, turning a blind eye toward the pain of bullied students as well as their diminished ability to perform in school. Adolescents are vulnerable because for the first time in their lives they can't afford to confide in parents. This age's core issue is to bond now with peers, so treatment by their peers carries an outsize effect. Without the solidarity of their peer group either, adolescents are easily stranded and set up as helpless targets. Researchers at Yale School of Medicine who reviewed studies of adolescents and suicide concluded that the studies show that bullying victims are 2 to 9 times more likely than other adolescents to consider committing suicide. (For more information, see the work of Kim and Leventhal in the Resources section under "Suicide Prevention.")

How can parents help? One key is to give children the information they need ahead of time so they have the tools to deal with it. That includes letting them know that bullying is never okay. Early on in school, tell your kids that they have a right to be protected from bullying and that you will do everything in your power to help protect them. Ask them to promise that they will let you know if they run into this kind of trouble, and pay loving attention for signs of bullying and then caringly reach out and ask.

Another key is to advocate for emotional intelligence training in schools. Studies show that EQ programs dramatically reduce bullying and instill norms of tolerance and inclusiveness.

Make use of the excellent antibullying resources available online (see the Resource list for places to start). There you can find inspiring stories, parent-child school workshop presentations, self-study groups, and step-by-step activities to help your child prepare to confidently confront bullies. Share this information and advocate with school principals, concerned parents, and teens.

If adolescents do encounter bullying, a parent can say, "This is not okay. It is never okay. Even though you are your own person, this saps the energy you need to take full advantage of school. It is too much pressure to deal with alone. I am responsible for helping you during times of trouble. I am here with you." Parents can get their teenager's permission to find help, either online or face-to-face, and can solicit their preferences about who to seek help from. Consider changing schools. Parents and administrators can also band together and confront the situation collectively.

During adolescence, when kids are distancing emotionally from parents, many parents will have no idea that bullying is happening (as I didn't). Many kids being bullied do not speak of it because they are trying to handle it on their own or because the bullies threaten them if they do talk about it or shame them if their parent or an administrator intercedes. Sometimes the child feels so worthless they may even feel they deserve such treatment.

But being bullied is toxic and dangerous. Bullies may prompt their victims to kill themselves. Getting this treatment from peers hits an adolescent hard. Over time victims feel so beaten down, so worthless and hopeless, that they do attempt and complete suicide.

As with Jon, the evidence often appears in body language—sunken shoulders and chest, stunned or listless expressions, lack of energy, eyes that seem distant and disconnected from life, or else eyes that bore straight through you. When normal personalities shift and turn sullen, introverted, or fearful, or when adolescents isolate themselves or take no interest in activities they used to excel in or love, these are symptoms of trauma that may suggest bullying or other serious abuse.

What can you do if you notice these symptoms in your child? Let your child know what you are observing, and ask questions that will draw them into conversation: "What do you need right now?" Or, "How can I support you?" Or, "What's happening in your life to cause this shift?" (Avoid yes-or-no questions such as, "Are you okay?") Whether or not the child answers, they need to know that you are paying attention, that you care, and that they have your support. If they don't respond, let them sit with your questions, and bring it up again later. And then again.

If it feels serious, take action. Talk with your child directly about your fears. Ask them for some honest feedback so they aren't left alone and stranded. Get regular updates as needed, whether every day, every week, or somewhere in between. If you sense they could harm themselves, clear the house of all possible means: guns, poisons, cleaners, knives, scissors, razors, ropes, lines, drugs, and so forth. Ask friends and relatives to check in on and involve your teen. Take your child out of the situation: go on vacation, stay with relatives, travel. Does your teen need a new school? New residence? New hobbies or activities? Time off cellphones and social media? Psychiatric or psychological support? Fun or peaceful, calming distractions? New friends? New skills?

As appropriate, involve your relatives, friends, neighbors, pastors, priests, rabbis, religious groups, teachers, administrators, legal groups, mental health professionals, police, or community and youth leaders— and collaborate with teen groups. In a crisis, keep no secrets. It always takes a village.

When Deeper Healing Is Needed

Like Jon, some children need more help than emotional intelligence, antibullying coaching, and stories from their parents' adolescence. They may need to acknowledge years-long buried pain from traumatic events experienced earlier in life. In situations like these, when a child has repressed emotion from severe abuse, seeking professional help becomes essential.

Had I known in Jon's teenage years what I know now, I would have started conversations with him encouraging him to go to a therapist for help with these traumas, however uncomfortable it might have made him feel at first. At opportune moments, I would have shared my observations about his body language and unusual reactions. I might have said, "How you feel and react is completely understandable given what happened to you when you were little. At four you were alone and helpless, and in some ways your body probably is still reacting to that, especially when things happen that create the same feelings you felt back then. Yet all trauma can heal with the right support. There are excellent therapists who can help you through this. I'm guessing you may prefer to see a man. Is that right? Would you be willing to check out a couple of them to see if you can find someone you trust?"

If a teen is not open to therapy, I would keep bringing it up. However, I wouldn't go further than this unless I sensed imminent danger. Parents are exactly the wrong people to tell adolescents to do anything, especially about issues like this. It is important that teenagers not feel pushed, or they may dig in their heels just to assert their independence from you. If you are worried about your teen, be creative and try not to lecture. Movies, podcasts, and books are great ways to get the message across that healing is possible. In Jon's case, I might have asked the relative he trusted and sought out the most, his Great-Aunt Amelia, to speak to Jon as well. But any person your teen trusts and respects will do, whether older family friend, neighbor, teacher, or relative.

Regardless of a child's age or needs, reflecting back on what happened earlier in life, whether an hour ago or back at age four, is an important skill to practice with ourselves and our children. Making sense of what happened earlier helps us heal by integrating the past with the present. It allows us to release the effects of past trauma and gives us the power to make better choices now and in the future. We can also reframe a childhood trauma by looking back on it as the motivation for becoming an empowered adult who righted that wrong and became a hero.

How to Parent a Teenager

When a child becomes an adolescent, the role of parent changes. The work of teaching takes a backseat, with parents making it available only when sought. For teens are moving on, emancipating into their own sovereignty. If parents haven't done their job by now, trying to parent a teen now is too late and often results in the exact opposite effect than the one intended.

The right time to parent a teen is years earlier, at the beginning of grade school. Every child needs to be told the clear benefits of as well as limits to their freedom. They need to hear fair warning, some appropriate and simply stated consequence for a violation. *Make sure the child knows this limit will be enforced every time, not as punishment, but because parents love the child and will do all they can to help the child grow up safe, healthy, happy, and free.* If you come from that caring place, children get it; they can hear you, and they will respond.

In adolescence, parents can expect these rules to be violated. For that is what teens need to do—to defy parental sovereignty in order to assert their own independence and test parents' love and limits. If the parents early on have set the consequences fairly and with no rancor, when a child turns into a teen it is a simple matter of continuing to follow through.

Teens may protest, but they will respect you and are more likely to realize that it's for their own good. They will know they are loved and will be able to internalize the lesson to be more responsible in the future. The key is consistent, automatic, nonjudgmental follow-through.

After my mom gave me my freedom at age seven, on the condition that I tell her the truth about whatever happened, I happily agreed and followed through perfectly—until I was sixteen. That's when my friend Jackie and I, on a perfect spring morning, ditched school and spent the whole day talking, laughing, and walking around town, even passing by the courthouse where Mom was hard at work. At day's end, Jackie and I forged notes to give our teacher the next day.

I returned home with very tired feet. Soon Mom arrived. As she started dinner, she asked casually, "So, how was school?"

"Fine," I lied.

"That's interesting. Today I was eating lunch up at the courthouse clock tower and saw two very familiar girls walk by."

Uh-oh.

She continued quietly, "Tomorrow you are going to school and telling them what you did and take the full consequences. Now, give me your car keys." I had just bought my first car, a '55 Chevy Bel Air. I handed them over. She said, "I'll decide what to do with the car later."

Mom followed through as she had promised. I had to tell the truth at school the next day and was given nineteen demerits, the only ones I ever received. I also lost my car and, with it, my freedom. But I couldn't be mad. I actually respected her more. She had told me what she would do, and she did it.

Never again would I lie to Mom, or pretty much anyone else either, for the price of a day of truancy was the knowledge of all I had lost. Gone were Mom's respect, trust, and belief in me; gone was my freedom to do what I wanted. The disappointment in her eyes and the awful silence between us were far worse than losing my first car. But much later, I realized that Mom also showed me how I could be with my own children someday.

When my sons started school, I sat each one down beforehand and said, "I know you are a very good and smart boy. There will always be a babysitter here after school, but I must also trust you to be honest and do what's right while I am at work. It's important that you know that if I ever find out you lied or did anything illegal or took drugs, I promise I will be the first to call the police. For none of that will ever help you in your life. It will only ruin it and put you in prison. I am your mom. I love you and want you to be happy and have a wonderful life. There is no way I will let you or anyone else ruin your life if I possibly can help it."

If they made plans for after school, I also made them promise to call me at work or leave me a note to say where they were. If I got home and found them gone with no note or phone call, all too soon I would be frantic, sure that something horrible had happened. I couldn't wait, for long ago that's how I had left Jon alone to face Tommy. Crazy with fear, I would call the police and report them missing. Jon or Alan would arrive home to have to explain to an officer why he hadn't called home and would receive a lecture from the officer in return. Because I was a single mom, that kind of police support was my salvation.

Jon forgot only a few times to call or leave a note. The last time I called the police, it was only a few minutes before I heard feet racing up the walkway. In through the door burst Jon, panting, with a red-faced young friend a few feet behind. "Is—is it too late? Have you—called the police yet?" he gasped.

"Yes," I said dolefully. "I called the police."

Jon turned to his friend and said, "Told you she would!"

Setting the limits early on meant that as my sons grew through the teen years, they knew what to expect from me. This set us free to think and talk like real people together—to tease and inform, to question and confront each other, as well as to laugh and goof around. We were not stuck in some stultifying top-down hierarchy of the parent as supreme being forever trying to tell the teenager what to do. That would only have led to alienation and perhaps outright war, for no teenager is going to let you control them.

To parent teenagers, forget about trying to tell them what to do. Those days are over; they are young adults now. Instead, ask them questions and give the teens the opportunity to know the answers. Let your questions call forth their own good sense and their sovereignty. When parents tell teens what to do, teenagers are unable to own their own process because they are following their parents' direction—the opposite of what they need for developing an autonomous personal identity. Following parental directions means losing out on their own empowerment. To be independent and learn to lead, we cannot be told what to do.

Say Yes

Parents of teenagers need to lose the word *no*. As long as they are being safe and lawful, youth need permission to go ahead and try and be able to both fail and succeed. Use the word *yes* instead. *Yes* says, I believe in you, I'm behind you, I trust your process.

So what if they fail? Failure means they took a risk, and there are huge lessons to learn here, more so than if they succeeded. As long as they are safe, it's fine to fail. It's important that parents trust their children as they move into their own individuality and their own genius. When an opportunity knocks on the door, say yes—and figure out the ways and means later. Support that young adult! You need to be their staunch ally, their solid, trusted ground that gives them the ability to spring forward.

When Jon got admitted to Carnegie Mellon, I did the right thing and said yes. But I should have said something else as well. What I needed to add was, "Yes—on one condition: that you read books on social-emotional skills, that you take classes in social-emotional adjustment, that you find a life coach or therapist to see you through this process. You are moving far ahead with your intellect, and that's fine, but for your personal development, we need to balance that amazing intellect with training in social and emotional skills. People your age usually learn that by interacting with their peers. Since you are leaving your peer group behind, you will need to pay special attention so your emotional development moves in step with your intellectual development. Your path is steep, and you are going high, and there will be tough moments. I don't want you to be stranded; I want you to be happy. Yes, you have my full support to test your wings—and I insist that you do research, read books, and perhaps find someone to provide this extra support while you're doing it."

Emphasize the Positive

Parents of teens need to take every opportunity to notice where their child is doing something right and to join in and do it with them. Let them know how terrific they are every time they act in good, kind, fair, industrious, or responsible ways. Let them know you appreciate each incremental attempt they make at moving themselves toward maturity. What they don't need is to be bossed around. They are autonomous, capable, perfectly fine people who will take care of things on their own if given a chance.

Notice and reward each attempt to grow. "Wow, congratulations on excellent work!" "You really gave it a real effort, and if you keep doing just that, you can't help but succeed!" "Staying on track and doing your best and never giving up can only pay off."

It is easy, as parents, to come from a punitive point of view, but the positive is so much more fun—so much more participatory and freeing. Love is always the right approach. Loving children means giving them freedom within safe limits. Parents do have to police the limits, but this can be done by emphasizing your love and regard for your child. Always explain it in terms of their benefit: "You don't want to go to jail. You want to have a happy, free, and wonderful life. I will do all I can to make sure that happens." When we emphasize the positive, kids get it.

If we as parents have been doing our job in positive ways, we have been mirroring back to our children all along, ever since they were born, what precious, genius individuals they are. No matter how a child is acting, it is our job as parents to hold the image of the child's most loving, brilliant self and to encourage the child to be that self. Every parent can do this at every moment—reflecting back only the good, kind, beautiful, true, and precious pieces of their child. Such mirroring is far more powerful than any punitive consequences can ever be. You are mirroring love, unconditional positive love.

Your child will naturally have to test this positive image, but if you stay true to their positive potential, they cannot help but respond to it. When they do test it and make a mistake, they are doing what they need to do to learn. Mistakes may feel terrible, but they are right and absolutely necessary if teens are going to make their way toward maturity and success in life. From mistakes, whether their own or those of others, teens can harvest far more powerful, practical benefits than they will ever get from books or classes.

When Your Teen Makes a Mistake

When your teen makes a mistake, first of all follow through with the consequences. They knew them all along; now your job is just to reinforce those limits.

Then encourage your teen to simply stop, breathe, calm down, think, and write about what just happened. Encourage them to reflect on the lessons learned. Join them in reflecting. Tell stories from your own life that show how every problem, when we survive it, contains seeds for avoiding or solving life problems down the road. Let them know that the terrible times of adolescence are all part of the ocean of life, and their job at this age is to surf every emotional peak and dark abyss, simply riding each wave as it comes. Riding today's wave is how we move ever forward and acquire the resilience to survive all the waves that nudge us on into the future. Riding each wave is how we become ourselves and face forward with courage, hope, and perspective. The more we do this and survive, the stronger and freer we become to succeed, whether in love, work, school, or career.

Have Fun with Your Teen

One of the most powerful things a parent of teens can do is to be who you are and just have fun with them. Having fun with your teen helps parents to keep alive their own inner novelty-seeking kid. Joining with your teen in having some adolescent fun proves to you and your teen that becoming an adult doesn't mean sacrificing your youth or the ability to enjoy life by doing active or silly things. In his book *Brainstorm,* psychiatrist Daniel Siegel writes of skateboarding down tiers of empty parking structures late at night with his kid, then riding back up in the elevator and skateboarding back down, over and over. That's the beauty of being the parent of an adolescent. They don't need you to be their parent anymore; they can help you to recapture your own child and join in with them as equals in having fun. Why try to fit an old, tired, and narrow role when you could be reviving your own sense of fun? So give up the suffocating top-down parent role, and enjoy these years with your teen! We are any age we choose to be at any moment. Why encrust yourself in just one?

TEACHINGS, AIRBAGS, AND SAFETY NETS

- Erikson pointed out that the core issue of every adolescent's life is to form a unique, stable identity and avoid role confusion.

- Angst during puberty and teen years is normal. But increasing isolation, misery, or preoccupations with one's body or other issues are not teen angst but serious issues needing help and attention. These are a few of the many nonverbal cries for love.

- To parent teenagers, forget about trying to tell them what to do. Those days are over. Instead, ask them questions and assume they already know the answers.

- Give up the top-down role every chance you get. Instead, treat teenagers civilly, more like you would treat respected equals. And don't forget to bond with and just have fun with your teen!

- Support and trust your teen. Let your teen know you believe in them, and back it up by your words and thoughts. Say yes to your teen as often as possible.

- Reflect back to your teen the good, fine, beautiful, true, and amazing person he or she is. Reflecting only the good is far more powerful, bonding, and fun than any punitive consequence.

- Teenagers have a right to ask questions, to understand, to be heard, and to be responded to as authentically as possible. Listen to your adolescent's questions or challenges, and answer them honestly.

- Teens will test the limits. They must do so in order to challenge authority, learn the truth for themselves, and establish their own independence.

- If parents have early on set rules and consequences fairly with no rancor, when their teen breaks a rule, it becomes a simple matter to follow through.

- If your teenager makes a mistake, first follow through as promised, then encourage the young person to simply stop, breathe, calm down, and reflect on what just happened. Urge them to write about the situation and what they learned from it.

- If parents try to forget about or repress their own painful teen experiences, they may blind themselves to understanding their adolescent children's crises or dilemmas.

- Sharing difficult personal stories is one way parents can help teenagers face similar issues with more perspective, possibilities, and hope.

- Schools teach to intellect, or IQ, ignoring emotional maturation, or EQ. But this leaves teenagers clueless about how to move forward toward adult emotional maturity. Adding courses in EQ, such as how to listen to others, how to take care of oneself emotionally, how to weather disappointments, and how to relate to others as equals, helps reduce bullying and builds emotionally balanced, resilient, and successful adult citizens.

- Let your children know that bullying and hazing are never okay. Assure them that they have a right to be protected and that you will do everything in your power to do so. Get your teenager's permission to get help, and listen to the teen's preferences about who to seek help from. Then follow through in full.

- Teens advancing intellectually ahead of age-mates need special support and guidance in developing their socio-emotional skills so they can move smoothly into intense, competitive milieus with older peers.

- Parents need teens to help them stay young and to keep abreast of technology, mores, moves, and music. So let them teach their parents well at every opportunity!

The Red X

~

STAGE 6. YOUNG ADULTHOOD

Age	Virtue Instilled	Psychosocial Crisis	Significant Relationship	Existential Question	Significant Issues
18-26 years	Love	Intimacy vs. Isolation	Relationships: Mutual Intimacy, Friends, and Colleagues	Can I love and be loved?	Finding Fulfillment in Relationships with Family, Colleagues, and Friends

JON'S GRADUATION DAY in May broke brilliant and crisp at Carnegie Mellon in Pittsburgh, with the land glowing luscious green under warm, sunny skies. From California and Texas, both parents flew east to join in celebrating him. Today our impressive university graduate would officially be receiving not one but two degrees completed in just four years' time: his undergraduate bachelor of science (with honors), condensing four years' of requirements completed in his first two years, then his graduate master of science completed in the next two years.

None of us knew how Jon had managed to keep to the original schedule outlined by this accelerated program in theoretical mathematics. But thanks to his extreme efforts, today Jon was graduating on time. Through his diligence he had saved himself at least two additional years of study and saved Mom and Dad at least two more years of pricey tuition. Just two months earlier, we had celebrated Jon's twenty-first birthday, making these hard-earned sheepskins the best coming-of-age present anyone could give themselves—or their families.

In every way, Jon certainly had earned this moment in the sun. That's what made graduation day a no-miss appointment. Jon would become the lone graduate of his program and his entering class's only survivor to complete all requirements and walk at commencement. The program was so brutal that twenty-eight students had dropped out in the first two years. Four more had either fallen behind or exited the program in the final two years.

I flashed on the letter he'd sent the month before telling us that there were no other master's candidates:

> I am now the only one on track for the degree. Every one of the original 32 others has bailed. You can't imagine how guilty and lucky that makes me feel at the same time. . . . This is the reason I have been waffling so much when people ask me how the program is going. This entire time, I only had a 3.03 percent chance of finishing. I'm glad I've almost got [the degrees], but had I known the odds, I never would have started.

Nor would we his parents have let him! A program with a 97 percent rate of failure? Who would knowingly put their child into a wringer like that? But Jon had persevered, and today we would stand in witness and celebrate his triumph. There was only one question: What had happened to each of those other thirty-two classmates? That information was not available, and none of us thought to ask. All we knew was that Jon, against impossible odds, had proven himself every single day of four years in this rigorous and elite academic program. He was assured a job in the top echelon of mathematical careers. Today we would celebrate our hero.

Meanwhile, I had a little wringer of my own to face and overcome. Some old family dramas going on behind the scenes threatened to keep me from celebrating Jon's stellar achievement. Tensions between Jon's father and me had once again resurfaced. After our divorce seventeen years before, he had remarried soon after while I had remained a single mom for eight years before remarrying. Unfortunately, my second marriage of nine years had ended just a few months earlier, leaving me once again alone, vulnerable, and financially challenged. So Jon's dad, a senior airline official, chose that moment to distribute free (for him) standby airline tickets to Pittsburgh to every single relative on both sides of the family, including my new ex and his son—every single person, that is, who had ever been part of Jon's family—except me, Jon's mom.

I might have been stunned, but I wasn't. This was consistent with how he had treated me during all eight years I was a single parent.

However, this time there was one major difference. This time the whole family knew. Always before, for both my sons' sakes and my own— to simply stay on keel and not make waves—I had just sucked it in and remained silent. This time there was no keeping it quiet.

At first delighted to receive free round-trip tickets to Jon's graduation, all my relatives were shocked to learn that I had been excluded. Even my new ex was angry. He and others tried to pass their tickets on to me, to no avail. The tickets were nontransferable. So one by one my relatives, in protest, either trashed their tickets or sent them back, effectively boycotting Jon's graduation en masse.

Everyone was upset, especially Jon. This was, after all, his outstanding achievement. But on my own, I decided that even though this last potshot rankled, why get mad? The man was just being consistent. What mattered most was to be there to witness and celebrate my son. Nothing could derail me. So I charged a ticket to my credit card and informed Jon that I would be there. Busy scheduling details, I never thought of how my simply showing up for Jon's graduation might affect the other side of Jon's family. Jon and those relatives, I would soon discover, were aghast, certain that my presence under the circumstances would provoke a terrible scene.

On the plane from Los Angeles to Pittsburgh I considered the situation over a glass of wine. Though my latest batch of incendiary feelings had smoothed some, they were far from gone. Before deplaning, I knew, I needed to be bulletproof.

But exactly how? I mulled and mulled. *All we see is love or a cry for love. Right. Jon's dad was crying for love. Right. The answer to hate is love. Sure, but what does that mean?* Over and over my brain twisted and turned. Suddenly, in the middle of a sip, the solution struck—so repulsive I actually gagged. Every single time Jon's dad tried to push my buttons I had to— yes!—give love. I had to go up and kiss the man.

Nothing could be more hideous. But having a plan in place gave me self-control. Whatever he said or did to trigger me, I knew exactly what I would have to do. If I followed my plan every time, something would shift. Of that I was sure. The thought was as awful as it was hilarious.

At the hotel I had just lain down to rest when there was a knock at the door. I opened it to see a very tall young man standing before me.

"Jon! Come in. Oh, my. You're so tall! My graduate!"

He looked upset and uncomfortable. "I'm not going through it."

"Of course you are."

"No, I'm not. I am not going to deal with you and Dad scrapping and making me embarrassed. It's not that big a deal. I can live without formally graduating."

"Oh, no. I and everyone else didn't come all this way for nothing. Jon, look right at me, up here, in my eyes. I want you to really get this. There is no one—not your dad, not any person on Earth—who could make me feel, think, or do a single thing to ruin your graduation. This is the absolute truth and my total promise to you."

Jon looked at me dubiously. "Mom, you go out of control, and you know it."

"I know that's what it might seem like to you, and this is no time for a debate, but I can definitely make you this promise and keep it. I will have absolutely no problem with your dad or anyone else either."

"I'll think about it."

I watched him walk away, still a bit gangly but maturing into the finest young man ever. He better give this graduation a green light. It was his call.

Early that evening I was awakened from my nap by a phone call from Jon's dear Grandma Letty inviting me to join them for dinner. Hazy and surprised, I told her I would be delighted, and I quickly dressed. Downstairs I joined Jon and his dad's family at the hotel restaurant. I sat in the empty seat beside Grandma Letty's sister, wonderful and staunch Aunt Sophie. Jon's dad and stepmother faced me on the opposite side next to Jon, flanked by his grandmother, her husband, and her sister's husband rounding out the group. The small talk was familiar, easy, and fun. I had after all belonged to and loved this family for ten years and, ever since the divorce, had entertained my former in-laws in our home at every holiday and kid's birthday. By the end of dinner everyone was enjoying them-selves and now felt at ease. The waiter came in bearing the check.

Instantly I flashed on the perfect kiss. Yes! Give love!

"This is on me," I smiled brightly, taking the little black leather holder from the waiter. Every face went slack and turned in my direction. "Relax, you guys—it's no big deal," I laughed as adrenaline pumped. "This is a celebration!" Unable to face the total, I simply added an insane tip to whatever it was, signed, snapped the folder shut, and handed it back to the waiter. The ensuing shocked silence was the one thing I'd never, ever heard in this family.

Everyone but Jon's dad smiled and thanked me profusely. He looked sour, as if something he ate didn't agree with him. Jon thanked me too, with his usual formality and a hint of warm lighting up those blue eyes along with a slight crack in that reedy voice.

It was worth anything not to have to kiss that man.

The next day dressed in honor for Jon's commencement. Pittsburgh was flush in rolling, verdant green. From a vivid blue dome the spring sun shone down, bright and warm. Chirping birds sounded happy and well fed. A soft, whimsical breeze greeted us. Dressed in our Sunday best, we were excited and happy, ready to celebrate.

We parked at the university, and, with almost two hours before fes-tivities were to begin, Jon took over. "This way!" he commanded, turn-ing a tall back and striding across a long quadrangle of brilliant green. He would give us a tour of places that had been important to him during his four years on this campus. We trailed after like a gaggle of goslings afraid of losing their mother.

Lagging behind, I reveled in my son's transformation. The shimmer-ing, seven-pound, three-ounce infant tenderly lifted to my sight just twen-ty-one years ago now walked so firm and sure at six-foot-one. This young superachiever knew more about applied and theoretical math than 99.9 percent of the world's population. Joy and quiet pride filled me. From today on, Jon would lead.

Jon marched us past ark-like buildings crammed with students, then through a colonnade of archways. Behind stone façades, high ceilings were inlaid with long cuts of light. Broad, marble stairways led ever upward. This stately campus seemed a million miles from Jon's humble origins back on the Pacific Coast.

Keeping up a light patter, Jon wove historic campus trivia with personal asides as we walked and gawked. An hour later, we'd been both informed and highly entertained. The time for the ceremony approached, and we had walked nearly full circle. He stopped at what was to be the tour's finale.

But why here? Passing through the door he held open, we found ourselves standing in the stairwell at one end of a residence hall, the building's fire escape. What could possibly be of interest here? It was dark, and the cold gray concrete walls closed us in and smelled dank. Stairs and railings wound round and round, ghostlike, over our heads. What would Jon tell us about this place? We gathered expectantly. In the gloom, my eyes glanced at the floor while adjusting to the dark. Squinting, I began to see a large, red X crudely painted on the floor around which the spiral stairwell turned.

"This is where they do it," he said. Then he turned and walked out the door.

What? Who are "they"? What is he talking about? We looked down at the lurid X, glanced at one other a clueless second, then followed him out.

Back in the light, Jon squinted at his watch. "It's time for me to get ready," he said and left, waving us in the correct direction. Filled with anticipation, we merged with a retinue of other well-dressed families walking down the green and past a hedge to our seats.

The graduation began. It was serious, organized, and efficient. Black-cloaked students wearing caps with swinging, thick red tassels marched in single file up to the podium to receive their degrees. Jon, the only graduate of his program, walked solo to the platform so many times for all his awards I laughingly joked that everyone else must think him either lost or just badly confused. Jon's serial distinctions and success made not just me but all of us giddy. Proud and bubbling, reflected in his light, we celebrated our young graduate's dazzling success.

Erikson on Stage 6:
Intimacy vs. Isolation (18–26 Years)

Erikson's Stage 6, from eighteen to twenty-six years of age, represents a unique and critical juncture in a young person's development. Young adults' new challenge, he says, is to bond intimately with others or be at risk of isolation. After high school, most youth are moving out into the world, perhaps to marry or to enter the military, the workforce, or higher education. This is a tumultuous, exciting, and also scary and vulnerable life moment. Those entering this age find themselves between two worlds, one known but receding and the other one, largely unknown, lying ahead.

Young adults are freer than ever at this age, and they are expected to fly solo for the first time and somehow be able to fledge as independent, fully functioning, sovereign adults. Left behind, for better or worse, is the world of high school, with classmates sorted into categories of hero, jerk, jock, nerd, brain, clown, or loser. Often left behind as well, though still connected by strong invisible ties, are family and friends.

For some, leaving that old world can be a godsend, an escape from bullying or belittling peer group labels, and they begin to revel in their sudden freedom to redefine themselves. Others experience grief and loss over friends and youthful good times gone forever. For most, it's some mix of both. But beyond all emotions, this is the time to embark on their very own solo adventure, to explore their potential and find their place, their work, their people, and their love.

Yet any in-between state is uncertain, and the transition to adulthood is especially perilous. According to Erikson, the danger is that youth, intent on building their adult ties with others in friendship, work, and love, will become isolated as they forge forward on their own. Keeping open life-lines with loved ones, friends, and trusted allies is vitally important to remain connected and avoid isolation. The more young adults become isolated, the more apt they are to experience loss of identity, meaning, direction, purpose, and hope—the kinds of losses that set a person up for a psychological fall.

Though Erikson saw the challenge of this age as bonding in an intimate love relationship, today that interpretation seems somewhat narrow. As Freud famously said, "Love and work, work and love—that's all there is." Both love and work require relationships, whether building intimacy with friends or a unique significant other or bonding collegially with other students in school or in the goal-sharing relationships of business and other shared endeavors. All involve the capacity to affiliate, to communicate and cooperate with others, to be transparent and vulnerable, and to contribute a unique sense of self and personal value to a larger endeavor. That larger goal might consist of the shared hopes of a couple or a family or the shared pursuits of cooperative work relationships.

In Stage 6, love and work become the twin forces driving adult growth, happiness, and success. To function well at this stage, youth need to be stable and healthy and to have enough self-esteem to know they are of worth to others. They need the seasoning and skills to cope with and sustain solid relationships.

Dr. Erikson set the age of young adulthood as beginning at nineteen, following the traditional age when young adults graduate from high school and attain their majority. However, more recent research into the development of the mind shows that human brains do not in fact reach adult form until about age twenty-five. While society may treat eighteen-year-olds as fully mature, independent adults, neuroscience shows that adult maturity is still years away.

Thus, young people at such a pivotal stage may face all the expectations, stress, and responsibilities of being an adult while still lacking the mature neurological apparatus to actually become one. Society may thus be turning what is normally a perilous passage into such treacherous straits that tragedies become much more likely. In fact, statistical evidence shows that between eighteen and twenty-four is a critical period when psychological breaks, including suicides, are more likely to occur. (For more information, see Heyes and Hiu, "The Adolescent Brain," in the Resources section.) While serious mental illness and suicide have many predisposing factors, when young adults are expected to set out on their own and succeed in love, education, and work without a fully mature brain, they may be set up for an avoidable fall—and possible tragedy.

While this chasm between what we expect of young adults and what they are neurologically capable of imperils all youth in transition, certain individuals enter young adulthood already burdened by the residues of unresolved earlier developmental crises, and for them the likelihood of some serious psychological crisis is far greater. As in Jon's case, they become vulnerable to needless tragedy.

The good news is that with new awareness informed by neurological research, we can revise society's expectations of this age to align with cognitive maturation. We can learn to expect our young adults to be less experienced and less fully mature than we had thought and to need more adult support as they make their way into the world. And we can step up to provide that support and hold them more firmly as they navigate this transition to full adulthood. It's time to look more deeply at the part society plays in placing young adults in psychological risk, for it is never okay or normal for our young to choose to kill themselves.

Jon in Stage 6

Jon had certainly worked hard to bond with others during these four years of college. After the initial hazing, he went on to become a valued member of the Math Studies department and the campus student body.

Jon cared about his peers and did all he could to help them—as he had in high school. He sometimes gave of himself so freely that he needed to reassess his contribution. His first job at the college was to proctor tests for Psychology 101, a self-paced course. Jon wrote home to admit that it didn't work out as he hoped. "I soon found myself running the entire course: test-production, proctor-scheduling, record-keeping, and film-running for 350 students. I started falling behind in my classwork, and though the job was very challenging, I had to abandon it after mid-semester. I am afraid that my decision was not too popular with those who had to run the course afterwards."

As a junior, Jon joined the Student Advisory Council in Mathematics, a volunteer position that allowed him to express his views on what he saw as an excessively competitive program where students needed more support from their faculty. "I was able to communicate my views on education directly to the department head," he wrote dryly. "Next year, the committee hopes to distribute more tactful versions of our opinions to the professors and even make recommendations for new courses and curriculum requirements for particular majors."

In all these ways, Jon was getting involved and proving valuable to others, finding niches where he could belong and make unique contributions. His efforts to find a significant other were apparently less successful. Of course he never shared any of this with a mom he was emancipating from, but in his letters to others he was quite open—letters that were forwarded to me after he died.

However, over four years, the loss of every single one of the thirty-two other bright students who had entered this tough program with him became an increasingly heavy burden, one to which he bore solitary witness at his graduation. What had happened to all those students?

Jon's survivor guilt must have been an ongoing source of personal suffering, for he even mentioned it in a letter home prior to graduation. He had shared the daily process with thirty-two others and had kept connected to them, only to watch them fall behind and drop out one by one. To walk for his degrees meant at the same time to mourn every peer who would have become his colleague on graduation and a potential friend and ally forever.

But losing his entire university cohort was only one of the ways in which Jon's foundation for success in Stage 6 was being undermined and his isolation increasing. What neither Jon nor his dad nor I understood at the time is how we, his parents, were undercutting Jon's ability to trust and connect with others and were undermining his forward movement or "graduation" into adult life. The rift between his dad and me compromised Jon in more ways than just at his graduation. Jon may not have known the particulars behind these tensions while he was growing up—certainly he didn't learn them from me—but I am now sure that from the divorce on he felt stranded in the middle without knowing whom or what to trust.

This rift finally boiled to the surface and threatened to derail the most public and successful moment of Jon's life. Though during graduation weekend I managed to make good on my promise and contribute a sense of stability that helped the family members enjoy one another and function seamlessly together, Jon had been profoundly affected by the now-obvious tension and lack of harmony between his parents. He felt it so keenly that he was ready to bail on the celebration himself. This was the first time he and the families on both sides had witnessed his father's attempts to undercut me, and Jon understandably wanted to avoid the ugly scene he was sure would come. The tension between his parents, which was much more serious and long-term than he ever imagined, almost sabotaged the event for Jon. This was not the kind of support he needed at this amazing milestone in his life.

And in important ways, I was at fault. From our divorce on, I effectively enabled his dad's harassment of me by keeping quiet about it. My good intentions to protect my sons from acrimony only created an ongoing, ever-widening hole that both families eventually fell into. The suddenness of the fall made it many times worse than if Dad's harassment had been known to everyone all along. I now realize that every instance was harassment I could have documented and legally pursued but never did.

By merely ducking every serious breach of trust by Jon's father, I maintained a rift between Jon's reality and my parenting experience. That choice kept me a victim and may have helped to build Jon's loyalty to his father at the expense of his loyalty to me. By choosing to keep quiet about the pattern of disrespect, I may have given his dad carte blanche to take advantage of Jon's trust and love to disparage and perhaps poison his love for and trust of me. It certainly allowed his father to refuse to face his behavior and take responsibility for it.

Finally, at graduation Jon suddenly faced the explosive effects of this grating parental rift in full, and instantly he took mature responsibility for both himself and his parents—something neither his father nor I had done to date.

Jon's isolation kept increasing in yet another way. His being so bright created a separation between Jon and his age group. Entering the university already years younger than his academic peers also separated him from them and compounded his psychological risk, especially among such a bright, accomplished, and highly competitive cohort. Though he did manage to successfully find a place within that world, in so many ways his ground kept eroding out from beneath him. Being the only graduate of the program stranded him from the only long-term friends and colleagues he could have made there and could have continued to collaborate with.

In many ways I didn't see at the time, Jon was becoming ever more isolated from the generation of peers he was born to be part of throughout life.

Meanwhile, all his successes too acted to set him apart from most everyone else. At twenty-one he was intellectually on a par with the best minds in theoretical mathematics. He could engage with eminent others over the theories of Einstein, but that's a group few others can or want to join. His triumph in such a challenging major isolated him from the majority of human connections. While none of us saw anything but the cup half full, Jon might have been ever more intensely stuck in a cup half empty, and perhaps he either didn't realize it or know what to do about it.

One other factor contributed to his isolation. Jon's program was purposely designed to be intense and narrowly focused as a laser beam. Students learned mathematics, period. To succeed, Jon had little time to socialize. There was no academic space for developing perspective or for cultivating outside interests or talents. He had no time to learn emotional coping or life skills. The program's narrow focus cut Jon off even more.

A year or two after his suicide, I learned a most unwelcome piece of information. Around the time Jon attended, his university had the highest suicide rate of any American campus. Schools do not volunteer such crucial data to potential or current students. If we learn such information, we likely learn it too late. So even more years passed before I recalled the red X and finally understood. Jon was showing us where his suicidal peers had died. Did one or more of his friends or students in his program end their lives there? Were there times when Jon almost X-ed out too?

What Healing Might Have Looked Like in Stage 6

Finding and then building a network of mutually reciprocal, ongoing relationships in both love and work (or, in Jon's case, education) would have buoyed Jon up during this critical stage in his development. Here was this gregarious intellect, a brilliant and fine young man who needed like-minded connections to grow a solid network of relationships that would last through adulthood. Those relationships would have helped him navigate the challenges of fledging into a high-stakes future and would have acted as a human safety net to prevent falling into the dangers of isolation.

Staying Connected with Family

Being far away from their family and friends isolates and jeopardizes youth right when they need solid support the most. Jon, like other young adults, would have benefited from more regular, two-way contact between home and school.

Jon certainly initiated such contact, writing twenty-five-page, single -spaced letters, which he would copy and ship out to individual family and friends. Such long letters home are, however, most unusual; few college students write them. Had we, his family members, been really listening, we could have heard them as the terrible cry for love that they were.

Jon was starving for the same level of communication in return. In almost every letter Jon begged for letters—for connection and information on what was happening. He kept reaching out to us and relying on us to reciprocate. Yet few of the family had the time or inclination to come close to matching Jon in output or wit. We simply didn't write to him with the same depth of care with which he reached out to us.

Young adults may thrive on special assignments that use their developing skills to solidify their place in the family and strengthen their relationships with family members. At Jon's funeral, when Great-Uncle Leo, an uncle on his father's side and a highly successful retired businessman, came up to share that after first meeting Jon, he thought Jon the perfect relative to commission to do a genealogy of their family and was about to call and ask him, I went into shock. Too late, I knew that serving such a key role would by itself have saved Jon's life. How perfectly tailored to Jon! Researching his father's family's genealogy would have used his skills and not only served the family but also embedded him as a key person in all their lives. How immensely healing and stabilizing Jon would have found this! Every family can find some similar role to make sure their precious youth stay connected as they move out into the world.

Solidifying a Relationship with Oneself

Keeping strong and healthy connections with their family of origin helps young adults solidify their relationship with themselves. The first relationship upon becoming an adult is necessarily with oneself; and for that to happen, a young adult needs a coherent, unbroken story of "how I got to be me." Questions or unknowns in their story act to undermine a coherent sense of self. Hearing family members share personal stories helps a young person fill in missing pieces of their individual story. Building a personal story free of gaps and dualities gives young people a solid foundation for trusting themselves and others, which is part of building their own unique adult identity within the family network.

What Jon unconsciously had starved for ever since the divorce was a whole, united family to love unconditionally. Children are undermined by parental rifts, burdened by divided loyalties, and they can forever mourn all that was torn asunder. How critical it is for parents not to visit their issues on children in ways that leave them psychologically sawn in two! Young people need to love both parents and respect them equally. Only when divorcing parents respect rather than undermine each other can children find the solid ground they need to build their own coherent identity.

On this, the most successful day of his life, Jon needed both his father and mother to show their unconditional love and support for their son by showing each other respectful accord. What else mattered except being there for their son to celebrate his achievement?

When young people are going through a major transition such as graduation, knowing their parents are united behind them provides a rock of assurance, enabling them to move forward independently with the courage and confidence that can overcome every obstacle. Had Jon encountered such united support at his graduation, how much more seamlessly might he have been able to move out into independent adult life? Would he still be here?

Young people undergoing life transitions do not have to rely solely on parents to provide much-needed support. Each person can construct their own rituals to mark the endings and beginnings in life. With imagination and vision, ordinary items can be gathered together and enlisted to help perform a rich and indelible personal ceremony. It is in each person's power to create some truly special unique and meaningful "graduation" or ritual at any point of transition. Ritual acknowledges a moment of change; it marks off what was from what will be. It helps us navigate the cusp between past and future. Taken seriously, rituals can support us at any charged or fraught moment in life.

Finding Intimate Relationship

During young adulthood, an intimate relationship is a key issue—either a stabilizing source of love and mutual support or an enervating cycle of drama and distrust. While the drive for intimate relationship at this time is normal, it is also important to remember that young adults' brains are still immature. So although relationship is important at this time, a relationship doesn't have to be serious but can instead be viewed as more of a social experiment to learn and grow from.

Today people are experimenting with various casual and serious dating and relationship models, for good or otherwise. As young people begin to engage in intimate relationships, it is important to remember that sexual intimacy has consequences that are not to be treated lightly. One poor choice can cause many years of emotional or physical suffering.

From puberty on, young people need complete information about sexual and romantic intimacy. They need to know how to build healthy and fulfilling emotional and sexual relationships and how to recognize unhealthy signals or warning signs of danger. Providing complete information to young people and feeling free to tell their own stories of what worked—and didn't—in intimate relationships is one way that parents, relatives, and other caring adults can continue to support young people as they explore their newfound adult roles.

Making a Difference in Creativity and Work

Young adults like Jon also need structured ways to participate and make a difference in their emerging or chosen creative arenas. One potent way to build self-worth and efficacy is to give supervisors, teachers, or administrators feedback about one's experiences and have that feedback heard and acted upon. Jon did provide feedback through his department's student advisory committee but was dissatisfied by the response he received. By the end of his university time, he was appalled about ending up the sole survivor of his entering class. He saw that the program had pushed students too hard too fast, and he was furious at the human toll it had taken. Just before his graduation, he wrote everyone that he would never give a dime to such an alma mater.

Young adults also benefit from sharing their thoughts and experiences in creative ways. Jon had a special talent for writing poetry, narrative, and also incisive, funny plays. He had written his first play at age sixteen—a spoof on me and my new profession that he titled *Psychology Today*. The script was so good that both his high school and later his university seriously considered staging it. To broaden his university experience, Jon could have channeled his feelings, humor, intelligence, and experiences into publishing serial shorts, such as insider parodies of university life or else light or serious essays on his ever-prolific topics of interest.

But as Ken Robinson in his TED talk on creativity indicates, education primarily focuses on improving us from the waist up, with a special focus on the head and "slightly to the left," as he drolly puts it. That certainly describes Jon. But diversity, he says, is the creative key to life and growth. In the dark Middle Ages, all modes of brilliance burst in a Renaissance in only certain cities benefiting from diverse culture streams. The diverse, free mix of intelligence wrought in every form—whether in food, art, music, ideas, technology, dance, mathematics, language, or story—has always produced unpredictable spectacular human benefits. Each form is itself an entire universe revealing the whole universe the more we explore.

Being narrow, rigid, or homogeneous, in contrast, acts to stultify, demean, and discourage life. In our education system, Jon learned to be right too much. The A's he earned also held him in thrall to it. He needed to take more risks to be wrong, to be different, and to push himself into new things—with his mind, body, travels, companions, and interests. The intertwining of his own diverse choices could have woven a lifesaving net to continually enrich and sustain him.

Nature's diverse intertwining is what created the possibility of life on earth. Weaving our own creative, diverse networks and being okay with making mistakes and learning from them will sustain our own individual growth even as it sustains the continuing emergence of life on earth.

Changing the Curriculum

In this stage, as young people are beginning to test their mettle in the world of relationships, school, and work, it becomes important to help them develop the life skills that they will need to support themselves in their relationships and future careers. Occupational, government, and university programs need to be structured in ways that protect and support the young they are entrusted to teach rather than discourage and demoralize them with excessively strenuous, unreasonable workloads.

To help students succeed, narrowly focused program offerings can be balanced with courses emphasizing life skills. Some examples would be courses exploring emotional intelligence, intimacy, self-management, communication skills, leadership, and relational skills. Such courses can promote a campus environment of equality and solidarity and can equip young adults with skills that ensure success in both future careers and relationships.

Courses in writing, music, art, dance, sports, psychology, sociology, or theater arts could have aided Jon's social and emotional growth and also balanced the rigors of such a compressed and narrowly focused program in theoretical math. Creative courses can help students stay balanced by building right-brain functions. These activities give students space to take stock of their experiences during this time of life when changes are unfolding rapidly. Reflecting on their experiences through writing or some other art form helps to balance a left-brain academic curriculum and allows youth to naturally mature as they creatively express their own ideas, emotions, and experiences.

To help students succeed, schools might provide every student access to a designated socio-emotional adviser to consult regularly. A confidential peer support group can be helpful too, where feelings are aired and worked through with collaborative, compassionate support. Clubs or support groups like these could form in every dorm to help residents connect with one another and to create a protective cohort for any members being singled out for hazing or bullying. Such groups could also collaborate in creating new group norms and help to stabilize individuals as they move through college and then beyond. Regular courses for credit could be offered teaching socio-emotional life skills.

Finding Purpose

In this critical stage of life, young adults need outlets for their energies—a smorgasbord of options to immerse themselves in and to discover more of who they are and where their passions lie. They benefit from a range of real-world opportunities in which they can test and grow their skills.

Young adults' passion for life and purpose can be satisfied by enlisting in some activity with a larger purpose or mission, such as sports, work exchanges, environmental or nature adventure programs, or the military. Enrichment opportunities such as education abroad, the Peace Corps, Doctors Without Borders, youth camps, missionary work, backpacking, river trips, or sailing adventures as well as volunteer jobs overseas or nationwide can help ground students in real-world issues. Young people can learn humanitarian values and can practice community-building skills such as cooperation and egalitarianism even as they become connected to a sense of higher purpose. Between high school and college is a rich time for youth to volunteer in a world full of problems all begging for human solutions. These involvements can deepen youths' empathy and sense of solidarity with others, whether human or other-than-human, and inspire young people to commit themselves to humane, ecological, and spiritual ways of life.

With family and social supports such as these in place, young adults can move out into the world with greater solidity instead of shakiness. They can better sense that they are both powerful and precious—needed and valued not only by their families but also by the communities into which they move. With such assurance, they can then begin their journey to find their people and place in the world as they also contribute to society at large.

Teachings, Airbags, and Safety Nets

- According to Erikson, young adults' new challenge is bonding intimately with peers in personal or working relationships, or be at risk of isolation.

- If young adults become isolated, they can experience loss of identity, meaning they will lose direction and hope as well—all of which sets them up for a psychological fall.

- Most young men and women between the ages of eighteen and twenty-one have historically been regarded as mature adults and expected to handle life in this way, while research now indicates that the human brain does not fully mature until about age twenty-five.

- This gap between eighteen and twenty-five coincides with a historical spike in mental breaks and increased risk of suicide. Our educational and social institutions need to realign expectations and program offerings to provide more support for youth as they emerge into adult life.

- The first relationship on becoming an adult necessarily is with oneself. For that a young adult need a coherent, unbroken story of "how I got to be me." Having a continuous personal story free of discontinuities and dualities helps young people stand on a solid foundation, upon which they can then build a coherent adult identity and stable relationships.

- Split loyalties and other divisive dynamics between parents sabotage their adult children's relationships with others and hinder their progress through life. Only when divorced parents respect rather than undermine each other can children stand with both legs on the solid firmament they need to thrive and succeed.

- The more problematic a young person's upbringing, the more unresolved traumas they carry with them, or the more immature their brain is, the more vulnerable and at risk the young adult is.

- During young adulthood, an intimate relationship is a key issue—either a stabilizing source of love and mutual support or an enervating cycle of drama and distrust.

- While the drive for intimate relationships at this time is normal, it is also important to remember that young adults' brains remain immature. So although relationships are important at this time, they don't have to be serious, but can instead be viewed as more of a social experiment to learn and grow from.

- Youth who leave home for school have just lost their entire support system and often feel stranded, depressed, and overwhelmed in a new milieu among strangers. They can benefit from ongoing contact with relatives, friends, and home community.

- Family members at home need to listen for and respond to all cries for love and connection from their newly fledged young adult. Provide solid support in letters, emails, texts, phone calls, and in person as needed. To manage this overwhelming transition, a young adult may need individual therapy or medication as well.

- Schools have an obligation to help their students succeed. Toward that end, a narrowly focused curriculum can be balanced with broader offerings. Some examples are courses exploring emotional intelligence, intimacy or self-management and courses that build skills in communicating, studying, relationships, and leadership. Such courses can promote a campus environment of equality and solidarity and equip young adults with skills that ensure success in both future careers and relationships.

- Young adults benefit from having opportunities to make a difference in their chosen creative arenas. They may thrive on special assignments that solidify their place in the family and use their newfound skills as educated, full adults. They enjoy having a niche to belong to where they can contribute their unique perspective and be of worth to others.

- Vital outlets for young adults' energy and developing skills are altruistic service options—local, national, or international. Community service shows young people they are needed and helps them grow in intimacy, compassion, and resilience.

- Young adults may gain insight on their lives, be empowered, and heal by reflecting on their feelings and transforming their experience through journaling, story, art, music, or dance.

- Confidential peer groups are great opportunities to air feelings and receive compassionate solidarity and support.

- Embrace diversity. Weaving our own creative, diverse networks and being okay with mistakes and learning from them will sustain our own individual growth even as it sustains the continuing emergence of life on earth.

Perilous Passages

〜

Age	Virtue Instilled	Psychosocial Crisis	Significant Relationship	Existential Question	Significant Issues
26–65 years	Care and Contribution	Generativity vs. Stagnation	Family, Elders, Career, Workmates, Avocations, and Community	Can I make my life count?	Caring for Self, Family, Elders, Friends, and Colleagues; Contributing to Work, Community, and Earth

WHAT DOES A twenty-one-year-old, bright, and starry-eyed master's-level mathematical theoretician do out in the real world? Graduation brought this question into more critical focus for Jon. After watching all his class-mates drop out, fall back, or fail, this lone survivor just wanted out. Jon yearned to rejoin the human race, hoping to find a real-world job in which to use his expertise and to team up with bright people doing exciting things to benefit everyone, not just a few academic elites.

Halfway through his fourth year, at an on-campus job fair, Jon finally walked away holding a job offer and feeling some relief about his future. At a worldwide consulting firm in Washington, DC, Jon would begin in their actuarial certification program, using statistical probabilities to help determine insurance risks and rates for different populations. Once a fully certified actuary, Jon was assured of an excellent career with fine earning potential.

Following graduation, Jon moved to a small, inexpensive apartment in Baltimore and began commuting to corporate headquarters in DC. After just three months (half the usual probationary period), the company awarded Jon a special 7 percent raise for exemplary work.

While Jon remained sunny and enthused at work, his coworkers couldn't guess that work was all Jon had going on for him in Washington. Every night he returned home to an empty apartment. It was far too silent. Too dead, alone, and enclosed—like a coffin. As time went on, the silence and emptiness only grew worse.

Jon had never lived alone before. He was used to a buzzing dorm life or the conversation-filled homes of his family and friends. By comparison, walking into his apartment each evening was like dropping into a black hole.

When new neighbors moved in across the hall—a Japanese couple, the husband a visiting professor—Jon instantly invited them over for dinner. This was not only the first dinner party Jon had ever thrown, it was also the first full dinner he had ever cooked. Excited and somewhat panicked, Jon called me for the recipe for his favorite dish—my "white" lasagna, a complicated vegetarian dish featuring three cheeses, spinach, and a mushroom sauce. Then he had to buy the lasagna pan, the ingredients, and all the other equipment and accessories. And then decide what else to serve. How do you set a table? With what? Where does everything go? What to provide for drinks? The invitation was easy, the food, materials, and preparation, over the top. But Jon persevered and served the lasagna, and his first dinner party turned out a success.

But as the months passed, Jon became less and less enamored of actuarial work. It was nothing at all like theoretical mathematics. At school Jon had felt challenged and creative; actuarial work, by contrast, was dry and formulaic. In time Jon realized he would never be happy doing this for the rest of his life no matter how nice the people or how high the pay.

In despair, Jon wondered if he would ever fit in or find a place to contribute and be happy. His accelerated university program had elevated Jon years ahead of peers his own age. Still twenty-one, having been released into normal life in the real world, Jon felt like a social misfit. Possessing all the right expertise but lacking the maturity, social skills, and corporate savvy of his new cohort of thirty- to fifty-somethings, where on earth did Jon belong?

He resigned from his job, deeply disappointing his boss, who offered up several attractive alternatives he was forced to decline one by one. Feeling guilty for letting her and all those good people down, Jon set out to reunite with his family. Packing his car to the roof, Jon steered straight toward his dad's home in Texas. Perhaps he could find a job doing mathematics-related work in his dad's airline industry. In Texas, Jon found the barbecue hot and the guest bed ready. Jon was happy to be home, reconnecting with all that was familiar and feeling that he mattered and belonged. Right away he fired off a few résumés, but over the month that he stayed there, not a single airline responded.

During this visit one of his dad's cousins out in California's Silicon Valley called to catch up and, hearing of Jon's situation, suggested that he come out and apply to her high-tech corporation. "I'm betting that Jon could find a great fit in this up-and-coming company," she said. "And while he's getting interviewed and reestablished, he can stay with us in our guest bedroom. We'd so enjoy having him with us!"

With spirits lifted, Jon sent over his résumé and drove off to California and the promise of both a job and a welcoming family. Meanwhile, the company reviewed his résumé and was impressed by this young super-achiever. And just then, this company needed a transfusion.

A key position had just come open when the forty-something man who filled it committed suicide. Though stunned by his death, coworkers knew little more. Perhaps this kid could be the replacement to keep the company competitive and profitable. He was young, but he sure seemed to have all the right stuff.

They called Jon in and interviewed him. The head of the interview team would be Jon's direct supervisor. Instantly Jon liked him. Rick was a good man, competent yet kind, someone to trust. The interview went well. The confirmation job offer arrived shortly after, with great pay and all the perks. Jon was now point person on the company's development team. What a worthy position of trust and great opportunity! Jon felt as honored as he was thrilled.

He began the job, coming home at night to a sweet family he adored. He helped the parents out around the house as he could and in the evenings tutored their fourteen-year-old daughter, Anna, with her homework. Afterward, they would play pinochle, just as he used to tutor calculus or play chess, Monopoly, or other games with friends and family back home.

But as time passed, the parents began to chafe at having such a long-term guest, especially a now-twenty-two-year-old young man hanging out with their young daughter every night. A few weeks into his new job, with kind voices they suggested Jon find his own place.

Outwardly, Jon agreed with enthusiasm; inwardly, he was heartsick. Just when he felt part of a great family, and finally happy both at home and with this new, terrific job, once again he must return to a solitary life in another small and empty apartment. Quickly he found an inexpensive place and moved in. Depressed again, he took special note of one spot he drove by on the freeway to work, where, if worse came to worst, there was an easy instant out. All he had to do was drive down the freeway and quickly swerve into the slot entrance of a narrow freeway carve-out, then speed up all the way into the eight-foot-high concrete soundwall at its far end.

In his new position, however, work was going well. Jon quickly came to enjoy and trust his new boss, Rick. Under his supervision Jon had his new team conduct market research while he methodically analyzed the company's efficiency throughout the plant. With Rick as good shepherd, Jon was sure he could help make the company a force to be reckoned with.

A few months in, one Thursday evening at home, Jon realized he could relax. Finally, he was okay—working at a high-tech company in a pivotal job with terrific people, settling in, learning fast, and feeling great about the possibilities opening up. California in general, and Silicon Valley in particular, fit him well, all so familiar, much nearer his hometown, and high-tech, supercharged—in a word, perfect. Finally, his lonely, depressed, and arduous journey was over. In fact, each problem in its own way had helped him arrive here. He would help drive this company skyward and, in the process, prove himself. Confident, happy, inspired with his work, and secure, Jon relaxed. A wonderful new life had begun.

To celebrate the prospects ahead, why not buy a new car—a cool, zippy sports car—to reflect how he felt? Good Friday was tomorrow, then three days off over Easter. The family was expecting him for dinner down south on Easter Sunday, so why not go check out and perhaps buy a new Miata on Saturday? He couldn't wait to trade in that clunker Plymouth Reliant he had always hated for a real sports car to drive down scenic Highway 1 and surprise everyone. Thrifty like his dad, Jon had already saved more than enough for a good down payment, and with his new salary, the car would be all his in a year.

Thursday evening in his apartment, for the very first time since graduation, Jon felt elated—happy, settled in, finally home. Jon reached out and called the good friend he'd known since junior high, Todd, now busy at MIT finishing his PhD, and spent happy hours on the phone catching up.

Next morning, still buoyant and enthused, he drove to work. He had some interesting ideas he wanted to run by Rick. Opening the door to his office, he walked in, sat down, and took out a yellow notepad and began jotting down each point, adding subheadings he didn't want to overlook. Minutes later, Rick walked in. Jon looked up, ready.

Instead Rick said, "I need you to come with me." Nonplussed but expectant, Jon rose and followed him to a part of the operations Jon knew but had not yet analyzed. Rick introduced him to the supervisor and a few crew, then turned to Jon. "Here's where you'll be working from now on. You'll be reporting to him now. Your desk will be set up today. Jon, I know you'll be a great asset here."

Jon had no idea what Rick was saying. He asked for clarification.

"This is where you work now. He's your new supervisor—you've been reassigned, and he'll be describing your new duties. Of course, your salary must be downgraded to reflect this new classification."

In a daze, Jon slowly realized that Rick, the boss he idolized and trusted, had just fired and demoted him.

Suddenly disoriented and dizzy, Jon blanched—like he might pass out. His mouth went dry, his stomach cramped, and he almost retched. "What . . . what have I done wrong?" he stammered.

"Nothing. You've done nothing wrong," Rick answered briskly as he walked away. "I'll fill out the paperwork and bring it by to sign."

In shock, uncomprehending, Jon stood immobile as everything reeled around him. His new supervisor began to talk, but Jon heard not a word. Pale, Jon barely breathed. His skin turning damp, then chilled. He stood stiffly, remaining silent and polite while his mind couldn't stop racing. His hands trembled, and a sense of doom flooded his gut. He tried hard to get back in control, but nothing worked. The rest of the day was a whiteout. When Rick showed up with the papers, Jon numbly signed them while his fingers shook. Jon could only ask again, "What have I done wrong?" and hear again, "Nothing. You haven't done anything wrong."

Rick couldn't be telling the truth. Jon knew better. Of course something was wrong, and he knew what: he, Jon, wasn't good enough. Just months in and already a proven failure. Throughout his life, Jon had hardly ever gotten a B, yet now the company and Rick had summarily handed him a stunning F. This was intolerable, unthinkable, and what was worse was that he didn't know why.

What he did know was that all his schooling, all he'd done to be worthy—to earn his way up the ladder and have the intellectual skills to contribute and make a difference, to succeed—was for nothing. Dad's cousins had just kicked him out, given him an F too. No way could he stand another night in that miserable apartment. No way could he return to this humiliating demotion or bear the facts back in this . . . this old, unending, and futile existence.

After numbly signing the papers, he walked off and returned to his old office, locking himself in to try and face things logically. His head swam as his extremities chilled and his heart pounded. Panic rose and threatened to engulf him. Filling with acid, his empty stomach burned and his mouth dried until his tongue clung to the roof of his mouth. Jon pulled a Diet Sprite out of the bottom drawer, popped the top, and downed it—the only thing he would ingest all day.

What he most feared was true after all. He was a failure. Didn't fit anywhere. All his trying, hard work, successes, had gotten him nowhere. He was alone. With no peers, no friends, no family, and now demoted. Kicked out of the one job he'd deluded himself into believing he was doing great at and was so sure he fit. By the one boss he would do anything for. He could face no more.

In a stupor, he sat heavily at his desk with head bent, unseeing eyes fixed on a blank blotter. Outside the window, sunset gradually faded to darkness. Finally, around 7:00 p.m. he took a deep breath and with great effort picked up the phone and called his dad in Texas. Hearing Dad's calm voice, Jon blurted in strangled tones, "Dad, I'm out of control." To his father on the other end, the rest was incoherent—nothing he heard made sense or seemed concrete. This was so unlike Jon!

Dad heard but did not understand. Even if he had, like most parents, he would not have known what to do. He spoke with Jon a few minutes, trying to reassure him. "Take it easy," he said. "Shit happens. Calm down. It will all work out. You'll be fine in the morning." He said goodbye, hung up, and returned to watching TV with his wife.

But on the other end of the phone, Jon could not calm down. He wasn't fine then, nor would he be in the morning. With his hand resting heavily on the phone, he wept helplessly, finally quieting to a long, numb silence. With a final effort, Jon fished out his little address book, tried dialing other numbers. Friday night of a holiday weekend . . . nobody home, only recordings. He hung up at each beep. Finally, a live person picked up, an uncle he hardly knew and couldn't bring himself to tell the reason for the call. After a minute of awkward hellos, they signed off.

Now he had failed even at getting help. Jon was alone in a life crisis— far from home and out of energy, ideas, and hope. Panic grew along with his despair. A whirlpool of ugly, negative thoughts cycled uncontrollably. *There really is no place on earth for me. I've failed and don't even know how. I called for help and failed that too. Nobody cares, no one is here for me, I don't matter. All I tried to do doesn't matter. I am lost and at the end. There is no home, no job, no new car, no lover, wife, people, place, or future for me here.* The truth was there from the beginning. *I really am . . . too bad a boy.* Contempt and self-hatred hardened into icy resolution. The time had come. He could still be a success.

Stiffly Jon rose tall above his desk, stood a long moment, then walked out the door to his now-former office. He turned to close and carefully lock the door, oblivious that the lights were still on. Outside corporate headquarters, he walked numbly into the parking lot, deserted except for one car, his clunky old Reliant. How he hated that paint-peeled and faded brown car—almost laughed at how he'd been ready to trade it in, tomorrow, on a new Miata to celebrate his new life and career. What a joke on him! No more tomorrows. No Miatas. No more setups just to be demolished. He was done, out of here, with one last mission: to finish off—demolish—this pathetic, ugly vehicle.

Jon sank into the driver's seat, leaving his seat belt unbuckled for the first—and final—time. Revving the engine, he steered out of the parking lot and a minute later onto the Highway 85 on-ramp headed in the wrong direction home.

The night was clear and soft, with a huge full moon rising like a floodlight before him. He knew exactly where he was heading and precisely what to do. Quickly, his destination approached. Pressing his foot to the floor, Jon accelerated the Reliant past a surprised woman driving on his left who in moments would become his single, stunned witness. At just the right second he swerved abruptly, threaded the car through a narrow slot opening in the reflective metal guardrail edging the highway, and instantly corrected to realign the car before speeding all the way up this fire lane aimed straight for its end, a looming, eight-foot-high zag of concrete soundwall. Time slowed as he rocketed down a dark, dead-end corridor, gas pedal floored and his eyes on target. Headlights shone down, lit up, then whited out the looming wall. Seconds before impact, Jon came to—realized this was wrong, stupid, a total overreaction—too late. Panicked anew, screaming "Nooooooooooo!" Jon stomped his foot down but missed the brake, grazing it to leave black striations along his shoe's instep—a detail the coroner would take special note of.

The brown Reliant hurtled into the wall head-on, instantly smashing the engine into Jon's outstretched legs, tearing flesh and breaking long bones into pieces. His screams cut short as Jon's head clocked forward into the windshield, whipped back, then slumped to his chest amid screeching concrete and crumpling metal, shards of glass, white smoke, and the smell of hot oil . . . to still silence.

Horribly shaken, Jon's lone witness exited at the next off-ramp to find a service station and a phone booth. With quivering fingers, she dialed 9-1-1.

Officers at the scene filled in "Broken Neck" as cause of death. The officer recorded death as "Instant." Before filing the report, he printed *FATAL* in thick black marker across the top.

Erikson on Stage 7:
Generativity vs. Stagnation (26–65 Years)

Erikson described Stage 7 as "the link between the individual's life cycle and the cycle of generations." The existential question asked and answered in the seventh stage of adulthood, between twenty-six and sixty-five, is, "Can I make my life count?" This is the longest of the stages, where all the previous years of life culminate in being "generative."

For Erikson, generativity meant "the concern for establishing and guiding the next generation." It arises from an individual's intrinsic optimism about humanity. One vital way to contribute is by joining in a committed relationship and raising happy, secure, and resilient children. Children literally embody humanity's hope for the future. They give back to their parents in turn, giving them joy while helping their parents grow too and transform.

Generativity also means becoming financially viable and emotionally stable enough to offer support to oneself, one's career, family, community, and circle of friends. One sign of generativity is getting paid for one's efforts as real-world proof that one is contributing something of value to the larger community. We can also be generative through offering up good ideas to others, through sharing our unique creative talents, and through volunteering in socially beneficial roles.

Generativity is always possible in both work and love, the two "cornerstones to our humanness," which Freud defined as "all there is." One can express generativity by perpetuating solid family values or being the one to choose to end a family cycle of abuse. Being generative might mean developing personal creativity by journaling and self-reflecting or by being a good friend, the family cutup, a good storyteller, a great father or mother, or the researcher of the family genealogy. Or by contributing anything else, such as penning a play or writing a book—whatever promotes the happiness, understanding, or well-being of others.

At this stage of development, we have matured physically, neurologically, and hopefully psychosocially. We have grown up and are now ready to take responsibility and join with others in contributing productively to our personal identity, our sense of meaning, our family and society, and life in general. During the seventh stage of adulthood we are busy accomplishing goals. We are taking care of ourselves; maintaining careers and stable, happy relationships; raising responsible children; being personally creative; and caring for aging parents. As we produce and perhaps reproduce, we continue to regenerate our selves in new ways and to evolve.

Over this longest of all developmental periods of thirty-plus years, work is a principal avenue of generativity. Work is the communal form of reciprocal love, a way of contributing to the community while covering our basic needs to survive. By joining in some purpose larger than ourselves, each of us can discover new aspects of "who I am," exploring individual and communal answers to the question "what am I here for?" Being employed means being specially chosen for who you are and being trusted to contribute. It means being considered so valuable that you're worth paying for. It means being welcomed to join in and empower a team of people assembled for some productive community benefit. Employment helps to buoy one's self-esteem, confidence, and optimism. It adds new, substantive layers to our personal identity and our sense of meaning. It supports our emotional well-being and increases our vital sense of agency and efficacy. All of these things help a person discover more of "who I am," which is the essence of personal generativity.

In adulthood, if that inherent need to be generative is stunted or denied, a life crisis ensues. The immediate danger becomes what Erikson called "stagnation"—existence that is shallow, lacking in meaning or connection to others or in purpose or vitality. Feelings of despair or hopelessness set in, and we lose essential connections, momentum, energy, and purpose. Stagnation can be expressed in many ways, including chronic mental illness, cyclic antisocial or criminal behavior and imprisonment, addiction, major depression, chronic weight issues, or learned helplessness. These are all forms of stasis and desperate cries for love. Instead of watching our star rise, we see a flat or falling line.

If, in addition to feeling stagnant, we are carrying untreated PTSD or chronic feelings of frustration or rage, we can become a danger to ourselves or others. We can harm ourselves through self-mutilation, anorexia and bulimia, ongoing recklessness, imprisonment, drug overdoses, and attempted or completed suicide. We can harm others in physical or emotional abuse or through neglect or in acts of destructiveness, cruelty, criminality, and murder.

But however we harm self or others, the danger is always to both. For there is no danger to another that doesn't put ourselves in equal jeopardy, and there is no danger to self that won't equally jeopardize and devastate our friends, loved ones, and innocent others.

Jon in Stage 7

Jon's developmental age of twenty-three doesn't qualify him for this stage of life, but his academic achievements, intellectual abilities, and new work position gave him early entrée to this stage of mature, adult functioning. Jon's tragic end reveals much about how perilous the passage to adulthood is for young, bright, idealistic, but still-unseasoned individuals. It shows as well how desperately adults need to be prepared with socio-emotional skills and to have all their intimate others (family, relatives, friends, and lovers) standing by.

Encountering failure at any time in our lives, especially when it happens suddenly, can be a profound shock. It can send even a seasoned and capable adult into a black hole of self-doubt and despair. But at a key moment such as entering adulthood, failure can be catastrophic. It can trigger an existential, even suicidal, crisis in a person who is moving into a new niche and does not yet have the seasoning and maturity to cope with life's ever-shifting challenges. Mental breaks are common on the cusp of adulthood, when youth must transition into independent living. If their economic or social status is too tenuous or if their self-protective boundaries are easily bridged, the results can range from problematic to catastrophic.

Here Jon was—fresh, young, superbright, academically accomplished, highly motivated, and also psychosocially at risk in this critical life passage. At twenty-three, he was trying to negotiate the passage into adulthood several developmental years ahead of his true age and maturity level.

In addition, Jon was holding inside him unhealed horrors from decades before. This crisis at work had triggered the long-festering agony and shame that his four-year old self felt on being molested, followed by being seemingly rejected and left by his daddy because he was "too bad a boy." Had we his parents discussed and resolved that experience with him and corrected those misinterpretations, such a volatile overload of caustic feelings would have been mostly neutralized. Even if they were again triggered in the present, they would not have been so overwhelming; instead, he could have had the conscious perspective to remind himself, "These feelings go back to how I felt at four after being molested and rejected by Dad; they are not just about today's experience." But because those crises in earlier stages of life had not been kept conscious and were not resolved, Jon was set up in this moment to feel and react as he did.

Neither did Jon know what was going on behind the scenes at his place of work. On the fateful day when Jon thought he had failed, what he didn't know—and his boss, Rick, couldn't yet tell him—was that indeed there was a reason he was suddenly relocated to a different part of the firm. It took me twenty years after Jon's death to ask one crucial question about what was going on at that time with this corporation, but when I did, the answer was a quick and heartbreaking internet search away.

Online, I learned that shortly after Jon began working for this company, the firm entered into secret negotiations to be bought out and incorporated into a nationwide infotech company. By that year's end, and eight months after Jon's suicide, the merger was complete. But back in March, Rick was unable to tell Jon about those then-secret discussions. Neither could he say that though the merger would wipe out Jon's position, Jon was seen as such a valuable resource that they didn't want to lose him. They would instead transfer him to a job that was sure to survive the buyout. Rick was in fact being Jon's good shepherd. He was telling the truth. Jon indeed had done nothing wrong. Jon's original sense of Rick as good and trustworthy was correct.

But Jon had zero seasoning in corporate politics. He did not understand what a high-pressure job he had stepped into, despite knowing that his forty-something predecessor had committed suicide.

Having struggled in this perilous passage to adulthood, and just now beginning to relax and feel assured, Jon received the news of his demotion as a total shock. He instantly took it as proof of his personal failure. He had never in his life received a grade lower than a rare B. Jon's emotional brain leaped to the most self-protective (but always least likely), worst-case conclusion: he had earned an F.

For the first time ever, his body-mind flew into a full-blown panic attack. Unable to control these feelings, get an explanation he trusted, or raise help from those he tried to call, Jon was left on his own, stranded and unable to cope. Desperate, Jon truly was, as he himself said, out of control.

In a sudden life crisis with no hope of help or relief, he chose a permanent out to what truly was a temporary problem.

Answering the Call

All Jon desperately needed that night was to be heard and believed—to matter enough for someone to come and stand by him in his hour of need.

Here is what such a phone call might sound like: "You say you're out of control? Is this like a panic attack? Sounds like you've had a huge shock. Tell me what exactly happened." Let the person talk everything out in full. Really listen and repeat back what you are hearing. Repeating the person's words lets the person know they are not alone. Make sure they know you understand.

Keep saying, "Tell me more." This helps the person in crisis discharge the toxic feelings in words. It helps them slow down. It buys time. Asking for more assures them that you care.

Directly ask, "Are you thinking of killing yourself?" If yes, or the answer sounds ambivalent, ask the person to get rid of all means of harm, like giving their car keys to someone else for safekeeping or getting rid of knives, guns, ropes, or bottles of medication.

Keep assuring the person, "You matter," and follow up with, "I'm on my way. Promise to wait for me—do nothing except to stay absolutely safe."

Give them some calming suggestions: "Take slow, deep breaths. Let every single thought go by, because right now there is too much you just don't know. I'll be calling or texting you every chance I can. Until I arrive, call whenever you need." Encourage them to drink water and have a bite to eat. Make them promise to do nothing but rest and stay put until help arrives. "Okay? Promise?"

Urge the person, "Reach out to others and talk to them about what happened, too. If you need instant help, call 9-1-1 or write down and call the suicide hotline at 1-800-273-8255 and talk to them. That's what these people are there for. Meanwhile, I'll be seeing you very, very soon. Together, we'll see this through! Okay? I'm on my way. Love you!"

Err on the side of safety. Call 9-1-1 yourself and provide details. It's far preferable to have them upset with you than gone or permanently disabled. If you are confronted, simply say, "I couldn't bear the risk of losing you." Then alert everyone you can to call the person and stay connected with them until help has arrived. That's love! (See the Appendix for a wallet-sized foldout to carry, about what to do if you get the call.)

Worst-Case Thinking

Worst-case thinking is emotionally hardwired into all of us. It is left over from the days of saber-toothed tigers, when those who reacted the fastest had the best chance to survive and become our ancestors. However, with primeval living long gone, acting on our first, most alarming thought today can devastate or even kill. It guarantees more havoc and unnecessary drama; it does not support life and longevity.

Our automatic and most protective catastrophic thought is actually the least likely to be true. Such thoughts are true only about—or even less than—1 percent of the time. Acting as if the worst were true, as Jon did, creates needless tragedy over 99 percent of the time. (Of course, in that other 1 percent instance, if someone or something is imminently threatening you, yes, do take instant appropriate action to survive!)

High achievers may be more prone to worst-case thinking in a crisis. Because they have so often been rewarded for being right, they may tend to assume they know what is going on when they actually do not. But if we are really smart, when we suffer a shock and instantly feel sure we know why it is happening, we will bracket that first thought and calm down enough to wait and see. We will consider more likely, less drastic alternatives. Panic lessens when we just stop, quiet our mind, and breathe, taking essential time out to relax in order to restore our equanimity and allow the real information to emerge.

To repeat, in a crisis, wait. Breathe. Relax. Do not act, no matter how urgently you want to. Every storm passes. Once it does, it is possible to gain clearer access to full information. The truth is almost never what our catastrophizing mind thinks—"You're a failure!" The truth instead provides important information over time, which we can use to become our best selves—but only if we stay alive.

Give Yourself Time to Survive

Life will indeed challenge each of us. Throughout the long stage of adulthood, life will surprise us with bumps, shocks, delights, gifts, and tragedies. Our job, when encountering any crisis, is first to survive. Most often, we do that by slowing down and staying safe—giving ourselves the time to survive.

When crisis comes, remember that bad times are inevitable. But bad times and even tragedies, once survived, in time become our greatest teachers. Against all odds, problems and challenges in life force us to grow; they teach and season us. By simply suspending judgment long enough to survive, we can stay centered in the middle of every shock and remain true to ourselves. Only then can we learn from each challenge and experience the growth and empowerment that come afterward—sometimes long afterward. "What doesn't kill us," as the philosopher Nietzsche once observed, "makes us stronger."

What Jon didn't give himself was time and trust. Time for the adrenaline to dissipate. Time to calm down, breathe, and ask himself some vital questions about his first, worst-case thought. Time to reach out until he could receive help, if not from his support system, then by calling 9-1-1 or the suicide prevention hotline (always available) at 1-800-273-8255. Time to wait and find out that this job change had nothing to do with him. Time to reestablish trust in his boss and in himself as a singularly accomplished contributor to his community. Time to believe in himself and to trust that he had done nothing wrong and that his life was incredibly worth living.

Surviving a Crisis

When a crisis shocks us like it did Jon, it's almost impossible to think rationally. We're overwhelmed. We panic. It feels unbearable. But it's not what happened that's so terrible, it's what we're thinking about it. There is an old adage in psychotherapy, one to tell yourself over and over in a worst-case scenario: It's never about what you think it is. So to survive a crisis, it is crucial to turn off your thinking and stay safe.

The first thing to do, of course, is call out for help, and don't give up until help is on its way. While waiting for help, you can do critical work to reestablish internal balance. Here is a step-by-step guide for turning off your thoughts and surviving.

1. Focus on your breathing. Slow it down. Lengthen it on the in-breath, and again on the out-breath. Count slowly as you lengthen the exhale, then do the same on the inhale. Breathe using your entire spine, lengthening and straightening it as you breathe slowly in, deep into your expanding belly. Then slowly and evenly round it over at the top into a conscious and equally slow out-breath, letting your spine and body round back down an inch or two as your belly empties. Keep doing this. It takes moving your body consciously through at least sixty slow, deep, and even breaths to feel the inner agitation begin to ease away. As thoughts pop in, just notice them, then allow them to pass on out and evaporate back into clear blue sky. Nothing is more important than breathing your mind and body into a calmer state.

As you focus on breathing, good things are happening inside your body. You are oxygenating every cell, nourishing the body while sending calming signals to your heart and brain. Your heart starts to slow, blood pressure lowers, and stress hormones such as cortisol and adrenaline are easing back to normal. Down in your stomach, the alkaline and acidic levels begin to mix and neutralize. You are spreading peace and comfort throughout your organs and limbs. You are strengthening your immune system and staying alive by slowly breathing yourself into a calmer state. This is required before doing anything else: we must be calm before our brain is able to think clearly and make good decisions about what to do next.

2. Take a body inventory, and focus on relaxing each muscle group one by one. Mentally pass over your entire body from the top of your head down to your toes, relaxing your scalp, face, neck, shoulders, arms, body, legs, and feet, feeling each muscle ease and soften before going on to the next area. You are continuing to breathe very slowly from your belly. Continue to allow your torso to undulate a little with each breath. Count as you inhale and exhale, lengthening the breath to eight or more slow counts both ways. There's nothing more important to do than to keep breathing and relaxing. Notice when thoughts or feelings arise, but do not attach to them. Simply allow them to float in, through, and out so you feel clearer and more spacious. Only your breathing and relaxation matter. You are restoring your body to calmness, equilibrium, and normal functioning. When the storm passes and the sky clears, you will be able to care for yourself more easily. That's when you can better reassess the situation and perhaps get help in addressing it.

3. Calm any remaining internal storms by using tools that have worked for you in the past. Do you have a racing heart, a stomachache, a clenched jaw, or tight shoulders? Do you have a headache, brain fog, or a general sense of anxiety or depression? Are you shaky or feel somehow out of your body, as if you were observing things from afar or above? Once you know your symptoms, use any tools that have ever calmed you in the past. For example, many people relax by soaking in a hot bath or going to a hot springs. Or they simply imagine stepping into a hot springs and feeling their muscles melt as they go deeper and deeper into the warm water. If your calming technique works even a little, keep doing it, and check inside to feel the shifts. The longer you pay attention, the more it will tend to shift.

If your usual calming techniques are not working, go through this list, trying each one until you find what does work:

- Tap your outstretched palm against your chest about twice per second for five seconds, then gradually slow the tapping. If you notice improvements in your symptoms, keep doing it and keep paying attention how it makes you feel inside.

- Rub your hands on your clothes or pet a beloved animal, and notice the sensations in your hands and in the rest of your body.

- Rock back and forth or side to side while holding yourself. If it helps, imagine you are being held by a beloved friend or relative as you rock.

- Imagine being in your favorite place where you feel safe, or imagine your favorite animal companion, and notice what happens inside. Make the experience vivid by noticing what you experience in each of your senses—what you see, smell, taste, feel, hear.

- If your body feels shaky, let it shake for as long as it needs. Amplify the shaking through your whole body, and shake out the shakiness. The shaking releases fight-or-flight energy and helps us revive and then restore equilibrium.

- Walk up a hill, ride a bike, bounce on an exercise ball, turn on music and dance, drum to your emotions, or move your major muscles in some vigorous manner to simulate fight or flight.

- Squeeze the thumb of one hand with the other hand more and more tightly until you are using two-thirds of your strength, and notice what shifts as you hold it. Switch thumbs when your hand gets tired, and keep paying attention to the sensations.

- Wrap your arms around your torso tightly and hold as hard and long as you can. Release. Feel the shifts. Repeat. Keep noticing the sensations, and repeat as necessary.

The more you pay attention to how your body and mind are responding to these techniques, the more you will tend to relax.

4. Reach for a larger perspective. In a crisis our focus narrows into tunnel vision and our internal balance disappears. We can feel light and disembodied. At this moment a larger perspective becomes critical. Thus a good question to ask is: *Ten years from now, how much will this situation matter to me?*

However it feels now, this is really just a moment. Even if it feels like the end, it's not. Do not act on catastrophic thoughts. Just breathe through a crisis. Down the road this horrible moment might look entirely different. It is even likely to have been of benefit. Give it time. Stop. Breathe. Rest. Relax. Wait. Get help. Repeat. This moment will pass. Another will arrive. The worse a moment is, the better the next moment will likely be.

Ask yourself: *What would I prefer to see, feel, and know about myself ten years from now as I look back on my role and choices in this moment?*

In any situation, there are many possible responses out of which to select a best choice. So really think through the options you have, and focus on the one that will make you feel best about yourself when you look back at yourself in hindsight. Choose well.

5. Question worst-case thinking. If you notice your first thought is a worst-case thought (which it usually is), challenge it. Given that worst cases actually have the least likelihood of being true, what other scenario is more likely? Hint: there are many. Jot them down in sequence, from least to most likely. Consider each in turn. What is less likely? More likely? Best possible? Bet on probabilities greater than your worst 1 percent, and wait. Ninety-nine percent of the time, you'll be right.

6. Keep breathing. Keep slowing the breath way down. Keep releasing anxious, chaotic thoughts by breathing all the way from pelvis to throat and rolling it evenly at the top into a long, slow, and easy out-breath all the way out. Keep consciously relaxing every muscle from your forehead down to your toes, and then do it again. The breath can restore calm all by itself, for the slowness and ease tell the limbic system, busy pumping out adrenaline and cortisol, to stop, let go, and trust in the process of life itself. A calm and easy breath helps you reestablish trust in your Higher Power's wisdom and love and in your own creative, resourceful self. Only when we are calm and at ease can we think clearly and make good decisions.

Every time we survive a crisis, we build resilience and give ourselves the opportunity to look back on it from farther down the road. With time, we gain the perspective to learn from what happened and perhaps appreciate how this seemingly terrible moment actually worked out in positive ways that were unimaginable at the time. But this can only be realized if we stay alive and safe, if we calm down and restore our internal balance.

Riding the Waves

When drama happens—and it always does—it's essential to just ride every powerful emotional wave. As in the sea, each crest grows to spill over and plummet into chaos and slowly dissipate, only to rise again. Trust the process, and ride each wave. Little by little, the waves move us toward new shores and undreamed-of possibilities.

There are many practices that can help us keep our balance in the midst of stormy seas. Meditation and mindfulness practices are two ways to stay connected to that inner balance. Yoga, tai chi, dance, being in nature, laughter, pets, making love, being creative in any modality, and following your passion all strengthen your inner resources. Participating in solo or team sports, improving yourself, helping others, and being of benefit— these and all the other activities that take us out of our heads will bring us back to our physical center in the body and heart. Coming back to oneself and the peace and equilibrium that lie at our center will help us weather every storm.

When we stay present and balanced through all apparent dramas, we gain access to the calm eye of the storm within, where it is safe and where all our senses can reopen and clear. By remaining aligned and in balance as we move through life challenges, we accrue more love, inner peace, and wisdom. For love, peace, and wisdom are the truth of our nature and the enduring truth of nature itself.

Addressing Problems

Problems are the seeds that grow us from the inside out. They often first appear to us as unwanted or even devastating shocks. But they are also learning opportunities. Once survived, they help to season us and make us stronger and wiser human beings, better equipped for living. Survive them by staying open, riding the wave, and seeking the lesson. Clue: the bigger the challenge, the greater the lesson. Life is a hero's journey. In every heroic story, some terrible wound or impossible quest sets the wounded one on his or her particular journey of personal transformation. The worse the wound or quest, the greater the transformation and triumph. So wounds, mistakes, or problems are all required for personal growth.

Why a problem showed up when it did is not as interesting as what we do with it. We have little insight into how something came to be and what part we may have played in it. But we do have all the power of our response—to not take what happened personally but instead to learn from it. We learn from it by staying open to what we can do to right the wrong, learn from the mistake, or turn what happened into something that improves our own and others' lives.

A couple I knew was on a scenic drive in the mountains when their car's bumper hit a boulder and popped out. Marty got out, looked at the boulder, then the bumper, then walked around to different angles and looked at both again. Without a word, he climbed back into the car and backed the car up while turning it just so, then shifted forward, and accelerated right back into the offending boulder. The bumper popped back into place, and my friends continued on their way. Still amazed days later, his wife, June, told me what happened. I heard from her story that our problems point to and hold their solutions within them. If we stay as open and unruffled as Marty and simply survey the situation from different angles, we too may learn how to use what created the problem to solve it.

Developing Our Networks of Support

We can weather the storms of life best when we have a solid base of support in a network of friends and loved ones. Yet building that support is best done when we are not in crisis.

Offering good, solid support to others on an everyday basis helps to create a solid core of support within ourselves. We can then use that inner core as a foundation for building supportive relationships. Spontaneous acts of goodwill, care, and generosity, especially to those we don't know, as well as to our perceived enemies, over time sows within us essential qualities that help to build a supportive network with others. Seeing with eyes of compassion, openheartedness, and love is always possible. It is our salvation and is what makes us humane.

What you want, first give that to others. If you want goodwill, give goodwill, and over time your network will grow and strengthen. If you want friends, be a friend to yourself and others. Treat others with respect no matter how they treat you, and never take what they say or do personally. If you hear unloving words from others, in a tragic, sad way you are hearing a cry for love. Give love.

Choosing Traits Wisely

One practice that can keep us centered and emotionally balanced is the practice of choosing wisely the traits we want to integrate into ourselves. It works like this: Every person around us is a compendium of unique qualities—some attractive, some not so much. As we interact with the others in our lives, we can choose which of their qualities we want to grow more of ourselves. Whenever motivated, we can pick a desirable core quality and practice being that quality. The more we keep practicing, the more that quality becomes part of who we are. In Alcoholics Anonymous a favorite expression is "Fake it 'til you make it." It works for sobriety, and yes, it works for moving into our ideal self as well.

Perhaps we have a friend who is bold when the situation calls for it. How does that quality feel inside? How does it change our thinking? How does it encourage us to react? How does it sound, and what does it tend to say? When we practice being bold as the need arises, even if we don't ourselves feel bold, in time boldness becomes a natural part of us.

Whatever you really want, consciously practice it and grow into it. Then you have built within you the qualities you most value. Moreover, this tends to center you in a chosen self you truly like and accept in full, and that helps to make you less dependent on others for your stability, health, and happiness. In an emergency, if nobody is available to help, as in Jon's case, you already have equipped yourself with all the right stuff to help you stay centered on your chosen course.

Being a Lifeline for Our Youth

No matter how seemingly grown up or educated our youth, they are still exquisitely sensitive and likely to take tough moments very personally. This is especially true when young people are starting out on their own. We who love and care for them must continue to remain available no matter what. Love is forever—it is never "over," never "enough," never "finished."

Being a lifeline means loving young people by sitting down with them and sharing how we survived the inevitable shocks of life. Long before a crisis, I wish I had talked to Jon of my own perilous passages. I wish I had warned him that he—we all—will be challenged in life, and it will often come as a shock, often when we least expect it, when we feel especially buoyant, finally in the clear, finally safe. Together he and I might have brainstormed ways that we could simply stay connected and stable during those times. I could have emphasized how every challenge that seems so insurmountable in the moment teaches us valuable lessons or sets us on a path that often serves us well. I might have emphasized the importance of staying present and conscious, of breathing through a crisis, of loving, trusting, and nurturing himself always and also extending love to others in need. He might have gotten a sense for how critical it is to stay in contact with loved ones, to be compassionate with himself and others, and to remember that in crises, what matters first is simply doing nothing but calming down, loving oneself, and surviving the moment.

I wish I had turned off the TV more often to eat, laugh, play, and share together with my sons. Together we might have created an open free space where each young man could be himself in full. I might have talked with Jon about freedom within safe limits and what that looks like. Together we might have created a realistic emergency plan for moments of crisis. We might have spun out the what-ifs: What if you are demoted because you failed at some unknown task? What if your company starts to inexplicably shift you around? What if your true love takes a hike? What if you're about to receive an offer for a better job tomorrow but you like the job you're in? And together, we could have brainstormed solutions to each. By doing this, Jon might have developed a surer sense of my love for him and a surer foundation and practice of self-love. He might have begun to understand that adult life will sometimes shock him, but that what matters is life itself—to love ourselves by being our best self in each moment and then trusting the process of life and our own evolving inner wisdom.

Being a lifeline for young adults also means being available to talk and to listen when a son or daughter or friend calls in a crisis. It means keeping them on the line until help arrives or the crisis passes—until it is clear they are not going to harm themselves or others in any way. Staying connected helps the person in crisis to balance themselves and restabilize and helps to forge a deeper, more enduring connection.

Being a lifeline means embodying love through caring, listening, and asking questions, then letting the person in crisis discharge all that destructive energy through talking. It means believing what the person says and being authentic ourselves, speaking from the heart, listening and asking questions, and giving hope while never denying their feelings or experience. It means sharing how you cherish and need them in your life. It means staying connected—and physically getting there as soon as possible and staying nearby to support them.

Remember to keep no secrets when life is at risk. If concerned, call 9-1-1 for a welfare check, and call anyone else you can to rally around the person in crisis. Being a lifeline means removing their access to all means of self-destruction—knives, guns, drugs or meds, ropes, and car keys. It means reminding them that while everything is important, nothing is that serious—certainly not worth killing yourself over. Instead it's an opportunity to evolve into more selfhood, which we will, in life. It means helping them reconnect with faith, time, perspective, and hope. Let them know that this is only a moment, not forever.

Had Jon reached solid, helpful support that night, he could have talked through his crisis while those on the other end of the line listened, asked questions, and took steps to get help to him and also get there in person.

Talking might have led to crying, and so he could have grieved this loss and drained out some of that self-destructive energy in tears.

Helping Young Adults Become Generative

Every young adult needs a solid base of support to help them transition into full adult generativity. Here are some ideas that could be implemented in schools, businesses, families, and groups of friends to help young people weather the perilous passage to adulthood safely.

Provide graduating students with transition-to-adult-life counseling as well as career counseling. As Jon's graduation approached, he could have been required to prepare for his transition through readings, tutorials, role-playing, and talking with available experts about any questions he had about adult life. Such life-transition counseling can help students transit knowledgeably and stably with an array of choices from the academic setting to city, business, and corporate life. Counseling and career services could house this transitional function.

Provide employee orientation and mentoring, especially to young adults just entering the workforce. Jon could have survived this moment had he understood a little more about corporate hierarchies and how to negotiate them. Employers could provide all new hires a tour of their corporate infrastructure, with flowcharts and protocols, in perhaps an interactive self-paced video tutorial. Human Resources could support new employees' successful transition into the company by assigning each hire their own go-to mentor. Such mentors could answer questions, interpret corporate culture, and troubleshoot as they track new hires through their initial weeks or months.

In the case of necessary transitions such as employee shuffles, demotions, or firing, helping the affected people stabilize should be the humane first priority. In Jon's case, Rick could have simply said, "Jon, I want you to know that circumstances beyond what you can know right now make this move necessary, and I imagine it may also be in your long-term best interest. Though this has to come as a shock, it has nothing whatsoever to do with your ability or performance to date. In fact, it is because we find you so valuable that I and top management are doing what we can to keep you. Things are in flux at this moment but should resolve very soon. In the meantime, please know that I and the management very much value what you bring to the table. I know that you personally contribute at the highest level, and I stand fully behind you."

Practice crisis management techniques. Parents, teachers, employers, and friends should learn and practice crisis management techniques, including suicide prevention. By knowing how to react when we get the call or see another in crisis, we can prevent the tragic loss of each irreplaceable person. (See the back of the book, "If You Get the Call: A Checklist.")

Draw up an emergency plan for use in crises. Knowing life will sometimes overwhelm us, families and groups of friends can draw up an emergency plan for how to stay in contact during and after crises. It can address various levels of crisis, from "feeling slightly off-kilter" to "feeling totally out of control." It should include a list of close relatives or intimate friends to notify if someone can no longer guarantee their own safety. It should also include a list of the most effective techniques a person uses to calm their own nervous system. We cannot know what crises life will throw at us, but we can give ourselves and loved ones the best possible chance of surviving if we are prepared.

If You Find Yourself Stagnating

Stagnation, as Erikson saw, is the lack of generativity. A feeling of stagnation can sneak up on us at any point in adulthood. If we can't seem to get up in the morning, or if we find ourselves sleeping too much, that's stagnation. If we find little to care about or do, that's stagnation. Or, if we allow ourselves to fixate on particular negative or riveting messages, media, or video games, we are addicting ourselves to our own adrenaline, which increasingly stultifies and numbs us.

When we find ourselves zoning out, when real life holds no interest, when we feel listless, depressed, or else easily enraged to the point of violence, one or more factors may be holding us hostage. It may be something in our external environment, such as unfulfilling relationships or work, that is inhibiting our growth and needing our attention. It may be that what we keep choosing to focus or dwell on is sapping our life force.

We may be copying debilitating patterns of behavior that we learned in our family of origin. All of these and more are simply challenges to face honestly and, as possible, to make informed choices about. Breaking free of stagnation means telling the truth about what is happening, first to ourselves, and then getting the support we need to move toward more creative and fulfilling ways of living.

What leads to stagnation? We are creatures of habit. Whatever we hear, do, or say repeatedly, no matter how true or untrue, over time feels truer. The more it is repeated, the more we accept it and act on it as fact. Any thought or habit strengthened with repetition turns into a neurological feedback loop in our brain, leading us to feel, think, and behave in these preprogrammed ways. So any messages we tell ourselves or expose ourselves to repeatedly matter—a lot! Beliefs or images we tune in to on social media or elsewhere keep building internal neural networks that increase our acceptance of those same images or thoughts—for good or for ill. So we need to be vigilant caretakers of ourselves and our loved ones to make sure our lives are not being co-opted by forces of stagnation.

There are many ways we can be lured into negativity. If we grow up hearing negative, critical, or hateful words, we may believe our elders and accept their views without reflecting on or challenging them. The more adverse childhood events we endure, the more likely our brains will wire themselves in negative, despairing ways that, if left unchallenged, can depress our life force so that we stagnate. We can get mired in the past by speaking in the past tense, as old people often do, which will lead us into believing and behaving as if our real life took place back in the past and is no longer vital now. And though life offers both crests and troughs of waves, we can stay stuck in the bottom of the cycle, seeing only darkness and danger, never trusting ourselves to surrender and move with the upwelling flow.

Stagnation is any bad habit that increasingly separates us from ourselves, others, and the vibrant, joyous, connected life that is naturally our birthright. Stagnation is toxic, and it is a signal. Moving into generativity means creating new habits—of movement, of thinking, of connection and involvement. It means cultivating honesty about our life and seeking to live with passion and vitality. Overcoming stagnation may take sustained effort, continuing to do the hard thing of moving from negative to positive by being involved in things that generate life. As we make hard choices to move toward generativity, it is important to always appreciate and reward ourselves in healthy ways for doing so.

If we get caught in a negative, enervating spiral, we normally need help to succeed in turning toward a new and life-giving direction. We can find help by telling the truth about what we're experiencing. We need to be courageous by admitting the truth first of all to ourselves and then being honest with others until we are heard and understood. Being honest is the first step in supporting our integrity and well-being.

Many kinds of support are available if we find ourselves losing psychological ground. Some people might choose to practice mindfulness or meditation to increase their mental clarity and quiet their minds. Some use breath meditation to calm down, center, and detach from unproductive, obsessive, or debilitating thoughts. Yoga can help a person move in conscious, healthy ways and become more present. Some people choose to listen to great teachers—to read books or attend workshops.

Mindfulness strategies are key in helping us manage negative emotional thought processes. Just a simple online search will lead you to many strategies for coming back to our own mind and heart. Dr. Marsha Linehan, Dr. Daniel Siegel, Jon Kabat-Zinn, Dr. Brené Brown, Dr. Srikumar Rao, and Eckhart Tolle are only a few of many wonderful teachers offering mindfulness and meditation practices that help people connect with peace in the present moment.

Doctors are a great resource when needed. Naturopathic, chiropractic, and allopathic physicians, among others, can provide help. Medications can now be matched with our DNA to increase the probability that they will enhance our own brain chemistry. Sometimes doctors or medications are exactly the lifeline needed to restore us back to positive functioning. New medications that target chronic depression and suicidality are often fast-tracked due to their lifesaving need and are but an internet search away.

For those mired in a stagnant, debilitating process, there are dedicated mental health, adventure, and nature programs as well as self-help recovery groups available in communities nationally and worldwide. These groups are tailored to fit every level of need, age, and personal situation. They may take place in person after work or school or might function as online support groups or might be structured as outpatient or inpatient programs. Some help is available for every level of need. Keep looking until you find what works for you.

Being Generative in Love and Work

In this seventh stage of life, we are seeking to contribute to the larger circle of life through both love and work, and to have our contributions recognized and valued in return.

If you seek for ways to increase the ease, happiness, and well-being of those you work with or love, you are acting in generative ways that will bear inner fruit, if not immediately then in the future. Care and respect are human values that each person is responsible for both giving and receiving. Show care always, in each relationship, and then respect the needs of others to pursue their lives as they see fit. Support them in their healthy choices.

Create trust in your relationships of love or work by being trustworthy. Without trust, there is no safety—for you or others—or ability to grow. Without growth, relationships stagnate and divisiveness reigns. So create trust by being true in word and deed and constant in loving-kindness. For as the Bible says, "That which you sow shall you reap."

Paradise can only bloom when there is an atmosphere of trust and safety, with equality, diversity, and the freedom to be all of who we are in both work and love. Wherever you are, in whatever you do, consciously sow the seeds that allow paradise to bloom on earth.

Staying Connected to Ourselves
Throughout Adulthood

Throughout our adult lives, we continue to grow and become generative by remaining in conscious connection with our higher self, with life, and with the greater good. So just be yourself as you grow, and keep noticing how you evolve into ever more of who you are. Stay conscious, reflect on and learn from the past, and confide in and listen to trusted mentors. Be your best self in each moment, and trust the unfolding process.

Know that you matter far more than you can imagine. You are the central core of an ever-growing human galaxy—surrounded by ever-larger concentric rings of family and children, friends, partners, colleagues, and others, on out to the horizon. Research indicates that each person is integrally connected to about 135 others, whether they are known or not. Each individual in your own living galaxy of others is able to exist in a stable orbit only because you exist as their gravitational center. Without you, a void replaces their unifying core, and a whole galaxy of wonderful others collides or careens off into space as the galaxy disintegrates. Without you, nothing can ever be the same. You are essential. You keep your galaxy intact and functioning.

As we make our way through adulthood, becoming more ourselves at each new stage, we may find ourselves at different times reenacting many different roles. We may become the innocent infant, the magic child, the good shepherd, the lover, the prince or princess. Or we may become— sometimes at the same time!— the hero, desperado, jester, scribe, idiot, sage, genius, lunatic, teacher, and cook. Each role owns a special genius and will reveal more of who we are. The years of adulthood give us the chance to enjoy each one, play each character to the max, and integrate their many gifts into ourselves as we segue from one to another.

Another easy and often inexpensive way to keep growing is to sign up for adult education courses in psychology and especially in socio-emotional learning (SEL). Building our skills in empathy, self-esteem, and communication will improve our lives and the lives of our loved ones. It has been long proven that SEL skills are more powerfully associated with happiness and success than is our intelligence quotient (IQ).

And when life challenges us, as it inevitably will, it becomes our responsibility as adults to save ourselves if we can and, if we can't, to honestly admit we need help and to stay safe until it arrives, no matter who the help comes from or how long it takes.

While we wait for help, we can breathe ourselves back down to a place of calm. We have the power to panic as well as the power to move toward center, calm, and peace. We can come back to our own mind and heart. We can return to our own good sense. Here is where sanity and logic reside and where all good decisions are made.

~

Teachings, Airbags, and Safety Nets

- The long age of adulthood from twenty-six to sixty-five is where we ask and answer the generative question, "Can I be useful and make my life count?"

- For Erikson, generativity meant "the concern for establishing and guiding the next generation." Today generativity might be ending a family history of addiction or abuse; being creative in any medium; helping others or being a good friend; or contributing to the community.

- If our inherent impulse to be generative is stunted or denied, a life crisis ensues with the danger of stagnation—loss of meaning, movement, and vitality. When we feel we do not matter, we slip into ennui, depression, addiction, mental illness, alienation, criminality, or suicide. Each of these is a form of stagnation—a living death or an actual death—and each one is a cry for love and life.

- Whenever we take initiative to make a positive difference, no matter how small, we regenerate energy and feel ourselves begin to matter. The generative impulse is ever within us; all it takes is remembering this and acting on it. The easiest way to practice this is to give others what you yourself would love to receive.

- Jon's tragic end reveals much about how perilous the passage to adulthood is for young people who might be intellectually advanced but socially and emotionally unseasoned, not yet fully mature.

- High achievers, who have so often been rewarded for knowing, may be more prone in a crisis to assume they know what is going on when in fact they do not. Thus they may be more at risk.

- In crisis, we are in shock and overwhelmed; we panic. Yet, our first, most catastrophic thought is always the most protective, and least likely to be true. Acting on it guarantees an impulsive attacking or fleeing overreaction. So stop, bracket that thought, and think up more likely scenarios, including those you would prefer. Meanwhile, get help, and do nothing else but breathe until a calmer, balanced state returns or help arrives.

- In crisis, keep breathing slowly, evenly, and deeply while continuing to relax every muscle from head to toe. Just wait. We can only make good choices in a calm, relaxed state once we actually have all the information.

- Use the calming techniques in this chapter to help you return to solid ground. And remember, in life, change is our only guarantee. Even if the worst case is true, if we just survive things can only improve.

- People in crisis desperately need connection, to be heard and believed. They need to know they matter, that others care and are standing by them. If someone you know is in crisis, send for help, stay connected, and show up in person to support them and prove their life matters.

- In any crisis, one generative question to ask is, "In ten years, how important will this moment be to me?"

- Problems are the seeds that grow us from the inside out. They are learning opportunities and choice points. Once we survive them, they season us and make us stronger, deeper, and clearer human beings. Survive them by staying open, riding the wave, and seeking the lesson. Clue: the bigger the challenge, the greater the lesson.

- Sign up for classes in socio-emotional skills, where you will learn key insights that promote happiness and longevity.

- Learn and practice mindfulness, meditation, yoga, breathing, and relaxation techniques to become that internally quiet, centering lifeline for yourself and others.

- Corporations should provide employee orientation and mentoring, especially to young people entering the workforce. Jon could have survived this moment had he had a defined, go-to person to talk to as needed and had he understood a little more about corporate hierarchies and how to negotiate them.

- Employees being reassigned or let go of in work require empathy, sincerity, due process, and transitional support. A message that in some way conveys "you don't matter" is inhumane and personally devastating. While never true, it creates chaos within the receiver.

- Be prepared; crises happen. We all need an emergency backup plan—a plan that can be written up in a short list and practiced to prepare for the personal emergencies that do happen.

- Stay close to this spiritual truth: that you were so loved you were given life, despite all the odds in the universe.

- Medication is available to help, and new, improved medications are always coming through. The right one for you is worth finding. It really can save lives.

One of the Missing

~

STAGE 8. ELDERHOOD

Age	Virtue Instilled	Psychosocial Crisis	Significant Relationship	Existential Question	Significant Issues
65 years on	Wisdom	Ego Integrity vs. Despair	My Life, My Kin, Humankind, Faith / Spirit	Is it okay to have been me?	Final Life Review, Being a Wise Shepherd to Younger Generations

TWO WEEKS AFTER his twenty-third birthday, Jon died by his own hand after receiving shocking news. There's no Jon to write about in Stage 8 since he never reached it—never came to know his true potential, find his true love…never arrived at inner peace or a mature integrity.

So what is there to say? What can be learned about this elder stage of life if Jon is not here to live it?

That has been my quest in the decades since his death. His suicide made it my destiny to move forward through the years without him. It was an impossible mission. Without him, who am I?

Now I have arrived at this final stage of maturation, and I have done so in his absence. From his birth Jon was my best and toughest teacher, and even after he died, he never stopped teaching. He forced me to learn how to survive a parent's most inconceivable loss. He forced me to learn what keeps life worth living after your child dies. He forced me on this search to reunite with him and somehow make sense of what happened in ways that might help others survive what he did not.

I had to scour every inch of our shared past to understand my son and his actual experience instead of my own rosy illusions of him. And Jon's life and death together forced me, as a new therapist, to learn how old shocks and hurts can be healed or avoided by simply knowing what it takes to resolve the core crisis in each stage of living.

Well into the last stage of life, I only now have the perspective that is impossible to have earlier in life. Not until now, on the far side of my becoming, am I able to identify the particular waystations that led to the person I am today.

I've lived a much harder, sadder life since losing Jon, though for me he's never an inch or a second away. I now know that he is part of me always.

For every day Jon still teaches. He and Dr. Erik Erikson tag along in every single counseling session, one young and one elder presence tuned to different cues. Each of them occasionally alerts me to delve into subtle emotional subtexts I might otherwise overlook. Jon sensitizes me to depression, trauma, and suicidality, while Dr. Erikson emphasizes a client's stage in life, helping me to identify and better guide the client through the internal crisis of that stage of life. Together they support clients' progress—like the two spiral strands of DNA weave life.

For the past twenty-plus years and because of Jon, I have been invited each year into classes at Jon's high school to teach communication and leadership skills to students, either those at risk or those in advanced placement. In these classes, magic happens. I always lead off with my own story—about growing up, then having a little boy named Jon, what happened, and what he taught me. At first there are laughs, then shock and tears. Then I look at them and say, "Each one of you has a story like this. We want to hear it!" Jon's story always inspires them to go way beyond their own fears of public speaking to share their own hard moments and what those moments taught them. Meanwhile, those in the audience learn how to speak in public, how to listen, how to give feedback in useful ways others can accept, and I coach speakers and evaluators to continue to improve.

Every year I am amazed at the students' sincerity and courage and, best of all, their fantastic personal growth. The entire class bonds as they offer one another inspiration, appreciation, support, and empathy. Every so often around town I meet former students who say, "That was the best class I ever had in school!" Then I ask, "Ah, but are you using the skills?" And they chorus back, "All the time! Everywhere!" Then I know, again, that Jon, through me, was their teacher, and he helped show them what they too could be.

One year I led an at-risk class in Virtual Enterprise. Their teacher greeted me with, "These kids will be lucky to get a job slinging fast food!"—words I was shocked to hear from a teacher. But over ten weeks, these youth were so inspired and involved in learning how to be effective speakers and communicators that all that energy pumped into their coursework. At the end, this class competed in Washington, DC, against 120 other nationwide schools' Virtual Enterprise classes. Out of the seven categories of competition, these so-called at-risk students swept five. On their return, their stunned teacher gushed, "This is impossible!" To which I said, "No. If your class could achieve this in ten weeks, this . . . is a failure of your education system." For all they really learned were social-emotional skills—something most schools don't formally teach. I left knowing that these kids had blown themselves way past some mimimum-pay job in fast food.

Since Jon's suicide, both within and outside of therapy, I have been able to help others survive what he did not. All I can do now is honor what Jon taught me by teaching and inspiring others with his story. For the only way to make Jon's story a tragedy is to do nothing about it. And the only way to survive our own worst shocks and arrive at the elder stage of life with hope intact is to take the moments of our lives and use them—to learn what we can from them so that we grow into our best, wisest version of ourselves. Then we can look back with no regrets, knowing we did everything possible to honor what life had to teach us.

Erikson on Stage 8:
Ego Integrity vs. Despair (65 Years On)

From the age of sixty-five on, Erikson said, we reach our last stage of maturation and begin to survey our past and come to terms with all that transpired—not for the first time but ever more surely for the last. With a lifetime of living behind us, we can look back on every twist and turn and review every choice that, for better or worse, took us here. We are also increasingly aware of life's finality as we continue to approach our expiration date. And with it comes the key puzzle piece that was earlier unavailable—how our story ends. Given all this, we face the core crisis of Stage 8, the final life review.

Here is the true age of reckoning, where we look back and ask: Was my life worth living? Did I contribute? What was my true life story?

The question is the same one we had at the beginning: Who am I? Except now it is phrased in past tense: Was my story one of success or failure? A hero's journey or pathetic tragedy? Did I go forth with courage and vision or make poor choices and operate by default? Was my life authentic and savory or pretentious, callous, and trite?

Erikson suggests that at this age individuals must somehow come to terms, taking their personal measure across a lifetime. As with each preceding stage, there are two possible resolutions. Either we will look back with quiet pride and see how we contributed to life on Earth, or we will find our life wanting. Were we productive, good, kind, and generous in our dealings with others and this planet? Do we feel fulfilled and loved and know peace as a wise, benevolent elder? Or do we feel alone and stranded? Or bitter, bankrupt, and in despair over all that is too late to change?

Elders who feel their choices and issues led to meaningful and positive outcomes will feel fulfilled and at peace as they negotiate this final age. At life's end, they can feel serene and unafraid of death. But those who harbor anger or bitterness and see only negatives will look back with agony and despair and will feel unprepared for or even terrified of what may lie ahead.

In this way, hell and heaven exist nowhere else but on Earth, as each of us arrives at one destination or the other at the very end of our lives, guided by the sum of our experiences and choices. Either we will feel at peace and fulfilled, in our own personal paradise, or we will toss in a storm of hell, bitter and beset from within and without.

The good news is, every moment we live we hold the key to where we will finally arrive—at the door of heaven or the abyss of hell, all determined not by what happens to us but by how we respond to what happens. Did we endure to learn from even the most terrible of experiences? Did we transform our difficulties to our own and others' benefit? As sovereign adults, we can choose, in each moment, how to respond.

This last age is the most important of all, because it ends in death. Death's finality is precisely what gives life meaning. If our lives were endless, what would truly matter? Because our lives are finite, our time here is precious, and everything we do has meaning and consequences. We live and die by the choices we make.

So, knowing we die is exactly what gives us the power to consciously live. At the end of our lives, will we be surrounded by love and feel joy, fulfillment, and peace? Or will we be alone and miserable, lost in bitter despair? That is our choice, in every new moment.

The Stage of Life Jon Didn't Live to See

If Jon had been able to survive his crisis—just breathing through it and remembering that a crisis is no time to make any important decision and that from any dark low, much can be learned and life will only get better—he would have reaped the benefits of the brilliant life he had begun. Since I survived his death, I was the one left to put those pieces together in retrospect and perform his life review.

Clues to the life Jon would have led began to appear almost immediately after he died. At his memorial service, shards of Jon's whole, aborted life showed up in the form of each mournful person who bore a piece of the wonderful future awaiting him. None of these pieces were yet known to Jon, but all were in place, about to manifest. The life that would have been was guaranteed to be immensely worth the living.

When Jon's Great-Uncle Leo, a retired CEO of a large, highly successful dealership, came up to me at the service to say, "You know, I only met Jon once, but after speaking with him for five minutes, I realized that here really is someone who really could save the world," I was stunned. Leo was never one to overstate a case. He had picked up on Jon's incredible potential, which other CEOs would have sensed as well. Had Jon lived and remained at his job, even after being reassigned to a less desirable position, he could have taken advantage of many desirable options in the world of career and work. Jon would have risen fast and high, just as he always did and always would.

But other careers that Jon didn't yet know about were already in the offing. After his death, letters of condolence arrived from every one of his previous employers—those he had worked for both full- and part-time. Each said that they had been actively searching for Jon to offer him high-level management positions uniquely tailored to his well-demonstrated abilities. One said Jon would have had his pick of where to live.

As described earlier, Jon also never knew that he was about to be asked to take on a special role in his family, researching the genealogy of his father's line, all underwritten by that same CEO, Great-Uncle Leo. Jon would have adored such a mission, and I know that role alone would have saved his life. He would have been terrific at the writing, storytelling, and historical research involved in retracing his family's saga. He would have found meaning, identity, and power in this new, extended-family role. By giving his relatives a sense of connection and solid identity, he would have been giving back to the family in a generative role. And who knows what else that work might have spawned.

Jon also never lived long enough to learn that he already had found true love. Instead, dear Laurel, the peer Jon had tutored in calculus at sixteen, had to attend an untimely memorial to honor the man she had always loved and hoped to marry. I was surprised to see her there since it had been almost eight years since I had last heard anything from Jon about her. But I poignantly recalled times she studied with Jon in our living room, and the one memorable time when he brought her to the house to show her our new puppy—and how adorable a pair they looked. Had Jon only known, the perfect woman was waiting for him.

When Jon's friend Paul said he expected and needed Jon to be in his life forever, I heard what Jon died too soon to understand: Jon was that essential. He was that loved. Jon was surrounded, though he may not have realized it at the time, with loyal, lifelong friends who knew him and needed him and who stood by as his very own staunch cadre of allies and personal resources, available to him forever.

Every piercing revelation at his memorial service also provided clues —clues to what might have gone so terribly wrong in a life that seemed to be going so very right. Sweet Anna shyly testifying that she just lost her pinochle partner—from those words, I later pieced together that Jon had searched for loving family life upon leaving his first job, and the welcome haven he found with Anna's family then became so difficult to lose.

Each piece of the puzzle that was revealed at his memorial is based on more of Jon's truth than either he or I knew while he lived. And each of those pieces helped me to fill in the larger picture of the lifetime of friendship, love, service, and fulfillment that could have been his had he only stayed alive. Each piece was a clue that this mother, a new therapist, had no choice but to follow and learn from, for they were all I had to help me find and reunite with my real son.

Now an elder myself, I can better see what Jon needed when he found himself alone and utterly stranded on the day he panicked and ended his life. It was the wisdom of the Wise Elder.

Wise Elders

An old Korean proverb says, "Birth is pain, sickness is pain, old age is pain, and death is pain." How morbid, you may say, but in life, change involves pain. It may be the pain of birth or disease, the pain of growth, the pain of bad news, or the pain of loss. Whatever form it takes, pain is normally unwelcome. We cannot see it for what it truly is. Pain is the intolerable signal of a new opportunity to survive and grow into more of our full selves. At birth and beyond, life is a necessary mix of contrasts—light and dark, grace and challenge, the dual aspects that guide us toward more life and deeper wisdom. Painful events are required to hone us throughout life into Wise Elders.

Only after a lot of living are we as elders able to see that what first presents in such rude form turns, in time, into the perfect intervention leading us to personal transformation. With time and reflection, we can finally appreciate whatever we survived for the function it really served. That ugly, miserable rock in the road we stumbled on, when we finally look back on it, is revealed a most timely gift—a change agent, exactly what it took to wake us up, shift our direction, create a passion, or teach an essential lesson that furthered our becoming. The most devastating loss can release us to meet the perfect partner, find a better situation, quit an addiction, or take up our lifework. Only after we've gained the greater perspective over time can we finally look back and appreciate what these initially unwelcome events made possible. In time the worst thing that ever happened to us is likely to be seen as one of life's finest blessings, cloaked at the time in the perfect disguise. This is part of every life story, if we simply trust life and trust ourselves.

As these challenging moments accrue over time and we simply survive, we learn to take nothing personally or at face value. Every no is a yes to something else. Every problem points us to solutions. Every choice is an opportunity to do our best. More and more we learn to simply conserve energy, reserve judgment, and remain open, alive, and present to the ways in which our worst moment can in time stand revealed as the best thing that could have happened. Staying open to how our view of events can be transformed over time is always possible; it is always in our power.

And even if we slip up, falling for a time into despair or refusing the lessons that life wants to teach us, the good news is that as long as we stay alive, the choice to heal and grow will always be available to us. At any point along the way, emotional or psychological damage done in the past can still be addressed.

We begin to heal the past once we take full responsibility for our role in a painful incident and reflect on what is ours to do about it, perhaps by collaborating with others involved to bring the situation to resolution. Listening to the wisdom that is within us and within others, and then working together to create more healing is what turns people into heroes. If collaborating with others is not possible, we can still take steps on our own to heal the hurt inside us. Every wound can be healed; every painful incident can become a stepping-stone toward a richer, fuller life if we simply trust and stay open to that possibility.

Those who fully accept what life teaches them and turn it to benefit arrive at the final stage of maturation as a Wise Elder. Surveying their whole lifetime of experience—no matter what it looks or feels like— they know they have arrived at a true place of power. Wise Elders stand at the destination they created with every conscious choice throughout their lives, reaping the benefits of experience and becoming fulfilled and vibrant human beings. Wise Elders know through experience what the young do not and cannot know. Wise Elders remember the events in the past full of critical information, events that became way stations on the way to here, the hard lessons learned all along the way that taught us how to live.

The cost of transformation may be impossibly high, and it may haunt us for the rest of our lives. But the more painful the loss, the more important it becomes to honor it by following the path it invites us to walk. What we will discover is that every crisis, as Erikson charted, is an initiation that perhaps none would wish for but that still holds vast potential for growth and for good. So take it slow, trust, breathe, and call for support as needed, from your allies and Wise Elders, those within you and those sharing your path. We are never alone.

Help from Wise Elders

What Jon truly needed on the night he died was help from Wise Elders. What if, for instance, he had reached his old but wise, sharp, and irrepressible Great-Aunt Amelia? I have no trouble imagining the conversation. After hearing him out about his seemingly hopeless job situation, she would have had an immediate retort. "Jon," she would have said, "I'm sure this must be a terrible shock to you, and I don't blame you for feeling all that you do. But no matter how devastated you feel right now, this will blow over. Until it does, there's nothing to do but keep safe, calm down, and wait. I predict that what seems so horrendous now will turn into the best thing that ever happened to you. You must believe me because I'm a lot older than you and I am absolutely sure of this even if you aren't. I happen to love and believe in you with all my heart. You are going to be fine. You've done an incredible job so far, and that's what you must trust and put your money on. Whatever happened is a random blip that has nothing to do with you or your future success! Never do anything rash or desperate. I'm right here whenever you need! Promise me right now, or don't even think of hanging up!"

Wise Elders have weathered every storm. They have seen past each pitiless frenzy to the sunny skies that always lie ahead. If Jon had received help from such a Wise Elder, he too could have arrived at his elder years, wiser for surviving all the ups and downs that life tossed at him. He died too soon to reap this hard-won wisdom.

The Wise Elder Within

Jon died too soon to learn this truth as well: our own Wise Elder is within each of us no matter what our age. What Jon needed to restabilize his emotions and to stay alive and on course throughout adulthood was right there inside him.

Look at a seed. Within it lives the entire potential of that plant, from tender seedling to fully ripened fruit. Just as inside a tiny acorn lives a mighty oak, so it is with humans. The wise self we can grow into over time is already present, within us; our Wise Elder holds our life's unabridged unfolding even before birth.

We arrive at the Wise Elder's full power only in this final stage of life, but even if we have yet to come to maturity, the Wise Elder within has all the resources we need for living. Those resources are present and accessible to us because they were instilled in us from the start. We can call on them at any moment in life.

Our Wise Elder self has the long view on all the moments that make up our lives. Through each moment of uncertainty, despair, and turbulence, our Wise Elder is there on the far side, having survived it all. Like Yoda, our personal Wise Elder possesses the full road map with all the landmarks in place to steer us forward.

If we reflect on it all, both the good and the bad, integrating all the lessons and learning from the pain, we are ever evolving into our resilient, clear-eyed, witty, and unstoppable Wise Elder. We can all grow up to finally inherit our Wise Elder as a celebration of life and a living treasure.

Recognizing the Voice of the Wise Elder

How can we recognize our Wise Elder and distinguish that voice from the babble of other voices that pipe up from time to time? Very simply. The Wise Elder's voice is calm, warm, kind, and if anything, a bit stoic. It rings with authenticity and is often tinged with humor. We hear the sounds of patience and fortitude always focused on the long view. If we check inside and hear a harsh voice, we are not hearing the Wise Elder. If we hear a voice inside that feels reactive or pushes us to do something urgent and dramatic, we are not hearing the voice of the Wise Elder. Most of all, if we listen inside and hear any hint of a critical or judgmental tone, this is certainly not the Wise Elder. The Wise Elder never speaks in ways that label, criticize, or demean.

Instead, the Wise Elder speaks with encouragement. The words might suggest whiffs of cooling apple pie, homemade chicken soup on the stove, or melting lemon and honey down a sore throat. They remind us of what we already know in our wisest, deepest selves. For the Wise Elder is us, the part of us that can see from the far distance what we are unable to see right now. Hearing the voice of the Wise Elder brings a sense of relief and increases our trust in our own deep knowing.

Imagine the kindest, wisest elder you know. Their words are true and serene. Their sentences are short but sure, and the silences between them ripple with meaning. They are apt to respond to any query by telling a true story from their life, often prefaced by a grin or slight chuckle. Their eyes are clear and sharp but kind. They are vibrant, never missing a thing. Those eyes are much more apt to twinkle at every challenge than to darken.

Wise Elders know that humor is a precious lubricant to inject into any problem. They never forget to head straight for the easiest and simplest way through any situation. They may encourage us to stay humble and relaxed. Elders know that what matters above all is to simply survive. What we survive in time turns into a power that, if wielded well, makes us stronger. It also gives us fantastic story material down the road to inspire and teach the young people.

Wise Elders know that the most powerful thing to do is often the hardest and also the most subtle: to do nothing at all. If, in the middle of a crisis, we turn inside to ask for help, often the Wise Elder will encourage us just to breathe slowly and deeply, to calm down and wait. Or perhaps eat something nutritious, sip some water, rest, take a walk, get to work, or go to sleep.

Following the Wise Elder's Voice

How do we learn to hear the voice of the Wise Elder? By slowing down and opening our focus of attention to see the long view. In any situation we can simply ask ourselves, How do I want to feel about what I did in this moment twenty, thirty—or a hundred—years from now? How important will this situation be to me then? What are all the choices I have, and which would make me feel the best about myself later on?

By consistently stretching to see the long view, we ensure our access to the best choices in our lives. By choosing the ones that send us in positive directions, day by day, we ensure the likelihood that we will continue to feel purposeful and buoyed, even through terrible moments. Eventually, we can cash in the ticket we have reserved for ourselves, the ticket to peace, to fulfillment, joy, and well-being.

What the Wise Elder Knows

The Wise Elder within knows that life is made up of waves, one after another, and that surviving means riding the waves until they bring us, wave after wave, to new shores. The Wise Elder knows that staying balanced requires keeping our minds open to whatever wave is taking us at the moment. Scientists tell us that though the body feels dense and small, within each cell is mostly space. Remain that spacious in your mind. Stay open and curious as the waves of life take you up and then down, as you ride every error, every experience or problem. You are far more expansive, powerful, and buoyant than any momentary issue or challenge. As life goes on, we learn that every error is the stuff of transformation, every experience has a teaching, and only problems have solutions.

Your Wise Elder within has surfed all of life's waves before you. Your Wise Elder looks back at them all and sees that each was the necessary and perfect ride to bring you to your final vantage point with clarity, seasoned resilience, and inner peace.

Every moment of life is an unexpected appointment. No matter what was on your schedule or what you thought you showed up for, be open to what shows up instead. Expect to be surprised. There are no coincidences. Humans simply have limited access to the necessary information.

The Wise Elder knows that a crisis is never about who we are. It is rather about something to be learned, something that can be transformed to bring us everlasting benefit. Tough messages come. When they do, it's time to get curious, stay safe and calm, and investigate what lies behind them and what doors they might open to a sunlit future.

The most important thing to remember is to always keep faith in ourselves, in our own worthiness, our good intentions, our choices, and our positive life path—to keep open and not prejudge. Through every high and low, bump and pothole, to simply trust the process and keep surviving. You will understand so much more at the end of your life.

Every problem or situation is a place of power and a wake-up call. It is time to consult with our inner Wise Elder. When consciously asking for help from this loyal best friend and sentient guide, we can bypass every dead end to arrive wise and vibrant at this mature destination.

Arriving at Wise Elderhood

We are all on a journey from birth toward our elder self, and it is what we do along the way that makes it a rich journey, allowing us to arrive in celebration at life's culmination. And on that far end, if you have done your job well, you will know something that no one can take away from you no matter what—the knowledge you gained from the journey you chose to go on. Thus it is imperative that you feel good about that journey and especially its destination—that you grow into the deeply informed, ideally seasoned elder.

With the clarity of hindsight, you look back and see how all that seemed so insurmountable at the time worked to make you stronger and happier. Holding this high elder ground, at peace with yourself, you stand in quiet triumph over it all as a model for others, available to steady those younger who travel behind you.

The journey of self-discovery culminates here—in our Wise Elder self. So why not be an explorer in the most conscious, empowered way?

Consider what kind of elder you want to become—some decrepit and hollow shamble? Or will you learn to live in the moment every moment, evolving into a vivacious and unstoppable Wise Elder who proves to every younger person that no one has to grow old to grow up?

If you reach Wise Elderhood in celebration, growing up only seems to add more and more to your potential until you overflow with possibilities. That irrepressible part of you radiates out as eternal youth. You say yes to life in every moment as a new growth opportunity, you keep learning, and nothing can stop you. Even death cannot stop that creative process because you will have become a model that others will take into their own lives.

At any age, you can tap into the Wise Elder. It's a choice you can implement every minute you live.

~

Teachings, Airbags, and Safety Nets

- Erikson said that with a lifetime of living behind us, in Stage 8 we have full perspective with all the information needed to review our past. The core crisis of this stage is the final life review.

- Every moment we decide by our choices whether we will end up inheriting heaven or hell: to know happiness, wisdom, and ease or misery, despair, and terror.

- Every moment of life contains unexpected appointments. No matter what you thought you showed up for, be open to what shows up instead.

- When drama happens—and it always does—just stop, do nothing but rest, feel, breathe, wait, endure it all. Ride the wave, and above all survive.

- As long as we stay alive, every wound can be healed, every painful incident become a stepping-stone toward a richer, fuller life.

- What each person needs when in crisis and utterly stranded and alone is the wisdom of the Wise Elder. This wisdom is alive and strong and within us all.

- Painful events hone us throughout life into Wise Elders. In time the worst thing that could ever happen is likely to be one of life's finest blessings, always coming to us cloaked in the perfect disguise. If we learn from the pain, we are ever evolving into a seasoned and unstoppable Wise Elder.

- By attending to our inner Wise Elder, we come to trust ourselves and our own compass.

- The voice of our Wise Elder is patient, kind, serene, and always encouraging. It rings with authenticity and is often tinged with humor.

- The Wise Elder knows a crisis is never about who we are but always about something to be learned that can bring us everlasting benefit.

- Tough messages come. When they do, it's time to get curious and investigate what doors they might open.

- The Wise Elder within you is irrepressible. It radiates out as eternal youth.

- When you keep learning, nothing can stop you.

A Call to Action

~

AFTER DOING ALL I could to understand what happened to my son, and after writing his stories in a way that can help others avoid his fate, I am now reaching out to you. For I am ever more clear that those we have buried still have power to benefit and save those here on earth.

Too many of us walk away from the suicide of a loved one and never return. Never reflect on what that person's untold stories might be. Instead, we simply grieve, do our best to survive, and move on. And in so doing, we contribute to our loved one's second death. That person's stories—the ones that cost them their lives—just might hold the keys to humankind's individual and collective salvation.

So I invite you now to honor your lost loved ones by telling their stories. What did their life experiences teach you? What did you too learn from their lost lives in the hardest, saddest way possible? Those who have died before us—children, parents, sisters, brothers, wives, husbands, partners, relatives—become our ancestors. Their lives still matter. Their experiences can help save the lives of those still living.

So please write up a story you learned from your loved one's life and death—a story that you feel matters and can help improve the lives of others. Please send your story to me on the contact form at my website, sallyaraymond.com. Together we can create a new book that honors our lost loved ones, telling our stories in order to educate others in ways that allow life on earth to flourish. For each story selected and published, there will be a small compensation.

Please join me in this mission. As my metaphysical guru, Cristiam, always reminds me, *Now is the Time and You are the One.*

God love and treasure the genius that each of you has always been and will be.

Sincerely,

SALLY A. RAYMOND

March 14 (my son Jon's birthday), 2019

Acknowledgments

～

THROUGHOUT THE MANY years since Jon took his life under that full moon on Good Friday, March 29, 1991, his book kept attracting rare and dazzling earth angels to help bring it to fruition. Right after his death these angels helped me survive; later they helped me rise above myself to take up the special mission Jon's life and suicide set before me. I must thank each of them, yet know I am incapable either of articulating or fully honoring each angel who flew in to assist with this calling. Still, I must try.

Thank you, Mom, for your sweet love of me, and for the loving welcome you gave to Jon and his brother from birth on. What an angel mom and grandmother you were and are! Though you preceded Jon in death, your grave by sheerest coincidence lies exactly seventy-five steps down the hill from his. On his birth and his death days, I visit you both, and as I clean your graves and beg for guidance, something new is always revealed. You and Jon are literally my touchstones here on earth.

Thank you, Dad, for holding on despite the agonies of pancreatic cancer until I could arrive with three-year-old Jon and his little brother, and you could see us again and kiss us goodbye. I was sure we had at least five more months together, but then you were gone. God love my genius angel dad. With your gifts, you taught me there were no limits.

Dear Aunt Amelia and Aunt Twila, thank you both for being different versions of the indomitable, staunch Wise Elder. Aunt Amelia, forever our family's clear-eyed sage and absolutely unstoppable wit, at Jon's memorial, you proved you so loved my son that you remained his champion even in his last choice. You staggered me then, as you did always. And Aunt Twila, at ninety-three years young, you are the angel aunt carrying on the spirit of my flinty pioneer grandmother. In different ways, each of you proved with your lives that no matter what, we never, ever have to give up, lose our vitality, or grow "old." You always showed me how to live and helped save my life.

Jon, my incredible firstborn son, thank you for the honor of allowing me to be your mother, then becoming that angel irritant forever forcing me past my limits all your life and ever since. In the time we had here, I don't think you ever knew just how much I loved you. I hope you do now. I have done my best with your stories, given what I came to know too late, as both your mom and a therapist. You were far too fine a son and too great a teacher not to allow your experiences to help others survive what we did not. Don't ever expect me to walk away or say goodbye.

Alan, my dear, surviving Lord of the Rings son, thank you for hanging in with me despite everything and for always being above and beyond this mom. I know my own mom and dad would be so incredibly proud of you, as they would be of Jon. I only wish you could have known them. More and more, I experience you as my dad's doppelganger. Mom always called him a genius, even after their divorce. Yes he was, and so are you. You and your brother made me the world's luckiest mom, and when Jon died, it was your life on earth that kept me here. I love you!

To Mike, the roommate who arrived in 1990 to help fund Jon's last year in Carnegie Mellon, an eternally grateful thank-you for becoming an indelible part of my life on day one. You moved into Jon's room, and somehow I noticed no difference—which was insane; Jon was an impossible act to follow. And after Jon died, despite your being at UC Berkeley, you checked in on me every Sunday with hours-long phone calls. Those calls saved my life, then and since. You are my "surrogate son" and world-class spirit. You gave me new life while being my ally, friend, buster, and personal Pygmalion. I don't know how I ever got so lucky. Thank you for the talks, the trust, the fabulous times, places, and people, for the trips during and after your documentary—and for making me ring bearer in your wedding. You two inspire, support, and push me past my limits.

N., thank you for showing up after that horrific postmortem call to stand by me, then taking me to faraway places where Jon kept showing up. Thank you for the sunsets, dolphins, whales, Maui, Yosemite, waterfalls, even for the shark and especially for the "gift to the Maui gods"—my earring lost on a hike in Hana on that worst ever Mother's Day after losing Jon and found again on that same trail six months later. Ever since, I wear this pair as proof that what is lost can be found.

Scott, my truest love and former husband, thank you for your unflagging support, keen wit, generosity, love, and loyalty—and for being the trusted ear I could then and still do pour my heart out to. Thank you for being the deejay for Jon's memorial, reprising in sequence the exact songs I heard at the time Jon died to serenade and inspire all gathered in his honor.

For the resplendent Dr. Jean Houston, profound appreciation for every Mystery School, lecture, and conference where you surprised and inspired me time and again. Thank you for your incredible shepherding and for that special gift on the "Night of the Gifting" so many years ago, giving me the name of "your perfect editor." Words fail to express my undying gratitude—for you, for your lifelong work, and last but far from least, for calling in my truly perfect and apparently indefatigable editor, teacher, ally, core spirit, and forever friend, Dr. Priscilla Stuckey.

Priscilla, you have believed in this book since the beginning. Your eagle eyes, heart, mind, and pure connection to Spirit helped to hone my ideas and written words over who knows how many edits into a unique, personal, story-driven self-help book. Without you—and I'm very clear, only you—this book would not be here at all, certainly not like it is or with the same gravitas. I sent you another manuscript entirely, and instantly you knew better. Through Jean, I believe Jon sent me you. Thank you for embodying hope and helping me make this pipe dream a reality.

Priscilla referred me to the "best" graphic designer, Ann Weinstock. Ann, thank you, deeply inspired art angel, for your calm patience, wisdom, and inspired graphics. Ann referred me to another "best," interior designer Sara DeHaan. Thank you, Sara, for your clarity in rendering such a difficult and complex topic! Heartfelt thanks go to my phenomenal readers Keely Meagan and Donnie MacLurcan, professor and inspired author of How on Earth; questions and suggestions from both of you helped to deepen the final edit. Thank you, Michael Klein, Esq., for your rigorous legal analysis and commentary; I am blessed to have such a high-caliber adviser angel on call as needed. Thank you, fabulous Phil

Johncock, for initiating me into book publishing. And special love and gratitude to Jude and Lacey, my in-house angel homies, feminine inspirations, and sisters-in-arms; I am blessed with you and your furry guides, Cody and Bella. Finally, last but never, ever least, thanks to a most special and intense former housemate, Florian—for every week while you were in-residence, checking in with me with either, "So, how many pages did you write this week?", or else "You'll never finish that book"—and either way, only increasing my resolve!

God love and keep each one of you. Fly high and shine forever bright! You're right in the center of my heart forever.

SURVIVAL GUIDE

WARNING SIGNS OF SUICIDE

The following signs indicate someone is at an increased risk of committing suicide. That risk rises if a behavior is new or has increased, especially if it seems related to a painful loss, experience, or change. But suicide is very preventable, so if you notice these signs in someone, don't hesitate! Call the Suicide Prevention Lifeline at 1-800-273-TALK (8255) for clarification and support. Then, err on the conservative side—on the side of conserving life. Review these warning signs:

- Talking about being a burden to others
- Talking about feeling hopeless or having no reason to live
- Talking about wanting to die or to kill oneself
- Talking about feeling trapped or in unbearable pain
- Looking for ways to kill oneself, like searching online or buying a gun
- Increasing use of alcohol or drugs
- Acting anxious or agitated or behaving recklessly
- Extreme mood swings
- Sleeping too little or too much
- Withdrawing or feeling isolated
- Changes in eating or socializing
- Giving away one's money or things
- Sudden relief or happiness following a prolonged depression
- Showing rage or talking about getting revenge
- Finding no interest or pleasure in formerly enjoyable pursuits or relationships

RESPONDING TO SOMEONE IN CRISIS

If you notice one or more of the warning signs of suicide in a friend or loved one, or if you get a panicked or weird call from someone who might be feeling suicidal, check it out! A person who is in a suicidal crisis feels driven to kill themselves, but part of them knows better and wants to live. In any crisis, being alone increases personal jeopardy, so this is the time to stand by your friend or loved one. Let the following steps guide your choices.

1. Ask! A person who calls you feeling suicidal may sound ambivalent because truly suicidal people are indeed ambivalent. If you get a call like this but aren't sure what the person intends to do, be direct and specific. Just ask, "Are you thinking of killing yourself?" They will answer. You won't be putting ideas in their head. Don't be light, falsely positive, or polite. Be real and caring. If they're not suicidal, they will simply say so.

2. Listen. Give your full attention, and keep drawing the person out. Let whatever sense of crisis they are experiencing drain off into a million words. Never deny their reality or judge them. Simply listen to understand. Notice and acknowledge their feelings. And as you can, lead to hope. For example, you might say, "Yes, right now I hear it seems impossible, but I know there's more." As possible, help them refocus on their own reasons for living. When someone shows real care and interest, people no longer feel alone, and that provides some relief.

3. Keep them safe. Don't leave them alone! If you're on the phone, take no chances. You or someone else call 9-1-1 on another line and provide the details while you stay connected with them. If you are with them in person, stay there while you get them help.

Try to find out how much jeopardy they are in. Have they tried to hurt themselves before? How? How many times? What happened? Have they got a plan? Are the means on hand? What substances have they already taken? To keep them safe, remove any means they have to hurt themselves, such as pills, knives, ropes, guns, and so forth. Help them calm down. Help them focus on their breathing by counting eight or more seconds to breathe in and eight or more seconds to breathe out, and keep that focus for at least sixty, slow, complete breaths. This will help restore calm and normal functioning,

Keep no secrets when life is at risk; disclose what is happening to anyone who might be able to help. It's better to have the person mad at you than dead or incapacitated.

4. Get a contract. If you are not physically with the person, ensure their safety until you arrive by getting a contract. Say, "You're in crisis, off balance. This is no time to do anything. Stay put, rest, and do nothing but breathe and wait. I'm on my way." Negotiate a verbal contract in which they promise to do no harm to self by any means, accidentally or on purpose, in the meantime.

Never disconnect from the person until help arrives or you have connected them to someone else or you are sure they will keep the contract you made.

5. Give hope. Every chance you get, help the person know that they matter, and infuse a sense of hope. Tell them how much you love and need them, and assure them that you are always available to talk to and help. Gently give perspective as appropriate—that life is change and that thoughts, feelings, and experiences are all temporary. That only death is permanent—which makes suicide a permanent solution to a temporary problem. Encourage them to resist self-destructive impulses—to breathe, trust, and give themselves time. Let them know that every experience is for surviving and learning from, not for killing themselves over. A crisis is always short-term and almost never is about what we think it is about. If we can just calm down, in time we get the information that allows us to learn from the experience. If, after everything, the situation remains impossible, well, tell them they can always decide to kill themselves later.

6. Calm their nervous system. Walk them through the calming practices listed in Stage 7, and remember to have them pay attention to what is happening inside them and to tell you about it. You can also do a progressive relaxation meditation with them, helping them relax every muscle group from their forehead to their feet. Also, focus on their breathing. Encourage them to let every thought pass in, through, and out their mind just as every cloud, no matter how dark, passes by so that blue sky always returns.

7. Keep working in their best interest. Work with the person to write up a safety plan that will help them remain stable over terrible, dark moments. Start with a list of things that help: useful distractions, fond memories, relationships, pets, activities, food, future hopes. Include suicide prevention numbers along with the names and numbers of everyone meaningful—significant others, relatives, friends, and neighbors. Then have them put the list in the best order so, as needed, they can just go down the list implementing each next helpful item until they get relief.

IF YOU GET THE CALL: A CHECKLIST

~

These calls often sound ambiguous, because truly suicidal people are ambivalent, but they *are* calling for help. So *don't* be ambiguous.

○ *Ask.* "Are you thinking of killing yourself?" They will answer. Don't be polite, be real!

○ *Listen.* "Tell me what exactly happened." Listen to understand, and repeat back what you hear. Keep drawing them out. Let them know you understand and feel their pain. Let their feelings discharge in words.

○ *Keep them safe.* Have them give keys, guns, knives, or ropes to someone else, and flush all pills. Check back: "How many pills did you take before flushing? How many did you keep in reserve?" If you feel any uncertainty, call 9-1-1 and report.

○ *Get a contract.* "Repeat after me: 'I promise to do no harm to myself by any means, accidentally or on purpose, until help arrives.'" Create a list of numbers of allies to call and things to do to keep them safe.

○ *Get help.* Don't do this alone. You or someone else call 9-1-1, call their family, and call close friends.

○ *Give hope.* "You matter, and I love you. You're in crisis. This is no time to do anything. Stay put and calm down until I or help arrives. Crises pass and even turn to blessings. We'll see this through together."

○ *Help them calm.* "Watch every thought pass in, through, and out, keeping your breathing slow, full and even. Every cloud, no matter how dark, passes and blue sky returns." Crisis thoughts are about fears, not reality. Help them relax every muscle group from head to the feet. Encourage them to drink water and eat.

○ *Stay connected.* Never leave them alone. Stay connected with them until you're there or help arrives.

RESOURCES

~

NATIONAL HOTLINES

911—Call if imminent danger to self or others.

211—Connect here to local centers where you can find many kinds of help: for addiction counseling, affordable housing, Alzheimer's assistance, child care, debt counseling, disaster relief, donation opportunities, education, emergency food, ESL classes, financial assistance, homeless services, job counseling, parenting programs, psychotherapy, senior citizen programs, suicide prevention, telephone reassurance and care for the elderly, volunteer opportunities, youth programs.

988—The 988 Suicide & Crisis Lifeline (formerly known as the National Suicide Prevention Lifeline) is a national suicide prevention network of over 200+ crisis centers that provides 24/7 service via this toll-free hotline. It is available to anyone in suicidal crisis, emotional distress, or disaster distress. The caller is routed to their nearest crisis center to receive immediate counseling and local mental health referrals. This Lifeline supports people who call for themselves or someone they care about. 9-8-8 supports calls, text or chat online at Lifeline.org. Veterans and Para Español speakers are provided specific numbers to press for specialized help. LGBTQ services and other languages' assistance are also provided.

741741—Crisis textline: Text HOME

SUICIDE PREVENTION HOTLINES

If you are suicidal, remember that most of the people who answer these lines are trained volunteers, not professionals, and the person who picks up may or may not be a match for you. If you sense a mismatch, simply thank the person, say goodbye, and immediately call another line. Continue dialing until you reach a helpful connection. You are worth all it takes to find a good fit and get solid help!

1-800-273-8255	National Suicide Prevention Lifeline (directs to 988 hotline)
1-800-799-4889	National TTY (Deaf and Hard of Hearing) Suicide Prevention Lifeline
1-800-784-2433	Suicide, Depression, and Crisis Hotline
1-800-442-4673	National Hopeline Network, Suicide, and Crisis Hotline
1-877-565-8860	Trans Lifeline (US), 1-877-330-6366 (CAN)
1-866-488-7386	The Trevor Project, Saving Young LGBTQ Lives
1-877-968-8454	Youthline: Teen-to-Teen Peer Counseling Hotline
1-800-273-8255	option 1: Veterans Crisis Line
1-877-838-2838	Vet2Vet: Veterans Peer Support Line
1-800-472-3457	National Graduate Student Crisis Line
1-800-773-6667	Postpartum Depression Phone Support for Moms
1-800-944-4773	Postpartum Support International Hotline
1-800-799-4889	StopBullying.gov

OTHER HOTLINES & HELPLINES

1-800-422-4453	National Child Abuse Hotline
1-800-786-2929	National Runaway Safeline
1-800-843-5678	National Center for Missing and Exploited Children Hotline
1-800-426-5678	Child Find of America
1-800-799-7233(safe) or 1-800-787-3224(TTY)	National Domestic Violence Hotline
1-866-331-9474	Dating and Young Adult Relationships Chatline
1-866-783-2645	SU FAMILIA National Alliance for Hispanic Health Helpline

1-800-736-9805	Families Anonymous (Addiction and Recovery)
1-888-425-2666	Al-Anon Family and Al-ATeen" (Addiction and Recovery)
1-800-244-3171	Addiction and Alcohol Hotline
1-800-347-8998	Cocaine Anonymous Helpline
1-800-622-2255	National Council on Alcoholism / Drug Dependence Hope Line
1-800-662-4357	National Institute Bilingual Drug Abuse Hotline
1-800-656-4673	Rape, Abuse, and Incest National Network (RAINN) Hotline
1-800-227-8922	Sexually Transmitted Disease Hotline
1-800-448-0440	AIDS Information, Treatment, and Research
1-800-799-7233	National Domestic Violence Hotline
1-800-222-1222	Poison Control Center Hotline
1-800-230-7526	Find a Planned Parenthood Center
1-800-366-8288	Self-Abuse Finally Ends (SAFE) Hotline
1-800-848-9595	Shoplifters Anonymous
1-800-931-2237	Eating Disorders Awareness and Prevention
1-800-985-5990 or text 66746	National Disaster Distress Helpline
Text 741741	Suicide Crisis Textline

ONLINE HELP

7 Cups 7cups.com
Connect with caring people for text chat, online therapy, and counseling.

BEBA: A Center for Family Healing beba.org
From the website: "BEBA supports families to resolve prenatal, birth and other early trauma, both physical and emotional, while facilitating the development of compassionate relationships, the healthy growth of children, and effective parenting."

Befrienders Worldwide befrienders.org
A worldwide organization of trained volunteers dedicated to preventing suicide. Provides free, immediate, confidential, and nonjudgmental support and also serves as a resource for loved ones desiring to help. Available by telephone, in person, and by text, letter, or email in ten languages and forty-one countries. Follow the links to the helpline of your choice.

Castellino Prenatal and Birth Therapy Training castellinotraining.com
Prenatal and birth therapy training for infants and parents. Offers the Womb
Surround Process Workshop for those of any age seeking to heal their own
birth traumas.

I'm Alive imalive.org
A live online crisis network with all volunteers trained and certified in crisis
intervention. Go to their site and click the Chat Now button to speak to a
volunteer.

Kidpower kidpower.org
An organization to help build safety in families and communities. It is
dedicated to teaching positive strategies to prevent and stop most bullying,
abuse, kidnapping, and other forms of violence against children. Workshops
for children and parents build confidence rather than fear. To date they have
centers in eleven states and fifteen countries.

LoveIsRespect.org loveisrespect.org
Chat live with an advocate 24/7 about healthy and safe dating relationships for teens, LGBTQ, and young adults. Both English and Spanish chat
available.

MOSAIC Threat Assessment mosaicmethod.com
An anonymous, computer-assisted questionnaire to assess the danger or
threat level from another person or persons in your current situation. Fill
out a free, automatically scored confidential questionnaire to evaluate your
immediate risk so you can take appropriate action.

The National Domestic Violence Hotline thehotline.org
To help those affected by relationship abuse to find shelters and reclaim their
own power.

Suicide Prevention Websites, Education, and Research

BeThe1To bethe1to.com
BeThe1To is a national suicide prevention lifeline helping people to "be the 1 to" save a life. They provide an outline of the five steps you can take to support someone you care about through a suicidal crisis. Includes resources, stories, a list of local suicide crisis centers, and an invitation to join this lifesaving movement.

CDC Suicide Prevention cdc.gov/violenceprevention/suicide/
National statistics and publications on suicide prevention from the Centers for Disease Control and Prevention.

Heyes, Stephanie Burnett, and Chii Fen Hiu. "The Adolescent Brain: Vulnerability and Opportunity," UNICEF Office of Research-Innocenti / For Every Child, unicef-irc.org/article/1149-the-adolescent-brain-vulnerability-and-opportunity.html
IHS Suicide Prevention ihs.gov/suicideprevention/
Suicide Prevention and Care Program from the Indian Health Service.

International Association for Suicide Prevention iasp.info
Founded in 1960, IASP includes professionals and volunteers in over fifty countries who work with the World Health Organization to prevent suicide. If you feel suicidal or know of someone who needs help, follow the Help link on their page for a crisis center near you.

Kim, Y. S., and B. Leventhal. "Bullying and Suicide: A Review."
International Journal of Adolescent Mental Health 20, No. 2 (Apr–Jun 2008): 133–54. Researchers at Yale School of Medicine reviewed 37 studies and concluded the studies say that children who are bullied are 2 to 9 times more likely to consider committing suicide. For more discussion of their study, see "Bullying-Suicide Link Explored in New Study by Researchers at Yale," *Yale News,* July 16, 2008, news.yale.edu/2008/07/16/bullying-suicide-link-explored-new-study-researchers-yale

Live Through This livethroughthis.org
An organization that videotapes the stories of suicide survivors to document narratives of hope and to show the many ways suicidal feelings are experienced over time and how they can be survived. "The most extensive catalog in existence of stories of hope and recovery after a suicide attempt."

Mankind Project mankindproject.org
A global network of men's charitable organizations that provide mentors for men at every stage of their lives and support men to reconnect with others and make a difference in their own and one another's lives.

Now Matters Now nowmattersnow.org
A group dedicated to helping those who have suicidal thoughts or have survived suicide attempts. Here you can learn simple coping skills in mindfulness and dialectical behavior therapy through watching videos and presentations by a wide range of people, including mental health practitioners who also have experienced suicidal thoughts or suicide attempts.

Protect Young Eyes protectyoungeyes.com
Protects children from online dangers through digital safety presentations and through familiarizing site visitors with parental controls possible on every kind of digital device. Provides reviews of dozens of social media apps and gaming sites aimed at children today, including those promoting suicide and pornography.

Speaking of Suicide speakingofsuicide.com
Suicide researcher Stacey Freedenthal offers resources and suggestions for those having suicidal thoughts, for survivors, for friends and family, and for mental health professionals.

Suicide.org suicide.org
Suicide prevention, awareness, and support through national helplines and education.

WHO SUPRE who.int/mental_health/prevention/suicide
supresuicideprevent/en/
World Health Organization (WHO) documents on suicide prevention in
several languages. Facts and figures about suicide plus resources to prevent
suicide.

World Federation for Mental Health wfmh.global
An international organization founded in 1948 and focusing on "the prevention of mental and emotional disorders, the proper treatment and care
of those with such disorders, and the promotion of mental health." Information, resources, and worldwide events.

THERAPIES FOR POST-TRAUMATIC
STRESS DISORDER (PTSD)

The following therapies have been identified as effective in dealing with traumatic experiences and PTSD. Though studies show that it is the bond between the client and therapist that promotes healing and recovery and not the technique per se, some therapies are linked to better outcomes for particular diagnoses. If you suffer from PTSD, you may want to check online to see what therapists in your area are certified in these techniques.

Cognitive-Behavioral Therapies (CBT)
Forms of talk therapy that address the links between thoughts, feelings, and behaviors. CBT helps clients identify and work to change their negative, distorted, or unhelpful thoughts or beliefs in order to feel better and behave in ways likely to increase overall quality of life.

Dialectical Behavioral Therapy (DBT)
A type of behavior therapy for managing painful emotions and minimizing conflicts, DBT helps people develop skills in mindfulness, distress tolerance, emotional regulation, and interpersonal effectiveness. It is the treatment of choice for the more serious mental health challenges, such as borderline personality disorder, depression, eating disorders, suicide prevention, PTSD, and substance abuse. It was pioneered by Marsha Linehan, a suicide prevention scientist. More info on her and on DBT in regard to suicide prevention can be found at Now Matters Now (nowmattersnow.org).

Eye Movement Desensitization and Reprocessing (EMDR)
Developed by Dr. Francine Shapiro, EMDR is a psychotherapy that enables people to heal from the symptoms and emotional distress that are the result of disturbing life experiences. EMDR uses eye movements and other processes to help traumatic memories resurface and heal. (See Shapiro, Francine, PhD, in "Books for Parents" in Further Reading.)

Gestalt Therapies
Children especially can benefit greatly from a therapist trained in Gestalt techniques of play, sand, or art therapy. A well-known proponent of Gestalt therapy with children is Violet Oaklander. (See Oaklander, Violet, in "Books for Parents" in Further Reading.)

Play Therapy and Filial Therapy
Play Therapy "uses the child's natural language of play in a structured and healing manner." Filial Therapy is one type of Play Therapy, and it teaches parents how to play with, understand, connect with, set limits for, and communicate with their child at the child's level. Through play, parents and children build a bonded, secure relationship that can flourish throughout their lives. Filial Therapy was developed by Bernard and Louise Guerney in the 1960s. For more information, see growththroughplaytherapy.com.

Sensory Integration Therapy
Based on the Sensory Integration Theory of A. Jean Ayres, this therapy works on nonverbal hypersensitivities and unconscious, or primal, trauma. Applying gentle sensory stimulation helps to integrate the reflexes and calm hyper-reactivity. For instance, gentle body-brushing therapies with young, highly sensitive children can help them reorganize their neurosystem and heal repressed trauma.

Somatic Experiencing
A therapeutic technique created by Peter Levine, MD, and designed to keep clients of any age conscious and calm as they are helped to gently reexperience and finally resolve traumatic life events. Involves therapists paying conscious attention to, or "tracking," a client's bodily (somatic) experiences from moment to moment to both slow the process and maintain psychosomatic equilibrium.

Thought Field Therapy or Tapping Therapies
Developed by psychologist Roger Callahan, tapping therapies use thoughts plus gentle tapping on acupressure points on the body to resolve traumatic experiences.

FURTHER READING

Picture Books for Young Children

Berenstain, Jan, Stan, and Mike. The Berenstain Bears Series. 1980s to present. A great assortment of books exploring children's problems and building coping skills. See, for example, *Trouble at School* (New York: Random House, 1987).

Brown, Laurene Krasny, and Marc Brown. Dino Life Guides. 1980s to present. A series of picture books helping children understand and cope with various life issues. See, for example, *Dinosaur's Divorce: A Guide for Changing Families* (Boston: Joy Street Books, 1986), a classic children's book now widely available in reprint editions to help children understand divorce.

Freeman, Lory, and Carol Deach. *It's MY Body: A Book to Teach Young Children How to Resist Uncomfortable Touch.* Seattle: Parenting Press, 1982. A book to help young children learn about and keep safe boundaries, how to distinguish "good" from "bad" touch, and how to avoid or respond to unwanted touch.

Girard, Linda Walvoord. *My Body Is Private.* Niles, IL: Albert Whitman, 1985. A book teaching preschool and elementary children about privacy, our private body parts, and how to stay safe and say no to uncomfortable touch.

Lansky, Vicki. *It's Not Your Fault, Koko Bear: A Read-Together Book for Parents and Young Children During Divorce.* Minnetonka, MN: Book Peddlers, 1986. Helping children learn what divorce means and how their life will change and reassuring them that the divorce is not their fault.

Masurel, Claire, and Kady MacDonald Denton. *Two Homes.* Somerville, MA: Candlewick Press, 2001. A comforting story about the reality of divorce.

Mellonie, Bryan, and Robert Ingpen. *Lifetimes: The Beautiful Way to Explain Death to Children.* New York: Bantam, 1983. A sensitive, caring book that helps children understand and appreciate that we and all other beings have our own special lifetimes.

Moore-Mallinos, Jennifer. *Do You Have a Secret? (Let's Talk About It!)* Hauppauge, NY: Barron's Educational Series, 2005. Helping preschool and early elementary school children distinguish between the kinds of feelings "good" secrets and "bad" secrets give us and which secrets to keep and which must be shared and with whom.

Olivieri, Laura. *Where Are You? A Child's Book About Loss.* Morrisville, NC: Lulu Press, 2007. A book sensitively written to help young children of all ages cope with a loved one's loss.

Schmitz, Tamara. *Standing on My Own Two Feet: A Child's Affirmation of Love in the Midst of Divorce.* New York: Penguin Books, 2008. An inspiring book giving children going through divorce hope in a dark time. How having two homes can bring unexpected blessings and benefits to their lives.

Spelman, Cornelia Maude, and Teri Weidner. *Your Body Belongs to You.* Morton Grove, IL: Albert Whitman, 1997. A book teaching young children that it's okay to say no to a hug, a kiss, or a touch, even if the person is a friend or someone you love.

Books for Teenagers

Cain, Susan. *Quiet: The Power of Introverts in a World That Can't Stop Talking.* Portland: Broadway Books, 2013. A powerful, well-researched book proving with real-life stories how introverts, whom society often undervalues, hold far greater potential for positive contributions than previously recognized—by either introverts themselves or by others.

Canfield, Jack, and Kent Healy. *The Success Principles for Teens: How to Get from Where You Are to Where You Want to Be.* Boca Raton, FL: HCI Teens,

2010. This book is the teen version of Canfield's *The Success Principles*, and it is shorter, clearer, and highly inspiring, driven by stories that model each of the techniques or tools presented.

Catherman, Jonathan. *The Manual to Manhood: How to Cook the Perfect Steak, Change a Tire, Impress a Girl, and 97 Other Skills You Need to Survive.* Minneapolis: Revell, 2014. Practical and specific how-to's across many life domains. For young men and in many cases young women as well who want to be adept and independent do-it-yourselfers.

Green, Gordon W., Jr. *Getting Straight A's: A Proven System for Achieving Excellence in High School and College, Becoming Test-Wise and Making the System Work For You.* Syracuse, NY: Kensington, 1993. How to read a book, how to take tests, and how to make the educational system work for you. Proven techniques for navigating school.

March, John S., and Christine M. Benton. *Talking Back to OCD: The Program That Helps Teens Say "No Way"—and Parents Say "Way to Go!"* New York: Guilford Press, 2006. The proven eight-step program that helps youth take their own power back from a disorder by using skills that help them tune out obsessions and resist compulsions.

Price, Catherine. *How to Break Up with Your Phone: The 30-Day Plan to Take Back Your Life.* Emeryville, CA: Ten Speed Press, 2018. The author shows that smartphones are designed to be addictive and lays out their human cost in terms of lost time and cognitive and relational deficits. How to customize apps and settings and how to adjust your mind-set to take back your life.

Schab, Lisa M. *The Anxiety Workbook for Teens: Activities to Help You Deal with Anxiety and Worry.* Oakland: New Harbinger Instant Help Books, 2008. Anxiety during adolescence is common, and this workbook offers readers activities that will reduce those feelings and restore their lives back to working order.

———. *The Self-Esteem Workbook for Teens: Activities to Help You Build Confidence and Achieve Your Goals.* Oakland: New Harbinger Instant Help

Books, 2013. Self-esteem is crucial for well-being, and this workbook helps teens to know and respect themselves while they steadily grow a healthy, balanced self-esteem. Exercises help teens resist self-doubt and rebalance after setbacks or criticism.

Shapiro, Lawrence E. *Stopping the Pain: A Workbook for Teens Who Cut and Self-Injure.* Oakland: New Harbinger Instant Help Books, 2008. Helps teens understand why they self-injure and offers a potpourri of practical ways to stop, including new ways to reduce stress and how to reach out for help as needed. For helping self-injuring teens move from a painful past to a pain-free future.

Siegel, Daniel J., MD. *Beyond the Blues: A Workbook to Help Teens Overcome Depression.* Oakland: New Harbinger Instant Help Books, 2008. Feeling depressed during adolescence is normal given all the changes going on. Practicing these activities helps teens cope with difficult feelings, lighten their lives, and move toward healing.

———. *Brainstorm: The Power and Purpose of the Teenage Brain.* New York: Tarcher/Penguin, 2013. Insight into the changes and emotions that teens and those in their early twenties experience. A great book for both teens and their parents or anyone wanting to make sense of a difficult and sometimes overwhelming life transition. Practical tools help both teens and parents navigate the emotional storms and relational dramas normal at this time, which Siegel notes as beginning earlier and resolving later than generally believed.

Simmons, Rachel. *Odd Girl Out: The Hidden Culture of Aggression in Girls.* Rev. ed. New York: Houghton Mifflin Harcourt, 2011. A best-seller when it was first published in 2002, this book revealed the often-invisible competitive and bullying dynamics between girls and showed how parents and daughters can effectively confront bullying and minimize the damage done. The revised edition includes strategies for overcoming cyberbullying and offers details of classroom antibullying initiatives.

Van Draanen, Wendelin. *The Running Dream.* New York: Random House, 2012. A powerful fictional story of hope and inspiration for all youth, especially at-risk, sensitive, and special-needs teens.

Whitson, Signe. *The 8 Keys to End Bullying Activity Book for Kids & Tweens.* New York: Norton, 2016. Workshops, quizzes, games, and skills to help readers stop bullying. A timely resource for teens that provides parents comprehensive information as well.

Books for Parents

Campbell, D. Ross. *How to Really Love Your Child.* Rev. and updated. Colorado Springs: David C. Cook, 2015. Too many children are sure they are not loved, despite all parents say or do. This book identifies the child's inner needs and provides parents with the words, the touch, and even the discipline that helps children feel loved and safe always—free to be all of who they uniquely are.

Cloud, Henry, and John Townsend. *Boundaries Workbook: When to Say Yes, How to Say No to Take Control of Your Life.* Grand Rapids, MI: Zondervan, 2018. Based on the best-selling book by John Townsend, *Boundaries with Teens: When to Say Yes, How to Say No*, this updated and expanded companion workbook offers practical exercises for setting reasonable and clear boundaries in career, parenting, marriage, and friendships.

de Becker, Gavin. *Protecting the Gift: Keeping Children and Teenagers Safe (and Parents Sane).* New York: Dial Press, 1999. Practical, positive strategies parents can use to enhance children's safety at every age level and in all kinds of situations.

Jurchenko, Ted. *131 Connecting Conversations for Parents and Teens: How to Build a Lifelong Bond with Your Teen!* N.p.: Amazon KDP, 2018. Why connecting with your teen matters, and how to build that empathic connection through conversing more and arguing less. Based on Christian principles.

Lythcott-Haims, Julie. *How to Raise an Adult: Break Free of the Overparenting Trap and Prepare Your Kid for Success.* New York: St. Martin's Press, 2015.

A mother and former dean of students at Stanford University gives parents a practical guide to raising children with increased resilience, self-esteem, and the confidence to grow into competent, autonomous adults.

Oaklander, Violet. *Windows to Our Children: A Gestalt Therapy Approach to Children and Adolescents.* Gouldsboro, ME: Gestalt Journal Press, 2007. A Gestalt play therapist writes about how to understand and work therapeutically with young children.

Pearce, Joseph Chilton. *Magical Child.* New York: Penguin, 1992. Based on the key teachings of Jean Piaget, this groundbreaking book suggests that every child's genius emerges when they are allowed to play and explore all the earth has to teach. Pearce suggests common errors in child-rearing lie behind the rise of autism, ADHD, schizophrenia, and suicide. Reclaiming that original creative intelligence and purpose through play is possible at any age.

Shapiro, Francine, PhD. *Getting Past Your Past.* Emmaus, PA: Rodale Books, 2013. The originator of EMDR shows the general reader how to apply this simple and effective technique for minimizing or healing the effects of PTSD.

Siegel, Daniel J., MD. *Brainstorm: The Power and Purpose of the Teenage Brain.* New York: Tarcher/Penguin, 2013. (See Siegel, Daniel J., MD, in "Books for Teenagers.")

———. and Mary Hartzell. *Parenting from the Inside Out: How a Deeper Self-Understanding Can Help You Raise Children Who Thrive.* 10th anniv. ed. New York: Tarcher/Putnam, 2014. From research in neurobiology and attachment theory, the authors show how interpersonal relationships affect developing brains. Parents learn specific tools to better understand themselves and help their children become more compassionate and resilient.

Siegel, Daniel J., and Tina Payne Bryson. *No-Drama Discipline: The Whole-Brain Way to Calm the Chaos and Nurture Your Child's Developing Mind.* New York: Bantam, 2014. Using research on neurological brain development, the authors provide practical strategies parents can apply to themselves and in disciplining their children to peacefully resolve conflicts, inspire happiness, and strengthen resilience.

———. *The Whole-Brain Child: 12 Revolutionary Strategies to Nurture Your Child's Developing Mind*. New York: Delacort Press, 2011. Using neuroscience, the authors help parents understand their child's developing brain. Simple, easy-to-remember strategies are given that help children think, listen, understand, and shift their emotions and behavior. Parents are encouraged to reflect on their own histories to be empowered personally and to share life stories with their children.

Townsend, John. *Boundaries with Teens: When to Say Yes, How to Say No*. Grand Rapids, MI: Zondervan, 2016. Shows parents how to apply biblical principles to set wise and healthy, reasonable limits with teens and help them take personal responsibility for their actions and emotions and build respect for themselves and others.

Suicide Prevention and Education, and First-Person Accounts from Survivors

Blauner, Susan Rose. *How I Stayed Alive When My Brain Was Trying to Kill Me: One Person's Guide to Suicide Prevention*. New York: William Morrow, 2002. A practical, down-to-earth suicide prevention manual written by a long-term suicide survivor. For anyone who is suicidal. Inspiration and simple, proven tools to save our own lives are scattered throughout in story form. Includes a full section of hotlines, websites, and resources.

Bolton, Iris, with Curtis Mitchell. *My Son . . . My Son . . . : A Guide to Healing After a Suicide in the Family*. Atlanta: Bolton Press, 1983. A gripping story of how the suicide of a teenage son forced a mother to search for meaning and hope. Appendixes include outreach and guidance for others who are similarly suffering, a list of reminders for the bereaved, a brief summary of the phases of grief, the experiential factors common to traumatic loss, and a valuable list of do's and don'ts for survivors and friends.

Briggs, Alan, with Sam Mellinger. *Guardian of the Golden Gate: Protecting the Line Between Hope and Despair.* Olathe, KS: Ascend Books, 2015. A man who has talked two hundred people out of jumping off the Golden Gate Bridge offers insights and help for despairing moments.

Fine, Carla. *No Time to Say Goodbye: Surviving the Suicide of a Loved One.* New York: Doubleday, 1997. The moving account of a husband's suicide and the author's nightmarish aftermath of grief and ongoing survival. Appended are lists of specific organizations, resources, and state-by-state support groups for survivors.

Hines, Kevin. *Cracked, Not Broken: Surviving and Thriving After a Suicide Attempt.* Lanham, MD: Rowman & Littlefield, 2013. Surviving after a jump from the Golden Gate Bridge, Hines testifies that on the life side of a bridge's rail, you're sure you want to die, but on the other side—and too late—you wake up and desperately want to live. Powerful testimony from one who knows.

McGugan, Peter. *When Something Changes Everything: A Companion and Guide for Recovering from Loss and Change.* Palm Springs: Potentials Press, 1998. Pithy and practical advice for a host of life problems, alphabetized for instant access. All together, a comprehensive guide to support each kind of recovery. Includes parenting guides and resources sections.

Quinnett, Paul G. *Suicide: The Forever Decision.* N.p.: Amazon Digital Services, 2012. For anyone thinking about suicide, and for friends, family, and loved ones who support and counsel them. Straight talk about suicide, and required reading for a person of any age contemplating suicide.

Shneidman, Edwin S. *Autopsy of a Suicidal Mind.* New York: Oxford University Press, 2004. A psychological study of one person based on his long suicide note along with interviews with his closest family members and friends. Eight different suicide experts offer their analyses of how this man's pain might have been healed. A broad and deep view of the deceased and the factors that led to taking his own life.

Erikson's Stages of Human Development

Erikson, Erik H. *Childhood and Society.* New York: Norton, 1950. Erikson's landmark compendium of historical, cultural, and social influences on childhood went beyond his mentor Freud's psychosexual analysis of infantile development. Erikson used an interpersonal, psychosocial frame to chart human development in eight consecutive stages. His theory and chart made clear that certain experiences are shared by all children, and it also explained how individual differences arise. It continues to be a powerful and useful reference.

————. *Identity and the Life Cycle.* New York: Norton, 1980. Three of Erikson's major essays in which he explored the crises and growth of the healthy personality.

————. *Identity: Youth and Crisis.* New York: Norton, 1968. Erikson explores in detail the adolescent identity crisis, defining it not as a crisis but as a pivotal moment of development. Though written in the sixties, it remains relevant for those who study child development and work with youth.

————. Joan M. Erikson, and Helen Q. Kivnick. *Vital Involvement in Old Age.* New York: Norton, 1986. The results of interviews with twenty-nine people over a span of fifty years. Now in their eighties, these interview subjects shed light on a final, eighth, stage of life, elderhood, with its challenges and joys.

Books for Healing from Trauma and for Living Well

Alcoholics Anonymous. *Alcoholics Anonymous: The Original Text of the Life-Changing Landmark.* Deluxe Edition. New York: Tarcher/Penguin, 2014. The Big Book of Alcoholics Anonymous continues to change millions of lives for the better. Used by individuals and in meetings to work through the steps of recovery and to support one another.

Bass, Ellen, and Laura Davis. *The Courage to Heal: A Guide for Women Survivors of Child Sexual Abuse.* 20th Anniversary Edition. New York: HarperCollins, 2008. The definitive and highly recommended work on a most difficult subject, updated.

Battenberg, Jane Rigney, and Martha M. Rigney. *Eye Yoga: How You See Is How You Think.* Minneapolis: Langdon Street Press, 2010. With exercises and scientific evidence, the authors show how strengthening the eyesight also helps to reawaken and strengthen brain capacities. A practical book for self-healing.

Davis, Laura. *Allies in Healing: When the Person You Love Was Sexually Abused as a Child.* New York: HarperCollins, 1991. Written for partners of adults who were sexually abused as children, this book teaches about the unique triggers, feelings, and needs of survivors and helps partners understand and support survivors' healing processes.

———. *The Courage to Heal Workbook: A Guide for Women and Men Survivors of Child Sexual Abuse.* New York: HarperCollins, 1990. A child sexual abuse survivors' workbook to accompany *The Courage to Heal* primary text by Bass and Davis.

De Becker, Gavin. *The Gift of Fear and Other Survival Signals That Protect Us from Violence.* New York: Little, Brown, 1997. How to tell the difference between true fear and unwarranted fear, and how to better protect yourself and those you love.

Firestone, Robert, and Lisa Firestone. *Conquer Your Critical Inner Voice: A Revolutionary Program to Counter Negative Thoughts and Live Free from Imagined Limitations.* Oakland: New Harbinger, 2002. How to counter and free yourself from negative thoughts, attitudes, and beliefs that interfere with building meaningful relationships and living a happy, fulfilling life.

Frankl, Viktor E. *Man's Search for Meaning.* Boston: Beacon Press, 1963. Incarcerated in a Hitler death camp, the psychiatrist Frankl somehow endured and found reason to live. This best-selling book is his testament to what he identified as the deepest drive in human beings: finding meaning in life.

Grossman, Dave, and Gloria DeGaetano. *Stop Teaching Our Kids to Kill: A Call to Action Against TV, Movie & Video Violence.* New York: Harmony Books, 1999. Presents the statistics and scientific research showing that media are teaching young people the mechanics of killing. Provides a foundation for parents and the public to address the effects of media violence on youth.

Hall, Alan. *Aspire: Discovering Your Purpose Through the Power of Words.* New York: HarperCollins, 2009. On the premise that words have hidden power to illuminate your path or, when used incorrectly, to undermine your best efforts, the author chooses eleven potent words and explores one in each chapter to help guide you toward success and inner peace.

Hay, Louise L. *Heal Your Body: The Mental Causes for Physical Illness and the Metaphysical Way to Overcome Them.* Carlsbad, CA: Hay House, 1982. The classic reference list of health challenges that identifies their psychophysical causes and offers a thought shift to correct each one.

———. *You Can Heal Your Life.* Santa Monica: Hay House, 1984. The author healed herself from cancer based on the belief that every thought we think and word we say programs our brain to create that same reality for ourselves. Here is that prescription in easy-to-follow steps for readers to heal their own lives.

Kahane, Adam. *Power and Love: A Theory and Practice of Social Change.* San Francisco: Berrett-Koehler, 2010. Based on his work with business and civic leaders, the author offers guidance on how to use both power and love to achieve positive ends and how to move fluidly between the two. A practical, hopeful theory that can empower people to move toward reconciliation.

Keirsey, David. *Please Understand Me II: Temperament, Character, Intelligence.* Del Mar, CA: Prometheus Nemesis, 1998. The updated and expanded guide for the most used personality inventory in the world, the

Myers-Briggs Type Indicator, helps readers identify their basic type and understand its strengths and how it influences their relationships.

Kipnis, Aaron R. *Knights Without Armor: A Guide to the Inner Lives of Men.* 3rd ed. Santa Barbara: Indigo Phoenix, 2004. This book is for men and for the women who care about them. Straight talk from men who are reenvisioning their lives and offering fresh, new perspectives on male psychology today.

Kübler-Ross, Elisabeth. *On Death and Dying: What the Dying Have to Teach Doctors, Nurses, Clergy, and Their Own Families.* New York: Simon & Schuster, 2014. The 1969 groundbreaking classic on the five stages of grief includes in this new edition a foreword by a leader in the dying well movement, Ira Byock. Provides for the living a map of how to understand and accept the realities of sorrow, grief, and loss.

Lodge, Elisa. *Primal Energetics: Emotional Intelligence in Action.* N.p.: Elisa Lodge, 2006. An educator in body work and expressive arts therapy shows how creative movement revivifies each person's life force.

Nepo, Mark. *The Exquisite Risk: Daring to Live an Authentic Life.* New York: Three Rivers Press, 2005. A teacher and poet's serious illness is the catalyst for a deep dive into quietness. How learning to listen proves that the only real risk in life is not to take every opportunity to learn and to savor each moment.

Ramos, Lizyvette. *Sexual Assault [Rape]: Moving from Victim to Survivor— Informative Guide.* Parker, CO: Outskirts Press, 2015. The author, a professional sexual assault advocate, uses a practical, holistic point of view to outline each step in dealing with sexual assault, from defining assault to addressing what happens immediately after an assault as well as long term. There is a comprehensive but concise treatment of legalities, finances, forensics, reporting, protective injunctions, and psychological and social components involved in survivors' healing.

Richo, David. *How to Be an Adult: A Handbook for Psychological and Spiritual Integration.* Mahwah, NJ: Paulist Press, 1991. A rich, thoughtful, and practical tour of adulthood using the hero's journey as a model to understand how we travel in life from fear and inadequacy to power and love. Read it little by little to best absorb its trenchant and vital wisdom.

Robbins, John. *Healthy at 100: The Scientifically Proven Secrets of the World's Healthiest and Longest-Lived Peoples.* New York: Random House, 2006. Bringing the wisdom of four of the longest-lived cultures in the world together with the latest medical science, the author reveals simple secrets for living a healthy, satisfying, and fulfilling life that grows in wisdom and happiness.

Rosenberg, Marshall B. *Life-Enriching Education: Nonviolent Communication Helps Schools Improve Performance, Reduce Conflict, and Enhance Relationships.* Encinitas, CA: PuddleDancer Press, 2003. The psychologist who pioneered nonviolent communication gives educators a practical, hands-on manual designed to create safe, mutually respectful, and learning-rich environments where "children love to learn and teachers love to teach."

——— . *Nonviolent Communication: A Language of Life.* 3rd ed. Encinitas, CA: PuddleDancer Press, 2015. The groundbreaking method now practiced worldwide to help people connect with self and others in more empathic and satisfying ways, laid out in a book and companion workbook. The method of nonviolent communication helps people hear their own and others' true feelings and needs no matter how the original message is phrased and then respond in an authentic, compassionate way. Helps people improve their communications, relationships, and quality of life.

Shapiro, Francine. *Getting Past Your Past: Take Control of Your Life with Self-Help Techniques from EMDR Therapy.* New York: Rodale Press, 2012. A pioneer in the field of healing PTSD offers the knowledge and techniques anyone can use to resolve traumatic personal experiences.

Tolle, Eckhart. *A New Earth: Awakening to Your Life's Purpose.* New York: Penguin, 2005. Tolle's second book suggests that humanity is living in an ego-based state of consciousness. Building a new and more loving future will mean shifting into a different consciousness in order to experience who we truly are, which is far greater than we have imagined.

———. *The Power of Now: A Guide to Spiritual Enlightenment.* Novato, CA: New World Library, 1999. This brilliant, healing best-seller takes readers out of their minds and into the present moment to help readers rediscover their true self. How to further personal growth to peace, happiness, and fulfillment by consciously living in the present—the only place and moment of power.

van der Kolk, Bessel, MD. *The Body Keeps the Score: Brain, Mind, and Body in the Healing of Trauma.* New York: Penguin, 2014. Using recent findings in neurobiology, a psychiatrist shows how trauma rewires the brain and how areas of the brain damaged by trauma can be reactivated and healed through innovative practices such as meditation, yoga, neurofeedback, play, and other therapies. How to go beyond trauma and mere symptom relief to reconnect mind and body in wholeness.

Witt, Keith. *Shadow Light: Illuminations at the Edge of Darkness.* Tucson, AZ: Integral Publishers, 2016. Without acknowledging or exploring our unconscious selves, we remain at the mercy of both constructive and destructive impulses, sensations, feelings, and embedded memory. This book helps readers access and constructively work with the wealth of material constantly in play within our psyches.

———. *Shadow Light Workbook: Recording Your Shadow Journey.* Tucson, AZ: Integral Publishers, 2017. The companion workbook, complete with exercises and space for responses and reflections.

Zimbardo, Philip, and Nikita Coulombe. *Man, Interrupted: Why Young Men Are Struggling and What We Can Do About It.* Newburyport, MA: Conari Press, 2016. A well-researched book arguing that young men are getting left behind by socially detrimental and addicting habits such as gaming and porn, resulting in a generation of socially awkward, hesitant young men who are increasingly unable to engage in real-world relationships, education, and careers. Research, anecdotes, and pragmatic suggestions are combined in this timely and ultimately inspiring book.

About the Author

~

Sally Raymond, LMFT, is a mother of two sons, suicide survivor, and marriage and family therapist in Santa Barbara, California. She is a speaker, writer, and educator and a passionate, devoted expert on the topic of suicide.

With six other therapists, she cofounded Children's Path Programs, a nonprofit designed to help children find and attain their passion and potential. As part of this effort, Sally leads an annual eight-week leadership intensive at an area high school, in which students learn to speak and listen with intention and emotional intelligence.

Sally is also board member and program director for Freedom4Youth, a nonprofit dedicated to ending the school-to-prison pipeline for at-risk youth. Through coaching communication, listening, and leadership skills, the organization helps incarcerated adolescents evolve out of gangs and drug addiction into successful students, peer mentors, and social models for their family and friends.

Sally was one of four principals featured in *Dialogue Project* (dialoguemovie.com), an award-winning feature-length documentary film dedicated to reviving a sense of community in public places. Across the nation, from Los Angeles to Washington, DC, the *Dialogue Project* sparked spontaneous, meaningful dialogue and new connections among casual passersby.

CPSIA information can be obtained
at www.ICGtesting.com
Printed in the USA
BVHW040556070223
658034BV00023B/307